JOURNEY TO HIGH PLACES

...A Spiritual Evolution

Shirley Ruiz

*You and I possess
within ourselves,
at every moment of our lives,
under all circumstances,
the power to transform
the quality of our lives.*

—Werner Erhard

SHASTAR
PRESS

P.O. Box 30186
Walnut Creek, CA 94598

The author would like to thank the following people:

Technical Advisor to Author: William Orlich
Cover Art: John Lykes
Illustrations: Kathleen Bruno
Editing: Kim Peterson, Matrix Productions
Word Processing: Kimberly Freeman, Matrix Productions
Back Cover Photo: Russ Fischella
Mt. Shasta Aerial Perspective Photos: CHM² Hill
Retouch/Photo Restoration: Michael St. James
Initial Word Processing set-up: Sandy Emerson
Typography and Production: Sharyn Abbott, Great Impressions
Printed by: R.R. Donnelley

Published by Shastar Press, P. O. Box 30186, Walnut Creek, CA 94598

Printed in the United States of America

Library of Congress Cataloging-in-Publication Data
Main entry under title:
Journey To High Places

   1. Spiritual Life. 2. Bereavement—Religious
   3. Ruiz, Shirley, 1933- 4. Bruno, Bobby d. 1981.
   I. Title.
BL624.R84   1987   291.4'2   87-23564

ISBN 0-944020-00-3
9 8 7 6 5 4 3 2

*** First Edition ***

This book is dedicated
to God, with eternal gratitude
for the love, strength, guidance,
inspiration, and Master Teachers
He continuously sends my way
and,
To Bobby, my son,
and all of the other
beautiful Soul-spirits
now dancing joyfully
in high places!!

Acknowledgements

Don't kill the dream—execute it!
Tough times never last, but tough people do!

—Robert H. Schuller

The longer I travel the spiritual path, the more I am aware that my life is a tapestry of ongoing acknowledgment to each of you whose path has intertwined with mine. Whether our relationship has been a physical one, or my life has been contributed to through your books, teachings, cassette tapes, channelings, or a shared mystical experience, I beam you a ray of love and gratitude. Each of you has held up a mirror in which I experience and know myself a little better.

Acknowledgements

Many of you Master Teachers will find yourselves acknowledged in the adventures of this book. To those many, many others, please know that our holy encounter lies forever recorded in my heart and in the ongoing Akashic records of our lives.

The writing of this book was verbalized into a commitment with God through the intuitive counseling skills of a beautiful Godspirit named Elaine Christine.

I lovingly acknowledge Jerry Ashton for allowing me to play in the arena of his Spectrum Workshops as Bay Area Director. Through those doors quickly came many of the teachers and tools in this book and several very dear friends.

An extra "thank you" goes to Werner Erhard. Through his extensive transformational gifts and personal commitment to "making a difference in the world," this loving heart of mine unburied itself, climbed "out of the manure pile," and glimpsed eternity.

To my daughter-in-law, Kathleen, a big "Bobby-Deer" hug. As our hearts and souls danced and cried together, we harmoniously did what needed doing. Her love and artistic gifts have enriched my life and this book immeasurably.

Thank you to Bill Orlich for his love and unwavering support and for so firmly believing this seagull could mend her broken wings and soar into the heavens, bringing her vision into a physical manifestation. And a big hug to Kimberley Orlich for her loving management of Bill's Printing Center. It freed me to complete this book and create Shastar Press.

"You name it, it's yours!" Thank you to my brother, Robert, and sister-in-law, Mae, for their open house, open checkbook, and open hearts as I made choices that would forever alter the course of my life.

To my Dad, Lou Ferrero, and stepmother, Teresa, goes my gratitude for the loving, nonjudgmental support given while I sometimes stumbled through the learning experiences of having, doing, and being; and, for the living role models they are of "age is a state of mind—who you are is more important than how old you are!"

Words alone can never express my loving thanks to Sandy Emerson. We both gratefully acknowledge Jesus for bringing together our loving hearts, talents, and resources to manifest our visions into physical realities. Without Sandy's loving computer expertise and teaching skills, I would have given up the Word Processor game the very first day of "computer kindergarten" when I wiped out my Wordstar Tutor. Her calm, cheerful, to-the-rescue techniques have taught me patience with my own learning processes and introduced my creativity to the magic world of computers and word processing.

Thank you to Gloria Schultz for allowing me to share "Gary" in this book.

My deepest heartfelt thanks to Captain Ken Jourdan and his heroic search-and-rescue team for their risky mountain-top mission on January 24, 1981.

When it became clear to me I was to form Shastar Press and self-publish *Journey to High Places*, a whole support team of "angels" appeared to add their energy and gifts.

Suzie Friedenthal, Georgia Kahn, Kay Snow Davis, Claudia Gvirtzman, Robin Blanc, Joanne Isert, Gloria Heidi, Lois Farrell, Tricia O'Hara and Kathryn Davi provided constant streams of love, encouragement, and enthusiasm that rekindled my energy when I hit a total burn-out phase. My body, mind, and spirit thank Meta Mergy and her multi-dimensional healing gifts for assisting me through the "dark night of the soul".

Thank you to Mark Allen of Whatever Publishing, Inc. for sharing his resources and expertise. My publishing consultation with him inspired me to *go for it!*

I am extremely grateful to Kim Peterson for the painstakingly sensitive editing of my "baby", and for contributing so many valuable insights and suggestions.

Acknowledgments to book designer Merrill Peterson for his creative recommendations.

A maze of typesetting specifications were translated by Sharyn Abbott and lovingly midwifed into the finished pages that signaled we were nearing the last stages of giving birth to this book.

Thank you to Mylo and Lillian Cox of Data Scan Typesetting for their open hearts and door when it came time for the midnight crew to swing into action!

A special thanks goes to my sister, Virginia Ferrero, who came in under the pressures of the "final hours" and helped us create deadline miracles!

Deepest appreciation to artist John Lykes who opened up his highest inspirational channels to bring forth the cover art. The telephone lines between Santa Monica and Walnut Creek hummed for weeks as we interacted on each element of it until our hearts mutually sang, "This is it!"

Ackmowledgements

Heavenly beams of love and gratitude to Sal A. Davi, who opened the "last door"!

Rainbows full of hugs and love to my supportive children, family, and golden network of friends—everywhere. We are "family" above and beyond any limiting boundaries of our physical relationships.

My eternal gratitude to the Masters, Angels, and Guides of the Light who have been channeling their infinite love, support, and wisdom through my opened heart and printed words; and, of course, to Bobby, the "Space-Master" catalyst, who opened my soul awareness to the Holy Spirit and my divine inheritance of immortality and oneness with God.

And to you who are reading these words goes my deepest thanks and love. If one little saying or experience I've shared inspires or assists you through a trying time, this book will have fulfilled the vision held in my heart while I wrote it. Thank *you!*

Introduction

The seed for this book was planted at the moment I was told of my son Bobby's death. It incubated in the depths of my heart and soul for fifteen months until my inner guidance led me to Ira Progoff's Intensive Journal Workshop. There, I experienced a dialogue with an unfinished work that had meaning in my life. *Journey to High Places*, a eulogy for Bobby, wanted to talk to me. The following dialogue took place:

ME: Well, here we are, together at last—I'm uncertain as to how our relationship should begin. The only thing I know for sure is that I want to do you justice. There's a little thought running through my head that there's a "right" way to write you.

BOOK: *Relax... Just let our relationship unfold. Don't structure it in your head. It is in your heart and through your intuitive guidance that I will be created. Trust yourself!*

ME: Thanks for the vote of confidence.

BOOK: *If you will look at the pattern of your life, Shirley, you will notice you have been guided to use writing as a means of self-expression at this time. There is a need for books like me. Weren't you searching the bookstores for books about grief written by people who'd been there? I can share your experiences and perhaps send out little loving rays of light to others who are hurting, too.*

ME: That's a *big* order.

BOOK: *You're up to it... Trust yourself, meditate, isolate yourself (if you must), and you will be guided in my creation.*

ME: I've never written a book before.

BOOK: *Isn't it great? You can create our style anew.*

ME: Death is a heavy subject. I'm not sure of the form you are to take. Though I'm learning a lot about expressing and processing my grief, I don't have any credentials to write a book on the subject.

BOOK: *Come from your heart and experience with love. What other credentials do you need?*

ME: When someone has come face to face with the death of a loved one, tears come so easily. How will I ever create a book so people can read it, perhaps through many restimulated emotions and tears, to the very end?

BOOK: *Did you not discover that your emotions, when fully expressed in a safe and appropriate way, led you back to a state of inner peace? Take a look backward into your own experience. Tears, and even brief periods of intense sobbing, were sometimes exactly what was needed to begin or further the healing process. Tears can be gifts, like beautiful love messengers, releasing the healing powers within you. When you suppressed your tears over a period of time, did they not "dam up" until they could no longer be contained? Then, you'd "create" some "reason" to let them flow. Remember when two weeks in a row, you fell in the same spot in the parking lot, breaking the same heel off your shoe, and twice ripping your nylons and your left knee to shreds? Busy, busy lady—you were too busy to stop and listen to the needs of your grieving body. Finally, you let yourself cry as you sat, picking all the embedded gravel out of your knee. Your deep sorrow over Bobby's death sent you searching for answers and support systems, did it not?*

ME: Absolutely! Through my seeking I've become aware of and experienced so much. How do I share it in a meaningful way?

BOOK: *Loss in general, including the specific loss of a loved one, is a part of life's journey for many others besides yourself. What you and others want most is to know that there are paths back to wholeness and a renewed sense of purpose in life. And, believe it or not, joy, love, and aliveness, too.*

ME: I know that now. But it sure didn't look like it fifteen months ago.

BOOK: *When you are in the Valley of Grief, it's so dark it's hard to believe there is light ahead in your life—anywhere.*

ME: It seems like a long, long road to travel.

BOOK: *Each soul is unique. The best path and timing for each person is also highly individualized. Just openly share of your experiences and the path you found.* Journey to High Places *is a journey open to all willing to go. Remember:*

> *"Ask and it shall be given you.*
> *Seek and ye shall find.*
> *Knock and it shall be opened unto you."*

ME: I have often heard these phrases, but I never before realized these simple truths were an actual road map to the treasures of life.

BOOK: *The truth is always simple. Keep seeking, Shirley, and share with others what you are learning. I'll see you in about a year or so. We'll see how we're doing.*

On January 22, 1984, the third anniversary of Bobby's death, I re-opened the dialogue:

ME: It sure seems like it's taking a long time to get this "plane"...I mean "book"...off the ground.

BOOK: *You always were a bit impatient, Shirley. It is one of the lessons in life you're here to master. No time has been lost. You have been seeking, asking for, and finding many valuable answers. Now it's time to sit down and share, in writing, some of the things you have discovered. Set it up like a "Smorgasbord of Experience" in which each person can read and choose the "morsels" he wishes to partake of for himself, leaving what doesn't appeal to his appetite on the "table" untouched.*

ME: Some of these chapters have been difficult for me to relive and capture in words. I think I couldn't have looked at it all so deeply even a year or so ago.

BOOK: *Exactly why you've needed to have patience. I'm sure you're aware the writing of me is also a personal catharsis and healing process for you, Shirley, as well as a journey into your self-expression.*

ME: Yes, more than just a few tears have trickled down my cheeks and onto your pages as I have been writing.

BOOK: *Tears, yes. Laughter, too! I heard you joking I was much like a pregnancy. Once impregnated, I have taken over with a will and life force of my own. Tsk, tsk, such a long pregnancy this is! Right now this fetus needs your undivided attention to its nutrition. Feed me your time and your love and watch me grow.*

ME: You are just like one of my kids—you have a personality, disposition, and sense of humor all your own. I want you to know I will create you with all the love I possess as you are dedicated to God, Bobby, and many other very special people.

BOOK: *Thanks. I know I'm a "love-child". That's why you've been chosen as my mother. One day I'll be ready to leave your heart and womb and come out into the world and fulfill my divine purpose, too. So, let's get on to the labor and delivery room!*

Table of Contents

The Phone Call

Flashes

The phone rings...a "bleep" on the radar screen has disappeared...an airplane is missing, presumably crashed...it rains...I rain...my son, oh no! Scared...*help*!! Prayers...what to do? A moment of absolute helplessness...then friends...phone calls...more phone calls...a frantic need to do *something*! Urge to fly to Mt. Shasta...it's dark and stormy. Wait...wait...weather's bad, winds up to 75 MPH! Wait...wait...can't get search planes out under these conditions... wait...wait...wait. Where is Bobby? What is he doing while we're waiting? Waiting...waiting...more waiting. Is he in pain? Freezing on the mountain? My heart pounds into eternity...the agony of more and more hours of waiting. The doorbell rings...a pilot miraculously appears and the weather lifts a bit. He files a flight plan for Redding...Mt. Shasta if the weather holds out...Bobby, I want to find you myself on that snow-covered mountain and part of me is afraid to. Please God...please watch over my Bobby! Bobby...we're coming ...*hang on honey*...we're coming!

1

Thursday, January 22, 1981

It was my oldest son Greg's twenty-eighth birthday. I was at work and anxiously awaiting 5 PM so I could go shopping for another last-minute present. The plastic surgery office I'd been managing for fifteen years had been busier than usual. Somehow I seemed to have an extraordinary amount of energy and focus to get things done. At 4:40 PM, as I was beginning to wind up my day, the private line on my telephone rang. It was George Olbur, my son Bobby's father-in-law. All I remember of our conversation was "...call California Air Charters in Los Angeles immediately."

I hung up the phone. My heart skipped a beat, then began to pound and race, sending streams of adrenalin through my whole body. My hands trembled. I could hardly push the buttons connecting me with the Los Angeles phone number.

A secretary answered. I identified myself.

There was a pause and then, "Your son Bobby's twin-engine Piper Navajo plane appears to have gone down about 9:28 this morning. It doesn't look good," a man's voice told me.

Bobby, a commercial pilot, was alone on a chartered flight carrying bank cargo from Redding to Yreka. The plane had disappeared from the radar screen in the vicinity of Mt. Shasta. "I'll call you when I know more," the voice promised.

The first storm of the winter season was nasty; it had played havoc with sending out any search planes. I looked out my office window at the thunderous gray clouds and cried. Nature was crying, too, large and stormy tears. Hours before I'd been elated with the heavy rainstorm because it was bringing much-needed moisture to our drought-threatened area. Now, I was frightened. With one phone call, the storm had become a cruel and devastating enemy force.

Panic set in: who should I call first? Where were their telephone numbers? Why wasn't anyone home yet?... One by one, I called the family:

KATHLEEN: (Bobby's wife)—not at work, off today, unreachable.

GREG: (my oldest son)—no answer at his Berkeley telephone number.

LAURA: (my youngest)—no answer at our Walnut Creek home.

MOTHER
AND DADDY: —unreachable; they must be out for dinner already.

KIM: (my daughter)—she was running our Walnut Creek office. Hearing her voice was reassuring as she said, "Dr. Ransdell is almost finished with our last patient. Hold on, Mom. You know if anybody could survive a plane crash, it would be Bobby! Do you want me to meet you at home?"

STEVE: (my son, living in Washington D.C.)—"Oh no, Mom?" he said. "No!! Stay in touch, *please!*"

RICK: (Bobby's father and my ex-husband)—dead silence on the other end of the line as I told him what I knew.

BOB: (my brother)—he was upset and offered help. *"Anything* you need, name it. It's yours! We'll find Mother and Daddy for you," he said.

Dr. Hale Tolleth, my boss, instantly absorbed my emotions at a gut level and the pain etched itself across his face. We'd been through a lot together in our fifteen years—our kids were a special part of our relationship.

Robin Burchett, our office secretary, a tear running down her cheek, asked, "What can I do?"

Susan Workman, our office nurse, turned as white as the uniform she was wearing when she heard. Sue, a recent widow herself, stood by silently in shock and disbelief. Just this past October, Bobby had flown her to Oregon for a final reunion with her husband's ashes. She had often talked since of that day and the tender loving care Bobby had given her as he chauffeured her, first by plane, then by car, to the little cemetery in Roseburg where Dick Workman's ashes were laid to rest.

The phone rang again; it was LaRena, my roommate and best friend, calling to say, "Take it easy, 'Ma.' I'll meet you at home as soon as I can."

Then another call came in, so startling me that I jumped a mile! It was Judy Boshart, a friend who immediately tuned in and deeply

3

connected to the goings-on. She was scheduled to fly to Europe that night but she didn't feel like leaving now. She could not change her plans and promised to "...stay in touch and I'll be thinking about you."

John Richards, Dr. Tolleth's financial consultant, milled around the office trying to put together the pieces of phone calls and conversation enough to know what was happening. Somebody told him and he looked visibly paler.

* * *

I raced home as fast as my little red car "Valentyne" would carry me. The traffic was heavy but Valentyne seemed to know when to pass and when to change lanes to get me from Concord to Walnut Creek in the shortest possible time. I didn't want to be out of touch with my telephone for an instant.

My body was chilled to the bone. The first thing I did when I got home was light candles. Being an avid candle lover, I had filled my house with every variety. I lit orange ones, tall ones, heart-shaped ones, rainbow-colored ones, and votive candles in lotus-shaped brass holders as I made a pilgrimage through every room. The last candles I lit were in my bathroom, one of my favorite rooms. The rust-colored carpet and copper hue of the foil wallpaper emanated a rich, cozy feeling. Whenever I felt cold, the infra-red heat lamp cast a rosy aura in the bathroom, warming me thoroughly.

I stayed in the bathroom and glanced at the beautiful postcards framed in dark oak that hung above thick rusty-orange towels. Each postcard represented a special place and time for me. Lots of beautiful sunsets—Carmel, the Golden Gate, Hawaii, the Washington Monument. A big lump formed in my throat as I focused on the picture of Mt. Fuji in Japan. Bobby and Kathleen had sent it to me when they lived in Japan while Bobby was in the Navy. They loved it there and Kathleen was even learning to write and speak Japanese.

I had always had an inborn fondness for Oriental culture, and its influence was apparent in my home. The porcelain statue of Quan Yin, the Oriental Goddess of Mercy, was radiating a quiet peacefulness from her place on the long marbled counter top. Her serenity filled the room as she reflected her essence in the mirrored wall above the vanity. She was a real "hanger-inner." With five children rough-housing over the years, many were the times she'd been broken and glued back together.

Dear God and all your helpers, I need your peacefulness so much right now, I prayed. My insides are going crazy! I repeated this prayer while lighting white votive candles in the golden candle holder hanging on the wall. I glanced up at the framed picture of a beautiful, velvety butterfly hanging above it and continued to pray: I light these candles and pray for strength for all of us. Most of all, Dear Lord, keep my Bobby safe and warm under a blanket of Your golden light.

The children began to gather. Kim, Greg, and my daughter-in-law, Kathleen, arrived almost simultaneously. We tearfully hugged one another and then settled down for our long wait. The telephone became our "hot line." We decided to use Kim's line for outgoing calls so mine would be open. The "call-waiting" feature on my phone ensured that we would be reachable at all times. Each time the phone rang, we sent each other strength as our eyes and hearts met. Still, no news came from the mountain. We kept telling each other to think *positive*. We kept the TV on in the background to obtain updates on the weather. Heavy gale winds—part of the pounding storm hitting California—kept planes from going out to begin a search.

Finally, a confusing report arrived: an explosion had been heard on the mountain and appeared to be coming from several opposite points in the Shasta area. The heavy cloud blanket had set up unusual lateral dispersements of sound.

"It's probably Bobby trying to signal us from where he is," Kim said hopefully. We were all hanging onto hope and to each other. Bobby was extremely resourceful, we reassured one another. If anyone could survive anything, it was Bobby.

The long night vigil continued. Friday morning arrived and we still had heard no news. Search teams were unable to get clearance to fly as the storm continued to dump heavy rains on Northern California. Snow on Mt. Shasta was falling below the 5,000-foot level.

Time lost its meaning and melted into one long now. The past was too painful to look at and the future was beyond our present knowing. Now was all we had. We did not know what to do next.

I called a friend, a psychic, who might offer us some insights. I was prompted to do this because Bobby and I had had deep philosophical discussions about life and its purpose the last two times we spent an evening together. They had been inspired by a book a friend had shared, *Messages from Michael*. I wasn't sure I "believed" any of it (the book says *not* to make it a belief system), but I couldn't put the book down until I'd finished it. After reading it, I found my perspective on life and the journey of the soul had been cracked wide open.

Someone had told me once, "The mind is much like a parachute; it works best when it's open." As I began peeking with an open mind into life from a higher point of view, I became turned on and fascinated beyond anything I had studied for a long time.

I'd given Bobby *Messages from Michael* at Christmas and he found it to be the same sort of turn-on. He had been looking at life from a "Divine Plan" perspective, questioning what his *role* was. My psychic friend was part of the original "Michael" study group, and Bobby had an appointment with her the next day. As I put in the call to her I prayed, Please, God, let him be found in time to keep his date.

"All I can 'get' when I tune into Bobby is that he's in a state of confusion," was the only information my friend could offer.

Oh, Dear Lord, *help me*! I can't just sit here and wait much longer, I cried silently. I've got to *do something*!

Kim called her friend Harry Stockman, weatherman on KRON-TV in San Francisco, to ask, "What do the satellite pictures show about weather for the next couple of days?"

"Very stormy and unpredictable, but...a chance for a break," Harry told her. Not very promising, but better than nothing.

Kim and Kathleen picked up a pizza they'd ordered earlier. It had been a long time since we'd thought of food. We gathered at the family "roundtable"—my mini-trampoline. When I wasn't jumping on it, I covered it with a thick foam coverlet. Its firm, leatherette surface made it perfect for "roundtable" dinners and meetings. It sat by the glass wall of my bedroom suite and on a clear night, you could see the lights of Walnut Creek and the Lafayette-Berkeley Hills from this vantage. Tonight was *not* a clear night.

As we gathered about the pizza the doorbell rang and Greg dashed down the staircase two stairs at a time to answer it. Returning to my bedroom, he brought in a young couple he introduced as Steve and Anne Higgins. Steve had flown with Bobby when they both worked for Bay View Aviation in Oakland. As soon as he heard the news, he came to offer his assistance. It seemed my prayers had been answered. Eagerly we asked if it was possible for us to fly to the Mt. Shasta area.

Steve and Greg made Kim's bedroom their pilot's headquarters where they spread out maps and began plotting while staying in touch with the changing weather conditions. The telephone conversations became a blur of pilot talk. Greg grew more alive with hope as a plan to get to Mt. Shasta, one way or another, started to form.

"I want to go to Mt. Shasta more than anything in the world right now," I told Steve. One look into his eyes and I *knew* I trusted his judgment, unconditionally, with my life.

"You're the boss. I prefer flying, but I am prepared to drive if it's the only way to get to the mountain," I continued. The spirit was contagious. Kim and Kathleen began packing a bag for each of us. They packed every bit of warm thermal underwear we owned; mittens, hats, and boots began piling up by the front door in case we had to climb the mountain with a search team. We wanted to be prepared for anything and everything.

The evening became a "weather-suspense game." My phone rang again; this time it was my Dad, also a private pilot since his Air Force days during World War II. My teenage years were filled with Saturdays when the phone would ring and Dad would disappear for the rest of the weekend. The call would be about a "downed or missing" plane and Dad would be off to join the Civil Air Patrol search team. Bobby and Greg, following in his footsteps, became members of the CAP team when each was old enough. Now I was beginning to understand where Dad's heart had been, weekend after weekend, as he went out on a search.

"Daddy, come join the search with us," I begged him.

"Honey," he said with a strange quiver in his voice, "this is one search I can't go on. Please understand." His normally strong and high-spirited voice broke. I could hear his heart crying with grief for his pilot grandson.

I called Don, my brother, in Redding, California. My brother, Robert, and I had very little contact with either of our half-brothers,

Don and Jack Douglas, while growing up. Still, there seemed to be an unspoken tie between us in times like this. Don and his wife Valerie invited us to be their houseguests whenever and however we got to Redding.

As I hung up the phone, I heard our pilot Steve shout from Kim's bedroom, "That's it! Grab your things, we're driving to Oakland Airport. Bay View Aviation is making a plane available to us. It'll be ready when we arrive. There's a break in the weather—enough to get us to Redding Airport. Let's go!"

While Kim and Kathleen loaded the car, I put a new recording on my answering machine: "This is Shirley. It is 9 PM, Friday evening. Kathleen, Kim, Greg, and I are flying to Redding tonight to join in the search for my son Bobby's downed plane near Mt. Shasta. We'll be staying at the home of Don Douglas in Redding and can be reached there at area code 916-555-4444. If you need to talk to a people instead of a machine, please call our other home number and talk to Laura or LaRena. We appreciate your prayers for us and for Bobby. Thank you and God bless you."

Listening to my message, I remembered thinking, who is this strange-voiced person answering my telephone? It didn't sound like the voice that usually answers my phone. Well, so be it—quivering voice and all—that's the way it was.

I hurriedly wrote a note to Laura, my daughter, telling her where we'd gone. There wasn't another moment left to track her down. I thought, "Laura will be heartbroken being left behind."

The Search

As Kathleen, Kim, Greg, Steve, Anne, and I climbed into the plane, we shuddered both from the cold night and the emotions we were feeling. Steve began his pilot checkdown while Kim, Kathleen, and I joined hands in a circle of warmth, strength, and prayer. What experience lies ahead of us, we wondered. The late-night flight was both eerie and beautiful. The nearly full moon peeked through big puffy gray-and-silver-lined clouds. We each buried ourselves in our own thoughts.

As we taxied down the runway after landing at the Redding airport, Greg recognized some of his friends waving. They'd come to lend support and offer lodging. Don, my brother, picked us up and took us to his home on Mountain Drive. It was to be our headquarters for the next twenty-four hours. My sister-in-law Valerie, a thoughtful hostess, filled the snack bar with hot coffee, tea, and snacks. The smell of freshly baked apple pie drifted temptingly through the house.

Search teams wouldn't be going up before morning, but Steve and Greg wanted to go immediately. Conditions were fairly favorable for a quick night flight around Mt. Shasta; the moon was shining brightly. Because of the 14,162-foot altitude of Mt. Shasta and the icy conditions, the weight of the planeload was a critical factor, so only three people could go. Steve was the pilot, Greg was self-elected as person number two, and one look at Kathleen's face told me she should be the third person. My heart played "tug-of-war" because I wanted to go, too!

An eternity passed before the three of them returned. We sat around consuming pots of tea and coffee, chatting and waiting...and waiting...and waiting. Steve and Greg came in first. Their expressions showed they'd found nothing. Their disappointed words verified it.

It was a different story with Kathleen. I looked into her eyes and *knew* something profoundly moving had happened to her on the flight. She spoke softly as she told us about it, "I can only describe it as a 'glowing light,' near the top of the mountain. It was a radiating light, not a reflection, shining outward from inside the mountain. Whatever the light was, it's connected to Bobby."

When Kathleen pointed the light out to Greg, he couldn't see anything. Greg thought Kathleen was experiencing the effect of hypoxia, an insufficient oxygenation of the blood. Flying at 15,000 feet, dipping and circling over the icy white mountain, could well provide ripe conditions for hypoxia. Inwardly, though, I questioned the diagnosis as a valid explanation for the light Kathleen had seen. She has an artist's visionary eye. I have often marveled at the things and colors she could see that escaped the average eye. The reverent way Kathleen described this "luminous white light, with an aura of subtle, effervescent blue light around its edges" touched my soul. Whatever the explanation, thoughts of a heavenly white light comforted me and allowed my mind to ponder other possible explanations for the light.

Rick Bruno, Bobby's father and my ex-husband, arrived by car with his wife Ann. We shared lots of warm hugs, tears, and an update of weather and search conditions. Rick looked tired and appeared to be in shock. Ann also looked tired, as we all did, yet, as long as I'd known her, there had always been a beautiful, warm, natural radiance surrounding her, an inner source of strength that always shone through. It felt good to have them both with us.

10

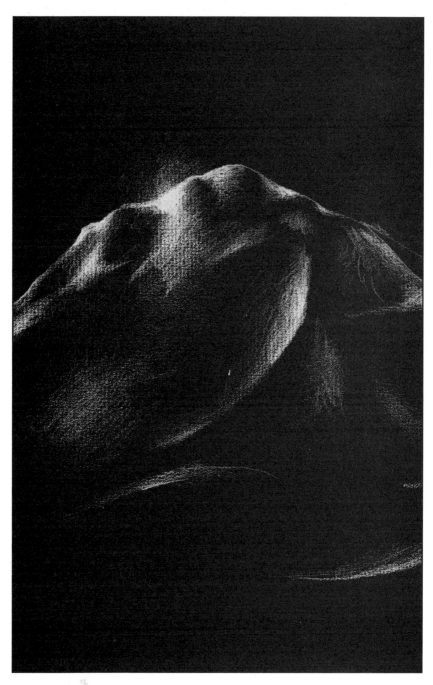

Luminous Light on Mt. Shasta

One by one, yawn by yawn, everyone bedded down. Although it was 3 AM, I was still awake, sitting on the couch wrapped in warm, comfy afghans. How could I sleep? How and where was my son? It was near freezing in Redding. What was it like on the snow-covered mountain? Was Bobby counting the seconds until daylight and rescue, wondering when someone would come?

I prayed to God like I'd never prayed before. Comfort, strengthen, guide, and protect my Bobby...wherever he is...whatever he's going through...right now! Please, God!

The moon finally sank from the sky and I found myself staring out the window into a black, cold night. I waited for dawn to bring its rays of light and hope. When the sun rose, my watch showed it was 7:25 AM. Valerie prepared a light breakfast for those who wanted to eat, but my stomach felt tight and I chose not to eat. I was anxious to go to the Redding Airport and get on with the search.

Heavy layers of clouds and fog laid a low ceiling on any visibility, dampening our hopes of getting an early-morning start on the search. Kathleen, Kim, and I went straight to the hangar where the Civil Air Patrol pilots were gathering. I felt grateful to see how many of them had come to help search. God love them, I thought, I sure do! It was a cold, early Saturday morning and staying in a warm, cozy bed must have seemed appealing, yet...here they were, volunteering their time and skills to search for a downed pilot. I could sense the beautiful, invisible link pilots have with one another; especially evident when one of them is downed or in trouble. My gratitude knew no bounds. I wanted to assist them in any way I could.

"Can I get you coffee or something hot to drink from the machines or coffee shop?" I offered. "Thank you for coming here to help search for my son. God bless you and guide you on your flight."

We introduced ourselves to each of the CAP members as we waited for word from the tower that conditions were clear enough to get the search planes off the ground. Kathleen and Kim were talking to some of the other pilots, while Steve and Greg were studying maps and keeping a close check on the changing weather conditions. "Let's go!" Steve's voice echoed across the hangar. We ran out to the airfield, where our airplane was waiting. We had to go in shifts of four, including the pilot, for the safest weight load. You couldn't have pried Kathleen, Kim, and I loose from each other with a crowbar. Greg, Rick, and Ann would make up the next planeload once we returned.

The pounding of my heart matched the intensity of our fully throttled engine as we lifted off the ground. At long last we headed for Mt. Shasta to begin the search. We rose up and up, climbing through and above the clouds that had kept us grounded for so long. Suddenly, straight ahead, like a magnificent jewel sparkling in the brilliant sun against a sky of blue velvet, shone the crystal-like snow-capped Mt. Shasta. Its majestic beauty took my breath away! No matter what was ahead of us, I felt a sacred reverence and love for this mountain as we flew towards her. An indescribable feeling welled up deep inside me.

We'd received conflicting reports about where Bobby's plane might be. We studied the glimpses of lush, green valleys through the broken cloud patterns beneath us. Something was calling us to focus our search on the mountain itself. We circled the mountain, straining to find any blemish in its smooth snow-covered landscape—*anything* that could be a clue to the whereabouts of Bobby's downed plane. From this height, the wreckage would appear as a small speck; because of Mt. Shasta's enormous size, we had to keep a safe distance. We would need a more powerful airplane to get a closer look. Flying so high, I began to lose perspective on size; there was nothing much to compare to up here.

The sun almost blinded us at times, bouncing its powerful rays off the pure white drifts of snow and ice. It probably had snowed up here again last night. Could it have completely covered the plane? My hopes fell a bit. The mountain was so huge. Which crevasse or peak was playing "hide and seek" with us? Please, God, please, I prayed silently, the pain in my heart is excruciating! Where is he?

As we were completing the last circle of our fruitless search, a voice announced over the radio, "We've located the wreckage."

"Oh my God, is Bobby all right?" I asked Steve.

"They probably won't put out any more information over the radio," Steve answered. I shuddered, not wanting to further explore all the ramifications and conclusions my mind was conjuring up.

"What do we do next, Steve?"

"We'll land briefly at the airport up ahead and see what we can find out."

13

As we landed, I vaguely remember thinking, "It's Montague Airport." No information was available here. We were advised to return to Redding Airport, as search-and-rescue efforts were being coordinated from there.

When we arrived at Redding, no one could—or was it "would"—speculate or give us a clue as to what shape the wreckage was in or Bobby's possible fate. They suggested we go home and get something to eat and stay in touch with them by phone. Eat? At a time like this?

We learned the wreckage was sighted somewhere on the north face of the mountain, above Whitney Glacier, at approximately 13,600 feet. Mt. Shasta had an elevation of 14,162 feet. Bobby was only 562 feet from the top. How many air seconds is that from clearing the mountain altogether? I decided it was torture to play the game of "what if." "Save your energy for more important things!" I scolded myself.

The Air Rescue Unit said it needed a large, specially equipped helicopter and rescue team to handle the climb to that altitude. None were available at the moment, but they promised to continue checking all known sources.

The Douglas household became a hub of activity. Old friends seemed to be coming in and out of nowhere to offer love and support. Several, whom I had never met before, introduced themselves as est 6-day graduate friends of Greg's. We began the all-too-familiar waiting game again—waiting for word of Bobby's fate. I began pacing. I couldn't sit still. This might have been a routine search-and-rescue mission for some, but not for me and my family. It was our Bobby's life in question up on that mountaintop.

I felt I had to reach him. The high energy that comes with the instinctive, protective parental drive began mounting up inside of me. My heart and voice cried out in unison, "I don't care what it takes. My son is not spending another night up there on that mountain alone!"

I became acutely aware of what I later realized was one of the greatest success secrets of life—an intense burning desire—so focused that everything else dims to the power coming through. I was experiencing that miraculous power which can enable an otherwise fragile mother to lift a 4000-pound car off her injured child. I knew I could climb that mountain myself if that's what it took. There had to be a way to get to Bobby and bring him down.

It was getting to be mid-afternoon. How many hours of daylight left? From the back bedroom I could hear our pilot Steve on the phone. Bless him! He'd been on the phone constantly, personally checking and rechecking each and every source for a special helicopter capable of reaching Bobby. He left no stone unturned, no source unchecked. No high-powered helicopters were available at the moment. The big California Highway Patrol helicopter was tied up with an accident down south.

California Highway Patrol...hmmm. A thought flashed.

I called my brother Robert at home in Orinda. Robert had been a Pittsburg City Police Officer, and then a California Highway Patrolman, before he decided to "go for it" and venture into his own business. An inner voice had coaxed him to cash in everything he could get his hands on and buy Ham Radio Outlet in Burlingame. The one operation had become a chain of ham radio stores and he was able to buy his own twin-engine plane, complete with a pilot on standby call, to fly him on his business ventures.

The Great American Dream can still come true when one discovers and develops his own unique talents and pursues them with integrity and everything he's got. My "baby" brother was living proof of that. His hobby-turned-business had also connected him to a worldwide network of "hams." I'd seen them in action in times of disaster—they are a dedicated and powerfully aligned group of human beings. Somewhere, someone would surely be able to help us locate a helicopter. My brother said he'd get to work on it immediately and check back with me as soon as he had something more we could go on.

At that moment, I was *clear* that if it took a call to the President of the United States himself, somehow, I'd find the line to get through to him.

Coast Guard...Air Force...Navy...all sources were being checked out. We knew the Air Rescue Services were checking, too. Personally contacting each source ourselves felt like an empowering thing to do.

Waiting...waiting...more waiting.

Glancing down at my purse, I noticed the yellow yarn ribbon tied to its shoulder strap. Somewhere in the world today, fifty-two Iranian hostages and their families were preparing for a joyous reunion and celebration—free at last. I'd been wearing yellow ribbons for several days. One was tied to my purse, one to the tree in my front yard, and one "flew" proudly from the antenna of my car. A world had prayed for the safety and release of these hostages and now they were free—miracles do happen. Please, God, please, let there be a "Bobby" miracle and a celebration for us too, I prayed.

The phone rang, jolting me back to the present. I didn't hear who the call was from; only the message: "A helicopter rescue team is on its way to the crash site. Bobby will be brought to Mt. Shasta Hospital at the base of the mountain."

Like a flash, we loaded into our cars and headed for the helicopter landing pad in Mt. Shasta City. As we made the hour-long trip we now saw the mountain from a new vantage point. It looked even bigger from the ground. We checked in with the Emergency Room personnel at the hospital. Someone pointed to the spot outside where the helicopter would land. We gathered there. The cold crisp air reddened our noses and frosted our breath. Emotion was rising and my tear ducts wanted to release some of the stress I had been accumulating. I looked at Kim, then Kathleen, then Greg. The same thing was happening to them. Our eyes scanned the skies for the first sign of a speck that could be identified as a helicopter. Our ears perked up for sounds that might indicate its approach. We paced and waited some more. Rick, Bobby's father, chain-smoked as he paced the far corner of the parking lot. No conversation seemed appropriate, as we feared it might drown out the sound of the approaching rescue vehicle. Suddenly, I felt restless. I asked Greg to check with the Emergency Room personnel to see what was happening.

"There's been a change of plans." Greg said on his return.

"What?"

"They're taking Bobby to Yreka."

"Why?"

"I don't know, Mom. They said the facilities are better there."

"We'd better hit the road if we're going to be there when the helicopter arrives."

"Go to the Siskiyou County Sheriff's Office. They'll direct us from there. I'll ride with Dad and Ann. We'll meet you there,'' Greg directed.

Steve Higgins drove my brother Don's car. Anne, his wife, sat in front with him. I nestled myself between Kim and Kathleen in the back seat. My heart ached more than ever as we drove farther and farther from the mountain. I couldn't question the "why" of it but I thanked God for the special carful of people riding with me. Anne and Steve were beautiful, beautiful souls. I had chuckled a bit when they first told me they lived in Soulsbyville, California. Of course— where else would "angels of mercy" live? Such a strange coincidence. All five of us seemed specially linked at the heart level. Though I couldn't reason it out, our souls also felt specially linked—very tenderly, very powerfully—in this shared moment of eternity. All human emotions were being deeply felt. And another part of us rose and connected above our human emotions to an inexplicable layer of blessed spiritual awareness that blanketed us with comfort every step of the way.

As we drove northward, I kept turning my head so Mt. Shasta was always in view. The sun was preparing for its late afternoon dip into the western sky. The white-capped mountain, reflecting the sunset, glimmered with tones of lavender, crimson, and gold. A small flicker of light caught my eye. I looked more closely—it was the helicopter—right behind us.

We followed the directions we'd been given and pulled into the parking lot of the Sheriff's office. Kim and Kathleen held hands tightly. They said they'd wait in the car to see where we would be told to go next. I raced out of the car. Steve gave my hand a little squeeze as we went through the front door together. I told the lady at the window what I was here for. She asked me to have a seat for a moment. I carefully investigated the face of each of the Sheriff's Department employees on the other side of the glass wall separating us. I was searching for a clue of what was coming. Working in medicine for over twenty years, I'd had plenty of practice reading faces and body language. So had they. As I looked them over, they immediately busied themselves. After what seemed an eternity, a uniformed female officer came through the door.

"Mrs. Bruno?" she asked.

"I'm Bobby's mother," I answered. "My name is Shirley Ruiz."

"Bobby's been taken across the street. I'll need some information before you go to see him," she told me in a compassionate tone.

I remember clearly the words I said, but though I said them, the meaning in them did not fully register; I was still in a deep state of hope. "I checked him into this world so I guess it's appropriate that I be the one to check him out of it."

I numbly answered the questions: full name, date of birth, address, father's name and birthplace, my name and birthplace, spouse's name. Just then Kathleen and Kim came through the outside doors, hand-in-hand. They looked at my face. No words were spoken. They both wept openly as Kathleen answered the rest of the questionnaire. The real impact and meaning of it all still awaited me.

The policewoman had said, "Your son is across the street." Kim and Kathleen had been sitting in the car waiting and knew what was across the street—a mortuary—but I was still in hope. Maybe I was expecting a miracle Medical Center to be there, like on TV.

This must be some kind of a mistake...a cruel joke...a bad dream, I thought. That's it! It's all a nightmare. I commanded myself with all my being to wake up.

I walked across the street and into the Girdner Funeral Chapel. This was not a dream. It was really happening. Coming to meet us as we came in the front door was a gray-complexioned man in a gray-colored suit. This man could use a little sunshine; grayness must be an occupational hazard, I was thinking when another thought crystallized: Oh, no! I don't have any control over the words this man is going to speak to me. The only choice I have is what I do with them.

With a fixed expression of sympathy on his face and in a voice that sounded a bit patronizing came the words he's surely uttered thousands of times before, "I'm sorry,..."

Help, God, help! This is my moment of choice, I silently wailed. In an instant, an astounding dramatization played itself out on the screen of my mind. First, a framed picture of a butterfly and a saying flashed. I'd seen that butterfly hundreds of times; it hung on the wall of my bathroom. A verse which adorned it said:

> You and I possess
> within ourselves,

> at every moment of our lives,
> under all circumstances,
> the power to transform
> the quality of our lives.

In that same instant of time, another picture flashed: I was riding a carnival-like train ride on the Boardwalk at Santa Cruz—the ride that plunges you into a dark tunnel and suddenly, dead ahead, you see the headlight and hear the sound of a locomotive engine fast bearing down upon you.

On the railroad track of my mind, two pictures were flashing for my attention. To my left was a vision of a "grief puddle." The message there was: Bobby's death...tsk, tsk...just another too bad. Ugh, that one hurt. To the right was a soft luminous white light and another message: commitment to finding a higher purpose and meaning in life through Bobby's death.

Hurry, Shirley, a voice within me urged. Hurry! You must choose...*now*!

I sensed my whole being jump to the light, away from the puddle of grief. What have I chosen so instinctively to do, I wondered. I didn't know how or what I'd do, but the commitment had been deeply internalized. It would have felt awful to choose "just another too bad" and the grief puddle—whatever that meant.

"I have some questions. Someone needs to identify Robert." The polite man in the gray-complexioned suit was still talking to us. Wherever I'd "spaced-out" to, I was back.

"Did Bobby suffer?" I had some questions, too.

"No. I don't think so," he answered. Greg volunteered to identify Bobby and followed the man down the hall. I felt emotionally numb and paralyzed. Greg returned.

"It's definitely Bob, Mom."

"I want to see him myself!" I answered.

"No, Mom—you really don't want to see him like this. Honest, you don't. Please, Mom, don't," Greg tried to stop me. That powerful part of me was taking command again. Words of comfort—"No, he didn't suffer"—were not enough for me. I had to see for myself. The gray man agreed with Greg. It would be too painful for me to view Robert. With that, I walked briskly and determinedly down the hallway towards the closed door.

No one or *no thing* was going to keep me from seeing my son! They tried. I heard voices pleading with me not to go through the door. Good advice for most people—but not for me. I'd been torturing myself with "what if": What if we could have reached him sooner? Would it have mattered?

The finality of death hit me in the gut like a "KO" punch as I passed through the dark wood door. Bobby's still-frozen body allowed me to view only what I needed to see to know that death had been instant. It was as though Nature was trying to soften the impact of the moment for me. She'd covered most of the grotesqueness of what I didn't need to see with mounds of pure white frozen snow. I studied the familiar soft-brown hairline. By now there was no sign of blood, just a jagged frozen skull wound that looked like Bobby's soul had made a quick emergency exit from the top of his head. My eyes dropped to the enlarged chest scar visible near the top of his opened shirt. Bobby had gotten the scar in a childhood accident. I wanted to hold him, comfort him, and breathe my own life-force back into the body of this precious child now lying so still. I cried quietly for some time. The next thing I became aware of were gentle arms on either side of me leading me out of the room. I glanced back over my shoulder for one last look at my son in his blue pilot's uniform.

I broke away from the arms supporting me and began rubbing my forehead. I blinked my eyes hard several times. Suddenly, I was running...I had to get outside...get some fresh air! As I took in a breath of the shockingly cold evening air, I let out a very long and very primal scream...coming straight from the depths of my grieving womb.

I'm sure anyone hearing the scream would be misled into agreeing people should be "protected" from seeing the bodies of their dead loved ones. Not always so. For me it was a necessary part of my grieving process. It had helped me to release forty-eight hours of stressful "not knowing."

"Why Bobby?" I kept repeating. "Why Bobby? He was in the prime of his life. Why Bobby?" Kathleen and Kim joined me outside.

"Do you think he really knew how much I loved him?" Kathleen was murmuring. We held each other in a triple hug and cried for a long while.

20

Decisions needed to be made. The legalities of a commercial plane crash made an autopsy mandatory. It would be at least Tuesday before his body could cross county lines and be returned to Contra Costa County for a funeral.

"Which mortuary do you want us to call for the funeral arrangements?" the man in the gray suit asked.

"Helyn Bryant in Concord," I answered, almost automatically. Helyn and I had worked together on the American Cancer Society's Annual Mardi Gras Charity Ball for years. I rubbed my forehead and closed my eyes as the man dialed the Bryant and Lough Chapel.

In my mind's eye I visualized Bobby and Kathleen on their first date. Kathleen wasn't quite sixteen yet—and such a beauty. I loved her, as had Bobby, from the moment I first laid eyes on her. Bobby and Kathleen were all dressed up. They were volunteer Junior Hosts and Hostesses for the festive Mardi Gras Ball being held in the Sun Valley Shopping Mall.

I opened my eyes. The memory tugged at my heart strings as the gray-suited man across the desk from me handed me the phone.

"Helyn," I greeted her, and then proceeded to tell her what had happened.

"You take care of yourself and your family, honey," she replied. "I'll take care of whatever needs to get done for Bobby. Have a safe trip home and call me on Monday."

Silently I thanked God for all the special people in my life who were now lovingly handling some of the details. We drove the long journey back to Redding in silence. Valerie and Don met us at the door. Valerie had done it again—a huge pot of spaghetti and french bread were ready for us. After dinner, we unanimously agreed to say our "thank yous and goodbyes." We reunited with our plane for a late-night flight back to Oakland Airport.

"I think it's pretty big of us to even think about getting into a small plane right now," Kim said, half seriously, half jokingly.

When we landed at Oakland Airport, Kathleen wanted to pick up Bobby's car. He'd left it parked at the California Air Terminal that fateful January 22nd morning, almost a lifetime ago.

"Steve might want to use it when he and Darsie fly in from Washington, D.C.," Kathleen thought aloud. As she got in the front seat, she saw Bobby's commuter coffee cup which he'd brought back from Japan. It was still half full. On the seat beside it was a "to do" list. On it was written, "Ask Kathleen about skiing Friday."

Kathleen picked up the cup and fondled it. She held the note close to her heart and stared blankly ahead. A teardrop rolled down her cheek, plunging into and merging with the half-emptied cup of creamy brown liquid.

The Arrangements

It was Super Bowl Sunday and the Oakland Raiders were playing the Philadelphia Eagles. Excited TV sounds formed the background for my somber thoughts. I seemed to be in another world, apart from "real" life as it went on as usual around me. Back in my quiet bedroom in Walnut Creek after all that had transpired during the past two-and-a-half days, I felt estranged. The kids were still sacked out; it had been exhausting both emotionally and physically for all of us.

I wondered what I should do first.

I stretched my aching body and started to mentally list what needed to be done. The "to dos" came so fast they overwhelmed me. I reached for a steno pad to capture and organize what had to be done, when, and by whom.

I let out a big sigh as I realized that life, unbeknownst to me, had already given me some dress rehearsals for this very moment. Susan Workman's husband Dick had died Memorial Day Weekend, 1980 in a boating accident on Lake Berryessa. His body finally surfaced after Labor Day that same year, following fourteen weeks of search, "not knowing," and anguish. Susan and Dick had been in the midst of a divorce so Dick's funeral arrangements were taken out of Susan's hands. Through a chance phone call she found out his body had been cremated shortly after discovery and the ashes were being taken to Oregon. She'd been torturing herself for three-and-a-half months. In spite of what the divorce papers said, Susan was deeply mourning the loss of the man she had loved and she felt left out of making the final arrangements for Dick's body.

In a moment of inspiration I suggested, "Why don't you have Bobby fly you to Oregon, Sue? It's not everyone who has a private pilot at her beck and call. He would be a great morale booster for you, too."

Bobby and Susan flew to Oregon two days later.

Afterwards, Susan told us of her journey: "This was a special trip for Bobby and me. He was so supportive of my emotional needs while he piloted me to Oregon, rented a car, and drove me to the little cemetery in Roseburg where Dick's ashes were laid to rest beside his father's. The flight was peaceful. We flew by a most beautiful mountain—Mt. Shasta."

Over the next few days, Susan grew increasingly restless. She kept saying, "Someone should have a memorial service for Dick here in the Bay Area. Would one be appropriate now? How can I set one up?" As we talked about it, I thought why not? She didn't really need anyone's permission to hold a loving memorial. Her questions continued: What would it take to put one together? How do I want it to look and feel?

PLACE: The shores of Lake Berryessa, of course. (Dick loved it there.)

DAY: Friday. (More people could come near the weekend.)

DATE: October 24.
(It was the day after what would have been their third wedding anniversary.)

TIME: 3 PM
(Gives people time enough to drive to the lake from the Bay Area.)

FLOWERS: Long-stemmed yellow roses in a vase on a table.

24

MUSIC: Elvis Presley (Susan's favorite) singing "My Way." (That sure fit Dick!)

HOW: We'll have to send out some kind of announcement or invitation. (Office co-worker Robin Burchett immediately began to layout some artwork).

WHO: Invite all the friends and members of his family who care to come. (Too bad—Dick's mother, Roma Workman, is physically unable to travel. Let's tape record it and send it to her!)

When we had completed our plans, Susan looked at me through tear-filled eyes and said, "Will you write and deliver the eulogy, Shirl?"

"I can't, Susan," I answered, avoiding her pleading blue eyes. "I'm trying to get this office in shape so I can be gone next week. We're doing another ASSET training. I still have all the logistics to pull together and equipment to pack." I was already taxing my physical strength and my twenty-four-hour day to the limits.

Susan continued to stare at me and, in a dead serious tone, said, "If you don't do it, Shirl, it won't get done. Dick was no marshmallow. Sometimes people misinterpreted his powerful manner and often their 'toes would feel stepped on.' You always saw the good in Dick. I know you'll know just what to say and how to say it."

I took a deep breath and looked at Susie. How could I refuse her? "I don't know where I'll find the time or the words, Susan, but I'll sure give it all I've got."

We all did. A touching tribute of love came together that crisp October day. You could feel peace come upon the shores of Lake Berryessa while the strains of "My Way" floated in the breeze.

As I reflected on Dick's memorial service, I recalled another accident that took place that same Memorial Day weekend in 1980 on Kirker Pass Road outside of Pittsburg, California. Though these two accidents happened many miles apart, they were now coming together in my thoughts and heart for a significant reason on this Super Bowl Sunday.

The accident on Kirker Pass Road claimed the life of a young man named Jimmy Dillon and his wife. I was so emotionally involved with Susan Workman's grief, I missed reading the newspaper account of the accident. I found out some months later when talking to an old friend, Kathryn Davi-Billeci. I was shocked. Kathryn, Jimmy's father Harry, and I had graduated from Pittsburg High School together. If only I'd know, I'd have sent my love and a note of support to Harry and his wife Barbara. My heart ached for Harry and his family, and I sent them a much-belated sympathy note. From this experience, I realized friends want to reach out to one another in times of trouble and sorrow. It brings out the best in each of us when we have an opportunity to communicate, care, and share.

As I pondered the love and empathy I had for Susan Workman, and for Barbara and Harry Dillon, I began to think about all of my friends. They were scattered all over the United States and to the far corners of the globe. Normally, I'd correspond with most of them in my next Christmas card, but to tell them of Bobby's death eleven months after the fact, at Christmas—ugh! And to telephone them all now would be an impossible, emotional task.

The seagull that had adorned Dick Workman's memorial card flashed in my mind. Then, I envisioned another card illustrated with a mountain top—Mt. Shasta. Perfect! By now, Kim and Kathleen had come into my bedroom and I described the idea. They agreed that a memorial announcement would be the best way to share our grief with special friends immediately.

Kathleen began sketching; the idea had clicked for her, too. Kim headed for the closet where we stored our huge box of family photos. She knew we had the perfect picture of Mt. Shasta for Kathleen to sketch from. We'd taken it a few years earlier on a flight to Bend, Oregon, with pilot friend Joe Gervais. Kim found the photo quickly and Kathleen sketched it. This daughter-in-law of mine is very talented; no question about it. Bobby always encouraged her to find creative outlets for her talent. He felt it was a crime to let such an artistic gift go unexpressed.

As I watched Kathleen's pencil shade in the crevasses and peaks of Mt. Shasta, I thought of a verse called "High Flight" that I'd seen as a sign-off on a local TV station. It had touched me deeply. I pictured Bobby in flight as the words and associated images flashed in my mind.

Up, up the long, delirious, burning blue,
　　where never a lark or eagle flew...

I couldn't recall the exact words. Then I remembered the last phrase:

Put out my hand, and touched the face of God.

The poem was perfect for the inside cover of the memorial card. I started writing the body of the announcement.

"Would it be all right to have donations in Bobby's memory be made to the Hunger Project?" I asked Kathleen. This organization is dedicated to ending hunger on the planet by the end of the century and I'd been a part of it since its beginning in 1977. Though I had worked for many charities over the years, this one seemed to be uppermost in my heart today. Kathleen said it was fine with her and excused herself and left the room. To my list of "to dos" I added: Call Hunger Project office Monday for appropriate donation information.

Kathleen came back and asked me to read a poem she'd written. Tears welled up in my eyes as I read her touching tribute to Bobby. "Can we use it on the back cover of the announcement?" she asked. I read the poem:

I sense a touch—your fingertips
　　The soft caressing of your lips.
　　I turn around,
　　But I see no one there.

The eyes that've seen a million years
　　Still fill with wet and warming tears.
　　I reach to hold,
　　But I feel no one there.

And of all the gifts that you gave,
　　I love the essence that you made.
　　You filled my heart with the richness
　　Of your sigh.

27

And though you are but sometimes there,
    Your soul stirs on earth and air.
    And then I know what others fear belie.
    For I move on my mortal plane,
    Our souls have touched, I stood the pain.
    You plucked it out like magic
    With your art.

As you led me and I bred you,
    Through hurt we sought to start anew.
    It brings me once again
    A place to start.

But forget you—no I never will
    The thought of you turns a nighttime still
    I feel you stir,
    But still there's no one there.

After reading, I replied, "Yes, it's beautiful."
The doorbell rang and Greg answered it.
"They're upstairs; go on up!" he said in greeting to Bill Orlich.
It was such a miracle to have a printer friend like Bill. I can't count
the projects the two of us had worked on over the past four or five
years.
"Perfect timing, Bill!" I welcomed him.
He asked what we needed done and suggested we use a rich, tex-
tured beige paper. "If brown was one of Bobby's favorite colors, why
don't we also use brown ink?" he added.
He said he'd pick up the paper and envelopes right away so we
could start addressing envelopes whenever we had time. That way
they'd all be addressed by the time we had the announcement data
finalized and ready to be printed. Bill was truly a "saint in jeans."
Everything for the announcement was falling into place perfectly.
The phone rang: it was a message relayed from Judy Boshart.
She'd called from England to check if Bobby's plane was found. The
last she'd heard was "no news yet." The message also stated she'd
said a prayer for Bobby at Westminster Abbey. A lump of grateful
emotion rose in my throat.

My son Steven called to tell us he and his wife Darsie had reservations on United Airlines, arriving in San Francisco at 11:40 PM. He sounded sad but thankful that we would all be together soon. At first it had appeared they would be unable to join us. Steve was in his last year of dental school at Georgetown University in Washington, D.C. His student money was tightly budgeted. In addition, Darsie was four months pregnant, so mounting medical expenses made every cent they had count. When my brother Robert found out the situation, he and his wife Mae quietly made and paid for the airline reservations. They called Steve and Darsie and told them the tickets to fly home were waiting for them at the airport. Another beautiful miracle!

I could thank them both personally at dinner; Bob and Mae had invited friends and family to come over around six for an informal get-together. We were all appreciative of the opportunity to see each other in person. We'd been in touch only by telephone since Bobby's accident.

The flower of love in my heart wanted to blossom and reign, but how could love walk hand-in-hand with grief? I felt an intense, unconditional love for everyone in my life and wanted to reach out and hug the whole world, so full of special people and miracles of love.

The thought—maybe not quite so much love for my ex-husband Bob's beautiful young wife—came filtering through my mind. Was I still harboring traces of resentment, jealousy, or not-so-loving feelings towards her? Hmmm...I wondered, heading for the shower.

The showerhead sent its massaging fingers of hot water over every inch of my body. No matter how tired or aching I was, "shower power" could send waves of healing energy surging through me—especially when I followed it with a rubdown of homemade "magic potions" and herbal lotions.

Getting out of the shower, I wrapped myself in the soft warmth of a king-size rust-colored towel and marched straight to the phone book on my nightstand. That by-now-familiar part of me was taking charge again. I dialed Bob and Suzanne Ruiz's home number and thought, I don't have the slightest idea what I'm going to say. One thing I do know is I can't tolerate shutting people out. If I find any of it in my world, I'm going to do something about it.

"Suzanne, this is Shirley."

"Hi, Shirley. I'm so sorry to hear about your son, Bobby. I was just going out the door to buy you a bouquet of flowers. My son Andrew and I were coming over to bring them to you." Her words triggered a flood of tears. How touching! I'd lost a son; she'd recently given birth to one. Mother to mother, there's no separation when higher, loving thoughts are allowed to take charge.

"Please, come along with Bob to my brother's house tonight," I invited.

Bob and Mae had laid out a beautiful array of colorful, scrumptiously prepared food. The smell of hot cider drifted from the kitchen. The fireplace crackled with warmth from big oak logs. Getting together with Bob and Mae and my parents was both painful and joyful. The doorbell rang time and time again as family and friends gathered. Hugs, kisses, food, love, and memories were being shared in every corner of the house.

The doorbell rang once again and I glanced down the stairs to the entry hall. I could see Bob and Suzanne had arrived. I saw shocked looks on the faces of my family and friends. It was as if I could read their minds and they were all wondering: God, why is Suzanne here? Shirley doesn't need any more stress or upset—not tonight. They had no idea I'd personally invited her to be here.

The spontaneous, intuitive part of me knew exactly what to do. I walked to the head of the staircase and embraced her with my whole being. She returned the hug. Tears swept down both our faces as she placed her infant son in my arms. I hugged little Andrew. A tremendous wave of sadness washed over me, immediately followed by one of love and gratitude. The whole roomful of people stopped whatever they were doing to witness our meeting—a moment of unconditional love. It was contagious and spread through everyone like wildfire.

"Welcome, Suzanne!"..."Hi, Bob!"...oohs and aahs, hugs and kisses for tiny Andrew.

Oh, the universal truths sorrow was teaching me. This lesson about unconditional love was crystal clear. The *pebble of love* one throws into the *pond of life* has a far-reaching wake. The power of love to transform life and relationships is unlimited.

In this lesson was a key to world peace, I thought, beginning with each individual handling it in his personal world first. The best thing

I could do for the world was to let love and peace begin with me, moment by moment.

The Raiders won the Super Bowl 27 to 10.

Yes, it had been quite a Sunday!

*   *   *

I was the first one up on Monday morning. Steve and Darsie had come in around 1 AM and were still sleeping. I checked Kim's room. Kathleen was already awake. There was so much to do today; together we began adding to the list in my steno book.

Our first stop was the Bryant and Lough Chapel. Helyn Bryant met us with a big hug and took us into her office.

Her first questions concerned scheduling the sequence of events. The best date seemed to be Wednesday, January 28th. A limousine would be bringing Bobby's body home from faraway Yreka sometime later tonight. The funeral chapel would be ready for friends to call and pay their respects to Bobby the next evening.

Helyn led Kathleen and I into a room full of wall-to-wall caskets. A strange sickening feeling swept over me. We surveyed the room and both headed for the same heavy oak casket. Kathleen and I were discovering a powerful harmonious alignment between us. When something was right, it strongly felt right to both of us. What a blessing to discover this bond during this decision-making time.

"You can drop off the clothes for Bobby later in the day," Helyn told us. "Who do you want to officiate at the funeral service?"

Kathleen and I exchanged a blank look.

"I have someone in mind who feels like the perfect person for your family. I'll have him call you this afternoon," Helyn said. With arrangements completed, we hugged her goodbye and thanked her again for making a tough task a little easier.

Our next stop was Oakmont Memorial Park. There'd never been much question about where we would bury Bobby. Oakmont was a very beautiful and peaceful place nestled high in the Lafayette hills. Views of Mt. Diablo and the surrounding valleys were usually spectacular from here. Today, the view was totally hidden by a dreary-gray overcast sky blotting out everything in front of us.

In the Oakmont office building we were greeted by a very pleasant lady who showed us into a private office and introduced us

31

to the gentleman who would be assisting us. He showed us a map and talked about the various "gardens" available. As he talked about each garden by name, one stood out to my daughter-in-law and me: "The Garden of Meditation" at the top of the hill *felt* like the right one for Bobby. The gentleman showed us a gridded map marked with lot designations—G-1, G-2, and so on. I was waiting for that special internal feeling I'd been getting when something clicked as the right thing. Sometimes a chill, with or without goosebumps, would clue me into my next move.

"It'd be nice to be near the paved road so if it's pouring rain, we could sit quietly in a car and be near Bobby," I said. "What's the number on this block of empty spaces?"

"This is section 8S/9B. B-lots: B-1, B-2, B-3, and so forth," came the reply.

"B-3, that feels like the one. Bobby was Bruno son number three." I looked at Kathleen.

"Can we see it?" she asked. We were driven up to view B-3. We could scarcely see twenty feet in front of us. Our Oakmont guide told us all about the view from the "Garden of Meditation."

"On a sunny day, you have a clear view of Mt. Diablo straight ahead, and to your left you can see Concord, Buchanan Field, and the Sacramento River." His words confirmed B-3 as the final resting place for Bobby's body. Buchanan Field was where Bobby took his first flying lesson on the very day he was legally old enough to do it. Kathleen nodded her vote of agreement.

"Oakmont seems to be in a flight path or something. Airplanes of all descriptions and sizes fly directly overhead," he continued. As if we needed a clincher!

Yes, Oakmont, "The Garden of Meditation," and B-3 were definitely our choices.

The Sun Valley Shopping Center was our third stop. A busy crowd of people all around us were continuing business as usual today, but for us the everyday routines had altered greatly. We had come to buy some new clothes for Bobby, and they, too, "picked themselves": brown pants and socks and a soft ivory-and brown velour shirt that felt cuddly and warm to the touch. We dropped them off at the Bryant Funeral Chapel and hurried home to meet Dr. Richard Wing.

Dr. "Wing" (the perfect name for the minister who would be spokesman for the family) was from the First Christian Church of Concord. He wanted to come over to the house and casually "hang out" with us awhile to gain his own sense of who Bobby was, his personality, and our family situation. Visiting with us informally would assist him in writing the most appropriate tribute for Bobby.

At Dr. Wing's suggestion, I made myself comfortable sitting cross-legged on the floor. It felt good to be sitting on the floor, hovered about the "roundtable," with a man of the cloth.

Dr. Wing asked what we wanted Bobby's life and death to represent. After talking with me a bit, he began to get a sense of what the funeral service message would be about, and he laid the framework for integrating it all.

The momentum was picking up, everything was coming together. I would write and deliver the eulogy. I didn't question the whys or hows of it; I "knew" what I was meant to do. Dick Workman's eulogy had paved the way. Bobby's eulogy would be easy—a "labor of love."

I gathered everyone in my bedroom for a family meeting. Laura arrived first in a deep state of disbelief and grief. She hadn't gone to Mt. Shasta with us and was feeling a bit left out. While we were awaiting the helicopter that brought Bobby down off the mountain, Laura had been at Oakmont Cemetery, attending the funeral of her dear friend, twenty-three-year-old Kathy Mooney. Kathy had died in an auto accident in the Sierras. After the funeral, Laura came home to receive the news that her own brother had not survived the plane crash.

"What's going on here," she cried as the news was broken to her. "The whole family seems to be falling apart. I've buried too many friends lately—and then, Kathy—and now, my own brother. I can't handle anymore!" Though she was present in her body, her heart and mind were still in a state of shock and numbness.

When everyone had assembled, I told them, "We have some things to discuss and plan for Wednesday's funeral service. First, we need to order our flowers."

"All I want is a single red rose on the casket," Kathleen said immediately.

The kids wanted a large, brilliantly colored wreath of mixed flowers with a banner that said, "Beloved Brother." I chose a large heart of white mums, severed obliquely by a band of red roses. The piece, called "Bleeding Heart," would have a banner saying, "Beloved Son."

We then went on to discuss the service. "I want to capture all sides of Bobby in the eulogy and I need each of your feelings and words to do it," I said. "I've been to funerals that weren't very personalized and always felt a bit ripped off when the eulogy didn't connect me with the life essence of that person. Let's keep going around in a circle, one by one, and toss out a memory or two, or any special feelings or things we want to say to or share about Bobby."

My children caught on fast as memories of times and places past with Bobby surfaced. We cried. We laughed. I picked up my pen and steno pad and found that the eulogy was writing itself effortlessly as I jotted down their phrases.

We finally came to the end of a very long day. We'd accomplished much. It was nearing 1:00 AM and Kathleen and I were in my bathroom talking, going over the events of the day.

"Wish we had a way to know when Bobby's body is 'home.' Wonder what time the limo will arrive from Mt. Shasta?" Kathleen asked.

"It sure would be nice to know, wouldn't it? I'll sleep better when I know he's near us, too," I said. "Too bad we didn't ask someone to call us when he arrives."

Moments later, as we were standing in my bathroom, the overhead lights quivered and trembled for about seven seconds. Someone or something was interfering with the electrical current. At the very same instant, the bathroom telephone echoed the flickering; it rang weakly with the same vibratory quiver and tremble. How could we explain it? We knew Bobby had safely arrived at the Bryant and Lough Chapel in Concord. We'd just been officially notified from some higher source.

*   *   *

Bill Orlich came by on his way to work early the next morning. It was Tuesday and the final copy for the memorial announcement needed to be proofread. Bill had done a beautiful job pasting up the layout for us. What needed saying had been said. The announcements would be printed, folded, and ready for mailing by early afternoon.

Another message came from Judy Boshart: a Faxgram from Paris arrived at Dr. Tolleth's office addressed to me. Robin, our secretary, called and read it to me over the phone. Judy had called her Palo Alto offices and had been told of Bobby' death. Her message said:

Dear Shirley,

    I lit a candle at Notre Dame in Paris for Bobby, you, and Kim. My thoughts are with you.

Love,

Judy

Well, Bobby, I thought, your soul must be doing okay. Prayers from some mighty high places are being said for you all over the world. You've got to be feeling the love we are all beaming to you.

Kim came into my bedroom just as the phone rang again. The only word she heard was my horrified, "What?"

It was Helyn Bryant who had called to tell me, "The funeral will have to be a 'closed casket.' Bobby's body arrived around 1:00 AM. After so much lapsed time, embalming is impossible." Helyn had determined that when she went to prepare him for this evening's viewing. She told me we could pick up the clothes we had brought for Bobby at a later time.

Kathleen had been keenly attuned to the unfolding conversation. "Please ask Helyn to make sure Bobby's wedding ring is on his finger. Lay his clothes in the casket beside him, anyway," she requested.

We asked no more questions. The answers might have been too painful to bear.

I decided to get the yellow ribbon that had been tied to my purse strap throughout the search and put it in the casket, too. I looked up to the mantel over my bedroom fireplace where a crystal-winged "Jonathan Livingston Seagull" figurine soared above a piece of driftwood from Monterey Bay. I picked it up and tied the yellow ribbon around the wire that connected the driftwood with the graceful crystal sculpture. I sat it on a mirrored tray belonging to my roommate, LaRena Maines.

It felt good to have a gift to leave in the casket for Bobby. It occurred to me that the rest of the family might like to think of something that had special meaning for them.

The idea proved to be great. The kids took to it like ducks to water. Our creative energy brought a busy "hustle-bustle" sound to my bedroom as "gifts" were created and placed on the mirrored tray. It was touching listening to each person speak from the heart about how his or her relationship with Bobby was signified by the "gift." The tray now held:

KATHLEEN: A hollow eggshell on which she had sketched Mt. Shasta and inscribed the message: "Please wait for me, Honey."

KIM: The scotty dog (Bobby's favorite piece) from the family Monopoly set. A tear fell beside it as she placed it on the highly polished mirror tray.

GREG: His guitar pick, a memento of their guitarplaying days, said a lot. He bit his lower lip as he placed it next to the scotty dog.

STEVE: A perfect miniature of Bobby's airplane made out of modeling clay. The tiny clay pilot with the "red-baron-style" flying scarf around his neck represented Bobby.

LAURA: A Hershey kiss tied in delicate netting decorated with hearts (her favor from Bobby and Kathleen's wedding), a jade box with a miniature lucky penny, and a seashell and a polished piece of green rock from a beach-combing trip.

GRANDPA FERRERO: A pair of Civil Air Patrol pilot wings and his Civil Air Patrol Captain's bar.

GRANDMA FERRERO: A heart locket with Air Force Wings that Grandpa Ferrero had given her at the end of World War II.

COUSIN KELLY: A folded note she had signed, "Love from 'Bum-Bum-Bumblebee'."

I added a small wooden airplane with a message on its side: "Bobby's Jet to Heaven." A smiley-face was drawn across its nose.

36

"Love Tokens"

Next to it lay *Messages from Michael*, the book I had inscribed to Bobby for Christmas in 1980. We invited other members of the family and close friends to participate in the "table of love." As I gazed sentimentally at the assembled gifts I realized they were all love tokens for Bobby's last flight—the one to Heaven.

"If anyone ever opens the casket, they'll probably laugh at all the junk we've put in," Steve commented, lightening things up. But the "junk" was very special to each of us and that was all that mattered today. I asked the kids to transport the "table of gifts" to Bryant and Lough Chapel and place it in front of the casket.

The doorbell rang again. It was Patricia O'Connor bringing by a steaming casserole. She told us to be sure and eat it soon. "It tastes so much better hot!" she added.

The doorbell rang yet again. This time it was my friend George Nelson, with a seven-course meal he'd lovingly prepared himself. I hugged him as I laid out the mini-banquet and called to the kids upstairs. "Chow time, come and get it while it's hot."

George confirmed the plans and the music we wanted him to play at the service. He also planned to tape record the funeral service for us.

"I think we've done this number before, George," I said. There was an affirmative nod as he smiled through closed lips, remembering—he'd been a godsend at Dick Workman's memorial service.

George Olbur, Kathleen's father, was given the seemingly impossible task of having a black-and-white photograph of Bobby from Kathleen's wallet blown up. It needed to be made into a glossy 8 x 10 we could frame and set on top of the casket. Time was getting short and we needed an "instant" photography miracle on this one. We got it!

Robin Burchett delivered the sign that was to sit beside Bobby's photograph. She'd done a great job! It read:

> He came into the world naked
> and he leaves swathed only
> in our love and prayers

All day the house was like Grand Central Station—a symphony of busy activities and doorbells announcing deliveries and many conversations that kept the telephone lines at our house humming. The kids were looking through their clothes, choosing what they would wear for the funeral tomorrow. Kathleen had definitely decided *not* to wear black. She finally chose one of Bobby's favorites: a silky navy blue-and-white polka-dotted dress. My teal blue silk dress felt like the best choice for me; after all, was there a proper funeral dress code? Who cares! It was our funeral and if Bobby's favorite color had been red, I might have chosen my red wool dress instead of this one.

Greg and Steve were talking with Steve Higgins, their stepbrothers Rob and Dave Ruiz, and cousin Robert Ferrero about the most appropriate attire for pallbearers. "Who has a navy tie I can borrow?" Steve yelled from across the hall.

In the late afternoon Bill Orlich came by to deliver the finished memorial announcements. Once again, I felt like I'd played the scenes from this movie before: Bill had also been the one to burn the midnight oil to get Dick Workman's memorial announcement into the mail three months ago. As I held the finished announcement card in my hand, I was deeply moved with gratitude for all the people who had contributed their ideas, skills, and love to pulling it together.

I had asked Steve to check with his Dad, Rick Bruno, to see if he wanted to sing "The Lord's Prayer" at Bobby's funeral service. Steve thought he'd really like to sing it along with his Dad. Rick returned the call saying he had a young friend who had offered to play a guitar solo. We all agreed that it would fit into the tribute beautifully, along with the taped music Kim was picking out.

Rick went on to tell us, "I'd like to...but, really, I just can't do it." He choked up when talking about singing at his son's funeral.

My mind flashed back to a late August day in 1955. I was nine months pregnant and attending the funeral of my generous and loving father-in-law, Frank Bruno. He was such a beautiful human being. He would have given you the shirt off his back. A relative, Dr. Cyril Bruno, sat beside me with his fingers on my pulse, telling me to breathe deeply. The sound of my husband Rick's clear, powerful baritone voice resonated throughout the whole chapel that day. It was taking a lot for him to sing his father's favorite song, "The Lord's Prayer." Rick's soul was demanding he give his very best in this final tribute to his dad and he came through with flying colors.

I had gone into labor as I left the funeral chapel and was taken to nearby Kaiser Hospital in Walnut Creek. It was false labor—my child was not yet ready to be born. Two weeks later, Robert Frank Bruno made his glorious entrance into the world—all nine pounds, four ounces of him. Now, it was time for the body of this child of twenty-five years, four months, and fourteen days to be laid to rest. I could certainly feel empathy with and understand Rick's pain as he declined to sing at his youngest son's funeral.

After receiving this news, Kim sat thinking pensively, then jumped up saying, "Steve and I will do it. It feels so right!"

I could sense their love for Bobby pulling at them, calling them to stretch and give of their talents selflessly. It didn't matter that they'd never sung it before—and they only had about an hour to find the sheet music and practice *a cappella*. They were unsure of how the timing, words, and music would blend with their voices and emotions but their determination soared above their mental reasoning—they would rise to the occasion.

Finally it was 6:00 PM and time to go to the Bryant and Lough Chapel. Bobby was available for "visiting." Nothing in this world can adequately prepare you for walking up to your own child's casket. My knees felt like they were going to buckle underneath me. The fragrance of gardenias overpowered the delicate scent of the roses and other flowers lining the sanctuary walls and surrounding the casket. I stopped to catch my balance and breath as the handsome oak resting place for Bobby came into sight.

From atop the casket, his picture radiated back to me a "knowing" smile of strength and courage. Robin's sign stood next to it. A single long-stemmed red rose lay beside the draped red, white, and blue flag that honored Bobby's "veteran" status. In front of the casket stood the little black oriental table, holding our mementos of love. Susan Workman had added her letter to the tray of gifts. Helyn Bryant had skillfully cared for every detail. The memorial announcements were on a table next to the Hunger Project donation cards. A beautiful hand-lettered placard sat next to them. It said:

Robert Frank Bruno

THE FAMILY OF
ROBERT F. BRUNO
REQUESTS THAT DONATIONS IN HIS MEMORY
BE MADE TO
THE HUNGER PROJECT.
HIS DEATH, AS HIS LIFE,
IS A CONTRIBUTION TO ALL HUMANITY.

I looked up and saw the "Beloved Son" banner on the "Bleeding Heart" floral piece at the head of the casket. A sob found its way up from my heart, through my throat, and out into the heavy stillness of the evening.

A familiar face came towards me—Ed Ruiz, my brother-in-law. We held each other in a long trembling hug. This must be a very difficult moment for him, too, I thought. A picture of a tiny angelic infant in a casket flashed across my mind. He and his wife Martie had stood in this very room eighteen years ago. A crib death had claimed the life of three-month-old Edward (Pee Wee) Ruiz III.

My brother- and sister-in-law, Manuel and Cathy Gonzales, planned to come to the Chapel the next day. They too, had been here to bury a son. A train accident had taken the life of twenty-three-year-old David Gonzales. It was unbelievable that three sisters-in-law had come to this same funeral chapel room—each of us to bury a son. How unfair and strange the Master Weaver's pattern of life can look when perceived only through the earthly, physical point of view.

I thought of the next day and wondered how I was going to make it through. The wheels of time and circumstance were already set in motion. There was nothing left for me to do now but pray for strength to transcend my sorrow long enough to deliver Bobby's eulogy.

The Service

*And ever has it been that love knows not
its own depth until the hour of separation.*

—Kahlil Gibran, **The Prophet**

The long, shiny limousine called for us at precisely 12:15 PM. We made our way slowly through heavy drizzling rain. Would it ever stop? Arriving at the funeral chapel, we were ushered to the special section reserved for the family. I could count my heartbeats as they echoed loudly throughout my whole body.

Stay focused, Shirley, I kept repeating quietly to myself. This funeral service is meant to be a meaningful and inspiring celebration of Bobby's life.

I could hear people clearing their throats. I sat staring at the podium I would soon be speaking from and felt a momentary faintness pass through me. Intermittent sounds of weeping blended with the soft organ background music.

I looked over at Bobby's casket. The whole front of the chapel was a tapestry of floral arrangements. The grief I felt was the most painful feeling I've ever experienced. I prayed inwardly, repeating, God, give me the strength and courage to do what I know I have to do.

I did not attend a church regularly and had no structured conventional religious affiliations or ties. At least, that's what I thought. Now, somehow, I just *knew* there was a God and I didn't need to go through anyone else to talk with Him. He was working through me directly, filling me with His inspiration and strength. "Please don't leave me now," I whispered.

The voice of Dr. Richard Wing filled the chapel.

"On behalf of the family of Robert Bruno, I would like to thank you for your presence here today.

"I see there are three reasons for our being here today. First, we have come to create a memorial to the life of someone whose life intersected with yours in many ways. I would venture to say that your life is distinctly different because of the way you knew Robert. We come to create a memorial to his life, and I'm sure we will fail at that. There will be nothing said here that will be good enough. There is nothing we could carve in stone, nothing we could say with stained glass windows that would really say what we want to say. The greatest memorial we ever leave a person is not the kind we put on plaques or design into windows, but the kind that is left in the hearts of those who knew and loved that person.

"Secondly, we have come here to be together. I can't speak for your experience; but in my own life, when someone close was suddenly not there any longer, we found that it was better for us to be together than to be alone.

"Thirdly, we come to find strength from God and from sources that have always been there but perhaps not always tapped by us. The greatest religious writing was done at the moment that a good person experienced a bad tragedy that could not be explained. "Robert F. Bruno was born in Walnut Creek on September 8, 1955. At his passing, he was twenty-five years of age. He was a member of the Civil Air Patrol. He is survived by his wife, Kathleen Bruno; his mother, Shirley Ruiz; his father, Richard Bruno; brothers, Gregory and Steven Bruno; sisters, Kimberly and Laura Ruiz; by his grandparents, Teresa and Lou Ferrero, Mary Edwards, and Ethel Hawkins; and by his great-grandmother, Cleo Meisenbach.

"At this time I would like to ask Shirley, Robert's mother, to come forward to share with you in this momemt."

I steadied myself as I slowly walked to the podium and adjusted the microphone height. I raised my eyes and looked out upon a full house. People were standing in the back of the room and overflowing into the corridors beyond where I could clearly see them. I scanned the sea of faces, lingering a second here and there. Relatives, old neighbors, old friends, pilots, doctors, nurses, new friends, the very elderly, and the very young had come from far and near this stormy January day to pay their respects. It was wall-to-wall empathy, love, and support that I could feel in every bone and cell of my body. My heart was racing and a huge lump of emotion rose and stuck in my throat. I tried to clear it. Please, God, please, I silently prayed. A warm, powerful, physical energy suddenly swept through me, more powerful than anything I'd ever known. The only description that came to mind was the Holy Spirit.

I took a deep breath, hearing the shakiness in my voice as I began.

"Kathleen, Rick, Greg, Steve, Kim, Laura, the whole family, and I thank you for being here with us.

"There is a poem called 'Bring Me Men to Match My Mountains.' Bobby was one of those rare kind of men. One had to search far and wide to find a person who had an unkind thing to say about him. He was a good, kind, loving human being. The family and I have sat around these past evenings remembering and sharing our deep love for Bobby. We'd like to share some of our memories with you.

"Bobby, at birth, seemed born with a peaceful old soul. As his parents—Rick, Daddy Bob, and I—if we had to judge parenthood by the time spent with Bobby, parenthood was a snap, no effort or hassle whatsoever. Pure love, pure joy!

"To Rick, Bobby was a son to give his love to and talk with and go fishing with.

"To Daddy Bob, his stepfather, he was someone to share exploring with, like trips to the Nortonville mines; and, to share his love of contact sports with. They loved playing 'King of the Hill.'

"To Greg, a brother to just hang out with, talking for hours. They loved strumming their guitars together.

"To Steve, a brother and best friend who shared a great love of creating things—small miniatures out of modeling clay—and filming homemade animated movies, a frame at a time.

"To Kim, Brother Bobby was an 'old soulmate.' He was stuffed animals and tons of brotherly love.

"To Laura, he was 'big brother,' lovingly leading and advising his little baby sister.

"To his grandparents, he was someone to be proud of and brag about. Especially to Grandpa Ferrero, who took Bobby for his first airplane ride and shared Bobby's great love of flying."

The quiver in my voice intensified. I could feel my Dad's pain as I heard him try to stifle the sounds of grief wanting to escape from his throat.

"To his stepbrothers, Robby and David, it was weekend jam sessions when the song 'Black Magic Woman' vibrated the whole house.

"To Cousins Kelly and Robert, it was Dillon Beach, sand dunes, sea shells, and running along the beach singing the 'BumBum-Bumble Bee Tuna' song.

"To his family and friends, he was all these things—a true friend, easy going, quietly loyal, and loving.

"For Kathleen, his wife, for whom he had a deep, deep love, he was a tender, loving husband. He was her best friend and wanted nothing more than to make her happy. Sharing skiing, flying, drawing pictures, and the poems and music they wrote together. They shared many cans of their favorite drink, TAB, in their years together.

"And to me, his mother, Bobby was a most loving, devoted, and inspiring son. Two weeks ago, his last words to me were 'Mom, I don't exactly know what our destinies are. I only know that you are a guiding ray of light for me.'

"Fate and time have reversed our roles. He is now a ray of guiding light for us.

"Bobby loved peanut butter and Karo syrup on his pancakes. He loved skiing with Kathleen at Kirkwood Meadows, staying with his Grandma Hawkins as she filled him with her huge hot dinners, strumming his twelve-string guitar, teaching Kathleen to play 'A Crazy Little Thing Called Love,' passing the family signal, 'Beep-beep-a-deep' which resulted in Kim, Laura, Greg, and Steve quickly piling on Daddy Bob to rescue me in a rambunctious and loving family wrestling match. He and Kathleen had a special whistling code with each other, used to signal when one of them came home.

"He loved the rock group Foghat and was forming a rock group of his own. He loved the earthy color brown and the clear blue color of the sky. He loved racing off to the beach with Kathleen to catch sunsets in Carmel, and at La Jolla, he loved jogging along the coastal sands. He loved his sister Laura's dill dip and playing Monopoly into the wee small hours with his family, awaiting Christmas morning. He chose the scotty dog as his marker, and many laughs were shared this past Christmas as he mockingly lifted his scotty dog's leg and 'pottied' on his brother's hotel when he landed on it. He was always helpful and available to Betty and George, his beloved in-laws, to run an errand or help them with whatever they needed to have done.

"He loved his mom's pumpkin pies, Kathleen's Japanese noodles, taking leftovers from 'Jack-in-the-Box' to feed to Ringo, the family dog.

"He liked pinching Frosty the cat's little white chin going 'Woooo!'

"Bobby's first real toy as a little boy was an airplane and he never swayed from his 'When I grow up, I'm going to be a pilot' dream.

"We are all comforted by the knowledge that if his young life of twenty-five years had to end at all, it ended doing what he loved doing most—flying!

"A majestic snow-covered mountain will stand forever as a monument to Bobby's quiet strength, his goodness, and his gentle, deep love for Kathleen, his family, and the well-being of his friends and all mankind in general.

"This glorious mountaintop cradled Bobby's body in the hollows of its peak as Bobby spent his last moment in his earthbound body. He is free now and at peace.

"He would want to have not died in vain. We, his family, have each looked deeply into our own lives and we are reaching farther than we have ever reached before to have our lives be about contributing to others, each in our own unique way. We ask you to do the same. We are all truly one, like continents connected deeply beneath the sea that hides the connection. Sometimes, people have to die before we get in touch with our great love for one another. Please join us in erasing any separateness that might exist in your life today. Reach out to those you love and express your love fully, *now*.

"Bobby's casket is closed today, leaving each of us with our own personal 'memory bank' of him.

"Please feel free to join the family at the home of my brother Bob and his wife Mae in Orinda. We invite you to come hang out with us; laugh, cry, and love with us.

"Thank you for being here and God bless you."

My voice started to break as I finished delivering the eulogy. I silently thanked God for giving me the strength to get through it as Dr. Wing walked back up to the podium.

"Shirley, I want to express appreciation on behalf of everyone here for your rare act of courage. Thank you."

Dr. Wing stepped down from the podium.

Kim kissed my cheek and whispered in my ear as she got up to sing, "I know Bobby is here watching us and he's smiling right now. I'll just look at his picture whenever I need a little strength."

My heart filled with parental pride and love as Kim and Steve approached and stood in front of the flag-draped casket. Kim picked up the microphone in her right hand and placed her left hand in Steve's. They squeezed hands as they both looked at Bobby's picture beside them. I could hear the strength come into Kim's normally soft voice as she began blending it with the clear powerful voice of her brother. Tears came to my eyes as their voices crescendoed into "for thine is the kingdom and the power and the glory, forever, amen."

As I looked at my family around me, there wasn't a dry eye amongst us.

Oh, the pain to lose a loved one so precious! Oh, the joy and privilege to have known a loved one that precious to lose.

The sound of a soft guitar lovingly flooded the chapel with a musical tribute to Bobby. As the guitar solo faded out, a very familiar taped voice faded in. Barbra Streisand was singing the closing memorial song from the movie "A Star is Born." The pertinent eulogy message, which asked if the departed was watching us now, drifted through our emotions. You could feel the upbeat pulsation of its finale lifting the overflowing chapel to new energy levels.

The whole family had previously chosen to form a "receiving line" in the hallway at the end of the funeral services. Parents, brothers, sisters, grandparents, and great-grandmother stood to personally greet and hug every single person who had come out this

48

stormy day to be with us. We didn't want to miss connecting with anyone. The reunions were a warm, blending round of tears and hugs.

The last mourner left, leaving just the family remaining in the room. It was time for us to have our last moments with Bobby's physical body. We held hands and formed a circle around the casket. For a few precious moments, silent prayers were said. Then, one by one, we each walked up for our moment alone with Bobby. It was a private interval in time for each of us. A time to put both hands on the casket and have a silent talk with Bobby and with God. We each were making a commitment to live life more lovingly and more fully, to somehow find a way to have Bobby's death and our lives be about love and serving others, each in our own unique way.

The pallbearers—Greg and Steve Bruno, Rob and Dave Ruiz, Steve Higgins, and young Robert Ferrero—gathered around Bobby. The meaning and the weight of the moment showed in each face as they lifted the casket tenderly into the waiting hearse. The American flag could be seen through the rear window as the hearse led the long procession of cars on its journey to Oakmont Memorial Park in the Lafayette hills. The rain did not let up one iota and was gaining an angry intensity as we climbed the long winding driveway to the "Garden of Meditation." The kids and I joined hands for strength and comfort as the gravesite with its protective awning and rows of chairs came into view.

We huddled closely together under the semi-opaque white awning. The rest of the procession of mourners were arriving and parking their cars. I turned around to see a huge roof of multi-colored umbrellas attempting to hold the stormy sky at bay. The words of prayer and blessing by Dr. Wing could be heard swirling and drifting into the soggy gray ambience of the day.

Six pallbearers laid their red carnations on the casket. The pounding sounds of rain and sobbing formed a weird duet of somber funeral music. The American flag was folded and presented to Kathleen.

Suzanne Ruiz hugged me and handed me a brilliant bouquet of yellow daffodils, a stark contrast to the blackish-gray of this wintry afternoon. My boss, Dr. Tolleth, came over and gave me a long trembling hug and slipped a note into my hand. I tucked it away to read at a more appropriate time. I knew it was time for the "tower of strength" in me to give way to the part of me that needed to grieve. All the way down from the depths of my womb an animal-like sobbing began.

Wet, I was soaking wet, with my tears and nature's tears. Inside and out, they were flooding me, trying to wash away the pain and deep grief. The saying, "Love knows not its own depth till the hour of separation," had taken on a new level of meaning.

* * *

After the funeral it was time to lighten up. If there's anything Bobby would have liked it would have been to watch us celebrate the love we have for one another. That was easy to do as we gathered at my brother's hilltop Orinda home. So many special people came to visit.

"Has it really been that long a time since we've seen each other?" was a familiar phrase. I was so glad to see my eighty-seven-year-old "Nana," Cleo Meisenbach. She still had that special sparkle in her eyes every time there was a chance for us to spend a little time together. Today was no exception.

Bob and Mae had done an outstanding job in turning their beautiful home into a reunion palace. Food and hot drinks were mighty welcome to our chilled bodies. Aunts, uncles, nephews, nieces, high school classmates, beach friends, and pilot buddies mingled into a house-full of people, basking in the warmth of love and reunion.

Gradually laughter began to trickle into the gathering. Soft at first, then more freely expressed as the photograph albums Kim had put together Monday night were passed around. They were triggering memories of crew-cut kids, Merry Christmases, adventure trips, first days of school, and "clowning around" times spent barbecuing and playing around in the family swimming pool.

Laura came over and gave me a big hug. She told me she'd gone back to the gravesite to rescue some of the red roses from the "Bleeding Heart" floral piece. "I knew you would want to save them, Mom, so I'll preserve them for you. Don't worry, the deer still have plenty of flowers left to eat at the cemetery tonight."

I noticed how very "alive" I felt in the depth of my grief and in the heights of my joy. Often times lately, both are present in the very same instant of time.

Shock

On my calendar I'd written one or two words that best described my feelings for each day. The day of the funeral, I wrote the word 'finality.' 'Emptiness' was written besides today's date. The funeral was over and the pace of my life had come to an almost abrupt standstill. All day I'd been writing personal notes on the remaining memorial announcements. My index finger ached where my thumbnail had cut into it. I stopped and shook out my fingers like floppy thermometers, rubbed the stiff places in my neck and leaned over and let my body go limp like a rag doll.

My body was feeling disconnected. Emptiness echoed through the cells of my being. I felt I was being drawn through a vacuum of nothingness. Did I matter? Did life matter? Did anything matter anymore? Help, God, help! I screamed from within.

Mechanically, I picked up the phone in my bathroom and found myself dialing Susan Workman's number.

"Sue, I can't explain...," I heard myself saying "I need you over here right now." I hung up and dialed another familiar number, Bill Orlich's.

"I don't know exactly why, Bill, but I need you to come over right now."

Neither of them questioned why I needed them. Both of them lived only a few blocks away and arrived simultaneously.

God, what have I called them over for? I wondered. What is this part of me that knows what it must do and does it? It seemed separate and different from the intellectual mechanisms I was accustomed to using for decision-making. This new force operating in me was sure and spontaneous, bypassing the arguments my mind may have wanted to toy with. Too much intellectualism seemed to "kill" or still the intuitive flow I had been plugged into since Bobby's death. My perceptions wanted to take shape spontaneously, ignoring rigid structures. They wanted to flow like a fluid river of inspiration. When I tried to analyze it all, my thoughts seemed limiting, leaving no room for the expansion of consciousness calling to me.

"I'm not sure what I am going to go through; only sure that I need to go through it and I want you two to be with me," I thanked Susan and Bill for coming.

"Please, don't disrupt the process. No matter what it looks like to you, stay with me through it," I requested.

Why had I so instinctively called for Susan and Bill to be with me? They both had tremendous compassion, love, and warmth that could be communicated to me through the heat of their healing hands, I thought. Hmmm...

I asked them to come into my copper-colored bathroom. The foil wallpaper seemed to intensify and reflect the heat of the infrared lamp. It felt especially delicious and welcome tonight. I was tired and cold to the bone.

I laid down on the thick rust-colored carpet. Like going into labor for the birth of a child, my body *knew* what it must do. Susan laid her warm hands on my upper torso, while Bill put his hands on my ankles. I realized I was about to fully experience something very meaningful. I began to tremble. Chills shook and jarred my whole body. My teeth began chattering beyond control. The chilling process continued while my body temperature felt colder and colder. The violent shaking increased. My mind drifted off...

Suddenly, I became aware that my point of perception was somewhere outside my physical body. I was above and to the right of my body laying below me on the floor. My sense of awareness was very clear and focused. Though no words were spoken or heard, I knew I was at a point of "choice" again. This time it was whether to leave or re-enter my physical body. The moment seemed to hover, floating in eternity. Then, like a flash of lightning, I knew that I had chosen to return.

I felt my body flood with warm and life-vitalizing energy as I stretched, wiggled my fingertips, and opened my eyes. I sat up and pondered what had happened. The following verse flashed in my mind:

> My soul watched the process;
> My physical body was in it.
> The struggle to surrender
> —And to choose.

Though my body had gone into shock, another part of me was clearly the observer of the whole process.

I hugged and thanked Bill and Susan for feeding their warmth into my body, explaining as best I could, the shock I'd experienced.

"I'm fine now; just need some sleep," I said, as I walked them to the door. "Good night, thanks again."

Alone once more, thoughts came rapidly. What was happening? Everything I had ever built my reality on was being shaken, opening me up to look at life through new eyes. A personal volcano was erupting deep inside of me, sending all my lifelong values and belief systems spilling out into the night like a fiery lava flow.

What was real anymore? I wondered. At times, I felt I was living on two different levels of reality simultaneously. Is this what happens to people when they crack up?

It seemed as though I couldn't fully comprehend a lot of things lately. I decided to scribble down some notes about what had happened to reflect upon at a later time when it all might make more sense.

How interesting, I thought as I stared out my bedroom windows at the twinkling lights of Walnut Creek, I had a choice whether to come back or not. It could be that people certainly do sometimes die when they're in shock. I wondered, does everyone have moments of choice at different times in their lives? Do we always remember them consciously? Why did I chose to come back? There must be a reason.

It had felt so good to be *a point of view*, drifting peacefully in space. That must be what Bobby is experiencing right now: a point of view drifting peacefully in space.

My bed welcomed my exhausted body as I laid down and pulled my favorite afghan around me, snuggling my nose into it to catch its newly laundered scent. In the silence of the night, I noticed an electric-like energy current dancing in my fingertips and throughout my whole body.

Wow, I thought, I'm plugged in. Go to sleep Shirley, go to sleep. Tomorrow is soon enough for any more thinking.

Back to the Everyday World of Nine to Six

the layers I have put
around the pain of
your going are thin.
I walk softly through
life, adding thickness
each day.
a thought or a feeling
of you cracks the surface.

—How to Survive the Loss of a Love

My clock radio went off; its whining alarm reminded me of a gendarme's patrol wagon from a World War II movie. It's sing-song, high-low, high-low, high-low tones matched the alternating message it was broadcasting. It was 6:00 AM, time to get ready for my first day back at the office, to the world of business and routines.

55

It would help if I could stay in this hot shower for an hour or two more, I thought. Early mornings in my warm cozy bathroom are luxurious "me" time. My mind usually flows in peaceful thought as I mechanically dry and set my hair in hot rollers. I almost smiled looking at the unmade face in the mirror.

"You again," I said out loud. "It's time to put on your colorful facepaint and go out in the world and do your thing one more time." Some days were easier than others: some days, there was a radiant glow on the face in the mirror; some days, like this one, makeup was the mask I wore until I could get the flow going and the radiance could shine from within once again.

Today seemed like a "let's pretend we're doing okay" day. I decided to put myself together and just take it one thing at a time.

Ten days had passed since the fateful phone call. Even though it was a hurting time, deep inside me there was a sense of a new strength, too. Not particularly a "hold-it-together" brand, but the kind of strength that comes from having stood a test, weathered it, and grown.

I reflected on the past four days since Bobby's funeral. There had been time to spend a couple of hours with my daughter-in-law, Darsie. She'd stayed quietly to the side and maintained a low profile during the funeral. Well, "high" profile might be a better description; Darsie was four months pregnant. Yippee, come July, she and Steve would present me with my very first grandchild. Appropriately, the baby would carry the middle name of Bobby or Bobbi.

Darsie and I had visited only briefly the one time we'd met six months ago. Greg and I had flown to Mannassas, Virginia, for Steve and Darsie's wedding. My new daughter-in-law looked very beautiful in her ivory-white dress. It set off her laughing green eyes and gorgeous red hair. At the end of the wedding ceremony, Steve took Darsie's hands in his and in front of the whole congregation serenaded her with a song that implored her not to change just to please him; he liked her just the way she was. Few knew of Steve's plan. Darsie was as surprised and pleased as the rest of us. Tears slipped down her cheeks and onto her gown. She wasn't the only one with wet eyes. Half a church full of people were dabbing at their cheeks.

Getting to know her better was very special. I discovered Darsie loved writing and was doing some stories for small children. It was nice to hear how lovingly my expected grandchild was going to be raised.

After the funeral, Greg and I decided Steve and Darsie had to see Carmel before they returned to Washington, D.C. This was Darsie's first trip to California and we had to do it up right. Viewing the turquoise Pacific from Carmel would be a special treat for her and for us, too.

Once there, I watched Steve and Greg run, tumble, and tackle each other on the mounds of white sandy beach. It was just like old times when my three boys were growing up. As I watched them rough-housing—a playful punching jab here and there—I felt a sharp painful twinge as the realization hit me. Bobby would never play with them in this physical form again.

My thoughts drifted to an evening after the funeral when we had gathered to watch home movies. My stepson David, his wife Cathy, three-year-old Tony, and two-and-a-half-month-old little Jamie joined us. Tony called me "Grandma Shirley" and gave me a big hug. Cathy handed me Jamie. She looked so angelic as she slept. Just then the doorbell rang. It was Bob and Suzanne Ruiz. I had invited her in a moment of spontaneity. Now, I wondered if I had done the right thing. It might be uncomfortable for her to watch her husband's past life parade before her on a movie screen. Oh well, it was too late now. Who knew who was going to feel what tonight?

Greg, Steve, Kathleen, Kim, Laura, Darsie, my mom and dad, and the rest of our guests spread out around the room with big bowls of buttered popcorn. I looked at little Jamie as she slept in my arms and hugged her closer to me. Jamie and I would watch the movies "heart-to-heart."

Reel after reel of living, laughing, and loving flashed across the screen. First we viewed a comic movie Bobby, Kathleen, and Steve had made. The special timing effects on our camera had produced something reminiscent of the Keystone Cops era. We watched lots of "first day of school" sequences with the school bus stopping on Olive Drive to pick up five freshly scrubbed shiny little kids. Scenes from Christmases witnessed the growing up of a family as sleepy tousle-headed kids opened presents and waded through mountains of ripped paper and ribbons. Robby and David were in many of them. Our five boys were crew-cut devils sometimes; crew-cut angels other times. There were also films of Bob and I on a belated honeymoon in Hawaii.

57

We laughed as we watched the digging of the gigantic backyard hole that was to become our family oasis. Reel by reel, the cement was poured, the pool was tiled and plastered. The big day came. Kim and Laura dove in when the pool was only three quarters full. They had waited patiently for five months and weren't waiting one second more. There were scenes of sunbathing, water fights, diving for colorful stones, and playing Marco Polo. Colorful beach towels draped the golden deck that surrounded the turquoise pool. Bodies were tanning beautifully and so was the turkey on the huge double-ovened barbecue pit.

Everything we were viewing on the movie screen was splendid, capturing all the good times we'd had in our years together as a family. My heart ached as the good times ended and the living room lights came back on. The loss cut deeply—Bobby, a husband, a family that had all gone on their separate paths for a new way of life. I glanced at the bouquet of roses on the table. We were like those roses in full bloom; the time had come for the petals to fall quietly to the floor.

Goodness! I glanced at my watch. I'd been sitting, thinking, fantasizing, and reminiscing for almost two hours. The notepad I always kept beside me during this early morning "me" time was filled with a mixture of today's "to dos" and sentences of fleeting thoughts I had jotted down. I completed dressing and headed off to work.

Back in my private office, it felt strange to sit in the chair where I had received that phone call on January 22nd. I glanced out my big picture window and gasped. My leaded-glass painting had fallen from the clear suction cup holding it to the window for viewing. I picked it up and stared at the Robert Browning saying painted on the flower-garden background. "All's right with the world" had fallen down. How symbolic!

I felt I was in the early stages of healing. Working in medicine and surgery for the past twenty years, I can attest to the fact that surgical wounds take a long time to completely heal. Plastic surgeons take "before and after" pictures to verify it. A closed wound with stitches removed didn't signal the end of healing. On the contrary, the softening of scars and the fading of redness from injured tissues took a year or longer.

Did I believe that now the funeral was over, that would be it for my deep emotional wound? Maybe to the world it looked liked that, but to one going through grief, the still waters of sorrow run deep.

I had a lot to learn. The gentle tugs at my heart would remind me, sometimes unexpectedly, of the fragility of the wound Bobby's death had made.

I opened my phone book. It fell to Bobby's address and telephone number. He doesn't live there anymore but I couldn't bear to remove him from my book—not yet. Again, I drifted into thoughts about the events of the past few days:

—Kathleen had started packing and storing Bobby's things. She brought me a handsome walnut-framed poem. Upon the ebony face of it, printed in gold, was the picture of an airplane and the poem, "High Flight."

—Film was developed, photos returned. Christmas. The last photos of Bobby. How precious they are!

—My sister-in-law, Mae Ferrero, called. She too, was feeling "tugs" of the heart. The check she'd sent Bobby for Christmas was in the bank statement that arrived in today's mail. She wanted to hang onto the endorsed check. The signature was a physical piece of Bobby she wanted to save.

—A friend called and in a cheery voice asked, "How have you and the kids been?" She hadn't heard yet.

—I looked at the Christmas present Kathleen and Bobby had given me: a book by Richard Dwyer, *The Sky's The Limit*. So many hidden and double meanings in everything.

—Bob Ruiz sent me a cassette tape with instructions to listen to the third song on the album. He heard it while choking back emotion when he found out that Bobby was dead. He strongly felt it was a message from Bobby, that he was okay. The song told of being in the rain, of keeping the world protected and making it through.

—A buddy of Bobby's returned Bobby's heavy jacket. Kathleen hugged it tightly, absorbing "the essence of Bobby" from it.

—Someone said, "You're lucky, at least you have four other children." What's lucky got to do with it, I wondered.

—The newspaper clippings from the Redding Searchlight

arrived. How strange to read about your own child in the headlines of a front page.

—Someone said, "Kathleen is lucky she and Bobby didn't have any children." How could she know how much Kathleen and I wish we had Bobby's child to hold?

—A telephone call on my answering machine from John Vanden, a member of Bobby's band, offered condolences. Bobby had spent his last night at a band rehearsal. It had been a good one. "He was an inspired musician, he'll be hard to replace," John said.

—Watching the movie *Resurrection*, I heard Ellen Burstyn speak the exact words I heard Kathleen utter when she hugged Bobby's jacket to catch a whiff of his essence.

—I watched Kathleen fondle, then play, Bobby's beloved twelve-string guitar. I could see the memories playing across her heart strings.

—I wanted to cling to anything that had ever been a part of Bobby—his ski sweater, his coffee cup, every card he had sent me. Kathleen handed me his pilot log books. Maybe I'd like to have them? Yes! The inventoried envelope of Bobby's personal belongings from the Sheriff's Office; would I like to keep them, too? Yes! I looked at the worn wallet. Its curvature fit the shape of Bobby's body. There was some money in the wallet. I tucked it safely away for the moment my heart would tell me *exactly* what the money should be spent on. It would be something special, for sure!

My first day back at work rolled by slowly in a blur of routine paper work and phone calls. Blowing my nose punctuated episodes of drifting off into a private world of thought.

The traffic was heavy on the way home and at one spot where two highways intersected the cars were backed up. I felt a need to empty out—talk, yell, or scream! Instead I picked up the mini-tape recorder on my front seat and began talking out my thoughts:

Life is like spinning my wheels—lots of energy expended but not getting anywhere. I feel like a puppet, dangling my feet, not quite able to touch the floor and go any-where. I need to get out of neutral and get my act in gear or I might freeze in this "nowhere" position, sink into the quicksand, and become immobilized to ever do anything worthwhile. Frustrated, restless, am I. My roles are changing, moments of lost identity. Divorce, death, an emptying nest. Where are my interests, where do I find my identity? Who am I? Years of raising kids, keeping house, running an office and being a wife; juggling the many roles like a circus performer. Now, everything's changing day to day. I feel like a heart-shaped peg in a pear-shaped hole. My edges don't fit within the confines of the old grooves anymore. I realized I don't appreciate how much I have until I lose it!

Pulling into my garage, I shut off the tape recorder. Enough thinking. I wished I could shut off my chattering mind as easily.

My heart and soul felt an urgency to clean up my life. I wanted to talk to people, write letters, balance my checkbook, and do all the other things I'd put off doing but my body wasn't interested in cooperating. It didn't want to play "clean-up" games or any other kind of game, either. It was a weary body and only longed to be rested, pampered, and listened to. I obeyed for once and put it straight to bed.

*   *   *

The next day at work, I took a longer lunch hour and drove up to the cemetery. Approaching the "Garden of Meditation," I saw a familiar car parked on the side of the road. Kathleen had come, too. I pulled a thick green quilt from the car trunk along with a funnel-like flower vase. Kathleen and I hugged each other silently for a moment. The colorful bouquet of mixed flowers cheered up the white temporary grave marker. It looked less lonesome there now that we had brought flowers and a miniature American flag. I reached into my purse and pulled out a wooden toy airplane and parked it next to the marker.

As Kathleen and I inhaled deep breaths of the crisp air, it didn't take words to communicate what we were feeling. The patches of green grass had been carefully replaced, but they couldn't hide the markings of a freshly laid-to-rest casket.

Kathleen was sad. She was also feeling anger. We both remembered seminar lessons about how undelivered communications can make you sick if they are not expressed. As if Bobby were right there in front of her, Kathleen began talking aloud.

"Bobby, you always handled the finances and I hate it! It's time to file income taxes and I don't know where anything is or what to do with it when I find it! I think it's pretty lousy of you to go off and leave me with all this messy paper stuff to handle by myself!" Her anger expressed, she shifted into tears, "I miss you and love you, wherever you are!"

Then it was my turn: "Bobby, this is all ass-backwards. Children aren't supposed to die before their parents. Now on holidays I'll be the one to bring the flowers to you. It's not fair for your life to be over at twenty-five," I cried out.

Across the hill, the workmen were setting up the chairs and an awning beside a neat stack of green turf squares. I felt a wave of compassion for the people who would soon be arriving for another graveside service.

"What if we came up here one day and someone had set up the awning next to Bobby, right where we were laying?" Kathleen voiced the thought that had crossed our minds at the same instant. Like homesteaders, we each had staked out the parcel of green grass on either side of Bobby as our territory. Kathleen had chosen to be on Bobby's left, and I had laid down my quilt on the right side.

The view of Mt. Diablo was spectacular from here. Occasionally, a butterfly would pass by and land on the flowers, and wave its "hello" before flitting on to the next vase of flowers. It was a beautiful place to visit with nature, God, Bobby, and the spirit world. We spotted a deer waiting quietly for us to leave so he could come out of hiding and feast on the tender roses and other brightly colored floral delicacies.

We knew we'd better make our homesteading legal. At the Oakmont Memorial Office, Kathleen purchased lot B-2 and I signed the papers for B-4. I could pay on the "time" plan. Bobby's time had run out, but I obviously still had some left.

Driving back from the cemetery, my inner dialogue began once again: B-4 is the place where my physical body will someday lay at rest beside Bobby. I felt a flush of inner peace, another letting go.

"View from B-3"

I was amazed at the amount of comforting and uplifting mail and loving phone calls I received. They filled my empty body with warm sensations. I wondered if a real live human being was still inside this aching mass of flesh and bones. One by one, I read each message and cherished it:

One of life's most difficult losses is that of a child. I want to share this quotation from Emily Dickinson:

> This world is not conclusion;
> A sequel stands beyond,
> Invisible, as music,
> But positive, as Sound.

Lovingly, Sande Hubbs

Shirley, allow this death to be a rebirth. Not only for your son, but for yourself. Allow yourself to be vulnerable and allow those around you to nurture you.

I love you very much,

Adela

Dear Susan (Workman),

Will you hand the enclosed sympathy card to the lady who lost her son in the plane crash? We have thought of her and her daughter-in-law every day since you called. There are so many similarities between our families that make it more than just another death.

Love,

Roma Workman

(Dick's mother)

Mt. Shasta is one helluva monument!

Love,

Kit

Dear Shirley and Kim,

Somehow in the darkest hour
The light comes shining through,
And memories of your loved one
Will still remain with you.

All our love,

Charlene and all the girls
at the answering service

Call me day or night to cry, talk or share.
May the Blessed Mother comfort you—
she, too, lost a son...

I love you,

Kathryn Davi-Billeci

'Crisis' in Chinese has two characters. One meaning is
danger; one is opportunity. Delve deep into your pain; you
will rediscover your strength. I send you my love and healing energy.

Karen LaPuma

There is only a handful of people in this world that can
keep a sense of happiness and laughter in the face of great
difficulty. Those that can do this have reached great heights
on what I guess you could call 'The Spiritual Survival Scale.'
These people have found the key to life and grow with leaps
and bounds as nothing can hold them back. You and your
family are among those people and are indeed blessed!
Thank you for allowing us to help. I know we have all
grown tremendously by sharing this experience.

In the Light and Sound
of Spirit,

Steve and Anne Higgins
Soulsbyville, CA

As I sipped tea and read these sympathy notes, I noticed the flowers that still bloomed on the tiny violet plant someone had brought over. People were so thoughtful and loving; their smallest expression meant so much at a time like this. Doug and Tacy Killingsworth had made a donation in Bobby's name to the Jesuit Seminary Association. The Mt. Diablo Hospital Volunteers had made a donation to the Doris Dengel Living Memorial Fund. A note from Greg's est 6-Day support group sent us love, and let us know a donation to the Hunger Project had been made in Bobby's name. I felt Bobby's energy applauding the mingling of God's Green Energy—money—to help so many worthwhile causes. A handlettered note from Werner Erhard conveyed his love and wholehearted support and love for what we were going through.

I picked up the note that Dr. Tolleth had handed me at the cemetery. It was filled with the words that would have been too difficult to say that day.

> Your pain, though worse than others before it, will, like them, temper and toughen you and increase your resolve to better spread your love and increase your ability to help others as they need help. I can't really give you sympathy—I can only wrap some love around you and grieve with you in your grief, as we are part of each other.
>
> Love,
>
> 'Papa Doc'

Silently, tears spilled from my eyes.

Ground Zero

From the time I filed for divorce from Bob Ruiz in 1976, I'd searched for the elements within me that caused me to feel like a two-time loser. As a young child from a broken home, I had firmly committed that when I became a parent, *nothing* would cause me to divorce the father of my children. This inner programming was so well done that it took a life-threatening illness before I could release myself from "I'll never do that to my kids." Although it was time for Rick and I to go our separate ways, I had made my childhood promise to myself more important than the inner voice which said it was time for me to look seriously at what was happening to Shirley.

As time went on, the mounting stress from suppressing my inner messages took its toll in my body—I suffered an acute attack of pyelonephritis. My kidneys did not want to function anymore. By the time I arrived at the hospital, I was unconscious and running a 105-degree temperature. The emergency room nurse couldn't get a blood pressure reading. At that moment, a most peculiar thing happened. I found myself hovering outside my body, watching and listening to the whole drama. I remember thinking, "I'm not dead, I'm right here and can hear every word you are saying."

My next memory was of waking up burning with fever to find a bottle of clear liquid dripping into a vein in my right arm. Five days later I was finally conscious enough for the doctors to talk to me. My prognosis wasn't good.

I prayed to God, if there really was one, Please let me live. I want to see a blue sky again, smell a rose, and hug my three little babies one more time. My recovery took an immediate and dramatic upturn from that moment. Life was indeed a precious gift and I wasn't about to waste it any longer. Six months later, I filed for divorce.

Sixteen years later, this time married to Bob Ruiz, the old symptoms appeared again. I was physically ill and emotionally torn, but I could not bring myself to file for divorce even though my inner voice was screaming for attention. Again, my body began talking loudly to me. I temporarily ignored medical advice to have a hysterectomy and a subcutaneous mastectomy. I didn't have the strength to handle the marital problems I was having, let alone any surgery.

I had a talk with myself one night: Shirley, here you are again, sick. Funny, but you are the only one who was present in both marriages. Somewhere within you, something is wired up wrong.

I realized that if I were the "sick" one, then the key to getting well again and feeling joyful and alive also dwelt inside of me.

The ongoing search to know more about myself on many levels began. I devoured books, took seminars, and kept many counseling appointments. If "know thyself" was a key to well-being, joy, and love, I would certainly give this path of self-discovery a try.

A friend and I signed up for a private relationship counseling appointment with someone who had come highly recommended. My first session with Elaine Christine, a few days before Bobby's death, did not disappoint me. It was a unique opportunity to look at my relationships and belief systems about men and marriage.

"Life is like a classroom: what you do not complete, you repeat," she said. No way. If ever I chose to be in a marriage again, I didn't want any of the unworkable attitudes I'd picked up still hanging around to haunt me. The week of Bobby's funeral I had cancelled my appointment for the second session. Finding Prince Charming no longer seemed a high priority.

I scheduled my appointment several days later. In her office, I made myself comfortable and prepared to look at my attitudes about different aspects of relationships.

"Lady, you're not here to talk about relationships or Prince Charming," Elaine said, looking me straight in the eye. "That will happen naturally, at the right time. I'm here to ask: what are you going to do with your gift? I was sitting at the funeral listening to you deliver your son's eulogy. A lot of people were deeply touched that day. I want to know what you are going to do with your gift."

I squirmed a bit. Elaine was too perceptive to accept anything but an honest and direct answer.

"I don't really know," I said. The story of choosing between the "grief puddle" or somehow having Bobby's death be more than just another "too bad" came out in our conversation. I had committed to myself, Bobby, and God to somehow turn it all into a contribution.

"Close your eyes and be still for a few minutes," Elaine instructed me. "Now, tell me what you are going to do."

"It feels like I'm going to keep a journal and write a book about sorrow and the healing process. I had a dream about a book with the title: *Journey to High Places: A Eulogy for Bobby*," I answered, opening my eyes.

"I'm going to keep reminding you just in case you might want to forget about your commitment," Elaine offered. Integrity was a big thing. How could I back down on an agreement made with Bobby and God?

I thought intensely while driving home. Write a book? That dream—I had had one like it just after Bob and I divorced. The book title in that dream was *Ground Zero*, and it was about the devastation of divorce. On the cover of the book was me, sitting in the middle of a target map. A "bomb" had gone off and my life was in total shambles around me. I awakened from the "bomb" nightmare at 3:00 AM one morning, wondering if anyone else in the universe was awake at this hour and hurting from a broken heart.

I started this book but then faltered, thinking: me—write? No, it was just another dream filed away on a shelf, forgotten. I had not grown in self-esteem or trust enough to follow the part of me that wanted to speak through writing.

When I got home, I retrieved the manuscript from the top shelf of my bedroom closet—an orange binder labeled *Ground Zero*. I felt fearful as I opened it. The wounds of grief were fresh tonight from missing Bobby. *Ground Zero* opened yet another wound, from another time and place. I decided to read the contents of the orange binder anyway...

GROUND ZERO

I awaken at 3:00 AM from a nightmare. I'm sitting in the center of an A-bomb type target. All my hopes and dreams lay shattered around me. I'm crying. The scene is imprinted on the cover of a book entitled *Ground Zero*. I begin writing my thoughts on the pad beside my clock-radio.

I stir, reluctantly surveying the holocaust of my life through narrowed eyes. I close them quickly. It's too painful. This must be a nightmare. Surely the alarm will soon shatter the long night's silence and bring me back from this bad dream into reality. Dawn comes. This *is* reality! The knot in my stomach aches. My nausea returns and my puffy eyes burn. Adrenalin charges through me. Its warriors quickly do their work! I want to scream. The endless tears start to flow again. I'm mad. I'm sorry. I'm strong. I'm a puddle of tears, a little girl waiting for someone to come along and kiss her "boo-boos" and make her all better!

I turn the stereo on to a quiet easy-listening station. *My Funny Valentine* filters the quiet of my early dawn world. Old memories stir. Will this unbearable pain ever go away? I pick up the book on my nightstand, *How To Survive the Loss of a Love*, and read about dealing with pain by being creative and writing a poem.

The book encouraged getting in touch with your creative energy, claiming that if you kept it up three or four times, "You'll get a poem, honest." I started writing.

YOU
are no longer
the center
of my Universe.
It scares me.
I know
I have reached an end...
or is it
really
just a beginning?
The future—
such an unknown.
So frightening
to be so
ALONE.
But, occasionally,
from this point of
GROUND ZERO,
I'm becoming aware
of a tiny spark of
creation,
deep inside me—
glowing and growing—
urging me on—
to a new lifestyle,
to a new ME!
There is
NO turning back!
I am a
rocketship,
seeking,
searching,
already launched
into my own
SPACE!

So much for poems. The message is clear!

Morning comes. Time for another day! I turn away from the reflection in my oversized bathroom mirror. "Oh, my God, who is this sad pathetic blob of red-eyed nothingness?" I said. "Someone's daughter? Someone's mother? Someone's secretary, and now someone's about-to-be "ex" something or other." The shaky have-it-all-together facade falls away.

WHO AM I?
Will the REAL me please stand up
and SHOUT!
I can't hear you.
I can't find you!
Life has lost purpose and meaning.
HELP!
SOMEBODY!
GOD?
Is anybody out there?
ANYBODY?
HELP!
Save an endangered species.
I'm the only ME left in the
universe.

I fire up and charge out of the house. I see an attorney. I demand the earliest court date and then procrastinate endlessly about signing any papers. One moment I'm captive in a martyred silence; the next, I'm a stream of woeful jabber to anyone with a sympathetic ear.

Shut up, Shirley! I'm so tired of hearing your story over and over again, I tell myself for the hundredth time. It's a broken record. Please, someone, please lift my stylus arm and get me out of this sick, stuck rut.

Searchingly, I pursue myself through the pages of *Passages*. Books are becoming my best friends. I arm myself with a stack of books on creative divorce and being an assertive woman. I disarm myself with a stack of books on how to be the perfect wife and save your marriage.

"You really believe in covering all the bases, don't you!" remarks the bookstore clerk as she tallies up the twenty-odd books I've chosen.

I see;
I saw;
I teeter;
I totter.

I reread *How To Survive the Loss of a Love* for the umpteenth time. I'm in *limbo*, a prison of nothingness. Without *choosing*, I'm going nowhere.

Self-inventory and evaluation: I'm one totally devastated human being, void of any feeling of self-worth or ability. My universe is at "ground zero." Where will I get the strength to rebuild it? Do I even want to?

Life was just getting to the point where the financial struggles of raising a family and career building would reach a comfortable plateau—dreams of a cabin in the mountains, vacations all over the world. Then Bob and I could coast. It's not fair for it all to fall apart now. I had forgotten that "coast" means to go downhill. Yep, that's what's happening, a downhill roller coaster!

I open my wallet to a small, anonymous clipping. I drink in its message.

Decision is a sharp knife that cuts clean
and straight; indecision a dull one that hacks
and tears and leaves ragged edges behind it.

So true. Just like the world of surgery. Many times I would schedule a patient for a "debridement of the wound" before skingrafting or other reconstructive surgical procedures could be done. Webster defines "debridement" as "...surgery, the cutting away of dead or contaminated tissue from a wound to prevent infection." Before healthy tissue can grow, the unhealthy tissue must be cut away. Sure seems true in the human psyche and self-esteem realms, too.

Hmmm...schedule Shirley for a major debridement procedure of everything in her life. It's time for her to let go! The divorce papers are filed.

73

My "little voice,"... Do I hear a small far-off cheering section? Time to make some changes!

I scheduled the two major surgeries I'd been postponing. First place to start is getting my body functioning at a healthier level. My surgeons questioned my wanting to have them both done at the same time. It entailed a lot of surgical hours and body stress. It would make better sense to wait three months between the subcutaneous mastectomy-reconstruction surgery and a hysterectomy procedure. My Grandma Ferrero had died of breast cancer. Watching the changing lumps and bumps, biopsies, and a partial mastectomy on one breast was making the breast surgery my first priority.

I felt so great after the five-hour surgery that I talked my gynecologist into moving up my hysterectomy surgery date. Two major surgeries less than two weeks apart. When I *do* make up my mind, a strong will and determination automatically take over to execute the plan.

After I woke up from the second surgery, I wondered if I hadn't outsmarted myself. I felt wiped out! Dragging my body around with a plastic bag attached to my side was a new experience. My surgeons warned me it would be a long healing process. I needed to have patience and be good to myself, but patience is not one of my foremost virtues. That is why I had scheduled it all to be done at once.

The day I was to be released from the hospital after surgery number two, Kim was having her singing debut at Northgate High School, and there was no way I would miss it! Bill Orlich, a fellow patient who had recently become a dear friend, picked me and my wheelchair up at Mt. Diablo Hospital. Bill carried me up the three flights of stairs in my condominium and set me down on my bed. He hardly puffed. I was exhausted and frequently breaking out in hot flashes, shakes, and sweats.

"You really ought to stay home and rest, don't you think?" Bill said with quiet concern. That fired me up.

"I am going tonight—whether it takes a fire truck, a resuscitation squad, a police escort, ambulance, or crawling there on all fours. *I am going to see Kim tonight!*" I shouted.

It took me over two hours to get myself ready. My hand continuously shook as I tried to put my makeup on straight. I still needed to be careful about raising my hands over my head or using my arms too much.

"God, how do I function with all these post-operative *don'ts*?" I cried.

In the middle of all the struggling to cope, something tickled my funny bone. I started laughing aloud, not at myself, but with myself. A thought that I might have to sneeze had started it.

"If I sneeze, all these stitches—from one end of my body to the other—might burst. I could unravel into a pile of pieces that used to be Shirley."

Bill shook his head and started laughing, too. I sat upon my "foam donut" as Bill pushed and parked my wheelchair in the center aisle. Kim was great. It was worth all the sweat it took to get there and watch her. I had the best seat in the house.

When I returned home, I found Kim and Laura had left a bumper sticker and a red rose on my nightstand. The sticker had a colorful rainbow on it and said:

Before every rainbow, there must be a storm.
Let's get onto 'rainbow' time
and let the storm be a thing of the past!

Healing, searching, seeking. A patient comes into our office. She looks and feels *great*! What has happened in the three months since we saw her? Whatever it is, I want some of it *now*!

"I took the training offered by the est organization," she shared with me. I enrolled in the next training and took three friends with me.

We drove to Santa Rosa to take the *first* available training. What an adventure Susan Workman, Alice Goble, Iris Oliphant, and I had! The first thing we did was to stick our watches in our purses. We'd forgotten in our rush to get there on time to leave our watches home as instructed. As we knew each other before the training, we also had to sit apart. We laughed a lot that training, mostly at ourselves; especially the wrestling with our consciences. We sat for two hours before we surrendered our watches to the table in the back of the room for safe-keeping. The watches themselves were not the issue we needed to look at but the attitudes with which we each played the game of life. Watches pointed out a "break the rules—get away with what you can" attitude.

It was an incredible experience. Custom-made for what I was doing with my life these days—debriding the garbage, physically, mentally, and emotionally. On the fourth day of the training, I had a very moving spiritual experience. We were doing a long process. My mind seemed like a computer. All circuits were full and then flipped over into overload. For an instant in time, my mind was silent and I had the first actual experience I could recall that God was no longer outside me, but was part of me! He was the part of me observing the whole process when the other parts of me were silent. I started laughing aloud. I heard other people laughing, too. Had they had the same moment of revelation? This training is not a religious or spiritual training. Words failed me when I tried to verbalize my revelation, so I quit trying and tucked the experience away deep within me.

One day I opened a friend's issue of *Playboy*. In it was an interview with John Denver. He'd had a similar God experience. Whew, it's nice to have some agreement. Enlightenment is lightening up about life!

I like it, I like it, I thought as I wrote myself a new description: *Ground Zero*—an incredible opportunity to rebuild the wholeness and integration of my mind, body, emotions, and spirit. They need to be connected, balanced, and flowing into an ecstatic state of well-being and aliveness. There is no right or wrong way. Each person needs to be dedicated to the personal discovery of that point of wholeness and integration. It is definitely a "do it yourself" process. *No one can do it to you or for you.*

*   *   *

I finished reading *Ground Zero* and closed the book. If God buries our talents and the blueprint for our divine plan within us, does He also stir up little reminders from time to time? *Ground Zero* was a book I never completed. Would *Journey To High Places* end up on my library shelf, too—a binder of notes, an unfinished dream, again? *No!* How could I back down on a promise made to Bobby and to God?

How and where would I begin? I'd heard that meditating regularly clears the mind for inspiration. Meditate. Do nothing. I didn't know how to do it "right." I said a prayer and closed my eyes in the silence.

Silence. That was a joke. My mind kept chattering a long series of "to dos" at me. I had programmed it well. It loved to mastermind the juggling of ten activities at once. Determined, I put on a meditative cassette tape of nonfrantic music by Steve Halpern. About ten minutes into the tape, my body and mind began to feel a beautiful kind of peacefulness. The cassette player clicked off.

My thoughts were questioning and philosophical. Is this the power speaking to me from deep within myself? I wondered. The Buddha taught that we are all buddhas. In Christianity, it's the Christ within — the spark of divinity given to each of us. Jesus, the Christ — His whole being was the Christ. Is the spark within the same essence referred to in all religions, though known by different names? Is this what I was experiencing the accelerated awakening of? Is this what "midlife crisis" is really all about — one day finding yourself so "off course" in life that something within you cries out for a change? Sometimes "time-for-a-change" signals look like frustration, burn-out, confusion, or a body that is falling apart. This inner guidance system whispers for a course correction. If that falls upon deaf ears, we experience discontent and painful restlessness. When this doesn't work, do we create crisis, a personal "earthquake" to shake us up and wake us up?

When I have released myself from old patterns and lifestyles, I've found myself in a state of "free flow" in the stream of life. I felt I had to stop using my energy to go against the current or row upstream. It is much easier to go with the flow. No looking for rocks to hang onto or hide beneath. That takes too much energy. Keep moving with the flow; life is change. Surrender to my inner spirit and where it wants to take me. Be in the moment of now, be joyous, and go with the flow!

I remembered Kim reading a bit of wisdom to me:

> He who can laugh at himself
> shall never lack for a source of material.

Pretty heavy thinking you're into these days, Shirley, I laughed. I remember when you searched for wisdom in a newspaper astrology column or a fortune cookie—looking for a clue that you would survive your own personal hell and find Camelot somewhere along the way to your future.

Write a book? I decided to sit on the hows and whens for awhile. But it wasn't easy; I had a lifelong habit of invalidating myself if I didn't do things right immediately.

Once I had wanted to be a pianist. Then I froze at my first recital and couldn't remember a note. The snickers I heard from the kids in the audience validated what was going on in my mind: guess I wasn't meant to be a pianist.

In high school, Jerry Davis and I were "Your High School Reporters" on radio station KECC. My big chance came when I sang "I'll Remember April." I did remember April but not in the right key. Oh, to be seventeen and survive your own embarrassment! Guess I wasn't meant to be a singer, either. At the time I thought all great people were born great. I never thought about how much work goes into making things look or sound effortless.

So now you want to be a writer, Shirley, I thought to myself. Will you give yourself permission to be a novice, make mistakes and keep on going anyway? A poem beneath a calendar picture of trees and birds suggested a good way of looking at apprenticeship in anything.

> Use what talent
> You possess;
> The woods would
> Be very silent if
> No birds sang there
> Except those that
> Sang best.
>
> —H. Van Dyke

For the time being I decided to save my thoughts in a journal and somewhere along the way, I'd see where all this was taking me. Tomorrow would be another day; soon it would be my favorite day of the year—Valentine's Day.

Valentine's Day

Valentine's Day had always been a special day for me, even as a young girl. It was a day to express all the love in my heart and be as sentimental and romantic on the outside as I am on the inside.

What in the world am I going to do with Valentine's Day this year? I wondered. A vision of the "Bleeding Heart" floral piece I'd chosen for Bobby's funeral flashed in front of me: deep red roses bleeding their color obliquely into the heart-shaped arrangement of white mums. "Beloved Son," the ribbon had said.

The phone jarred me back into the present.

"Hi, Auntie Shirley. How'd you like to go to Lake Tahoe and ski over Valentine's Day?" It was my niece Kelly. Our relationship had been special and close since the day she was born. She was often a part of our Saturday family outings.

Saturdays were a special time to explore and be adventuresome —kayaks on Lake Tahoe, barbecues in the sand dunes at Dillon Beach, "follow-the-leader" games in the moonlit paths of the snow-covered Sierras, making snow-cones in our foam cups out of freshly fallen snow and concentrated Hawaiian Punch, Giants baseball games and hotdogs, hiking on Mt. Tamalpais, Disneyland, Hearst Castle, Morro Bay, Carmel, the Boardwalk at Santa Cruz, the Wine Country, and on and on.

We explored every inviting beach we could find along California's spectacular coastline. One of our favorites was Dillon Beach, thirty minutes west of Petaluma. It had a clean mile-long strip of sandy beach and never seemed too crowded to enjoy wading in its tidepools, climbing on the rocks, or romping up and down its sand dunes. We loved the privacy and our own playfulness whenever we went there. The nearby resort store had *everything* we might need, just in case we had forgotten anything. It was always our first stop. I can still see and hear Bobby, Kathleen, Laura, Kim, Robert, and me running along the beach, with little Kelly being carried over our heads, kite-like, singing the "Bum-Bum-Bumble-Bee Tuna" song—so joyous, not a care in the world!

Had it not been for a TV interview with a movie star, I might have missed out on these joyous occasions. When she was asked about her relationship with her mother, she coolly replied, "I'll always remember my mother for her clean shiny floors."

The remark hit me like a ton of bricks. Our house had acres of clean shiny floors—even with five kids constantly running through it. Holding down a full-time job, all the hours left were spent shopping, cooking, doing laundry, and polishing the house to my immaculate standards. The movie star's words could have come from my own children's mouths. Was that the epitaph I would have on my tombstone if I were to die today? What a waste!

"Kelly, what a perfect way to spend Valentine's Day! Is it okay if I ask Kathleen and my friends Susan, LaRena, and Debra to come with us? I think Kim and Laura have already made other plans."

"Sure, we'll have a great time!" she replied.

80

The trip came together quickly and effortlessly. We couldn't wait to get on the road. At 11:05 PM on Friday night we departed for Lake Tahoe; waiting until the daylight on Saturday was a waste of precious hours. My brother Bob's big Blazer was packed to the rooftop with skis, luggage, and the six of us. We had brand new snowtires, so we wouldn't need to fuss with chains if we hit bad weather. Whoopee! No wonder we were so willing to brave the fickle mountain weather this time of night. It was a wet chilly night, but the trip proved to be rather routine. We sang and told stories and enjoyed the precious uninterrupted time to talk "girl talk." One by one, sleepy heads quieted down and dozed off. As we approached the drive up Echo Summit, rain began to turn to sleet, followed by snow.

I lurched forward to see more clearly. As I went around a big curve, suddenly, in front of us I could see a vehicle stalled crosswise in the road. People were milling around, at a loss for what to do. I had only a split second to make a decision. I turned the Blazer into the snowbank on my left, avoiding the sure tragedy of hitting the people standing in the middle of the road.

"*Hang on!*" I yelled as we came to a safe but abrupt stop. Thank God for a strong vehicle, snowtires, a soft snowbank, and His heavenly protection. My sleepy crew was now *wide* awake. The people in the middle of the road began to move their car over to the shoulder of the road. It was a miracle no one was hurt or killed as traffic began to swerve and pile up behind us. We backed out of the snowbank and proceeded up the short distance to the top of Echo Summit with *great* care. It obviously wasn't our time to "check out."

The snow lightened to flurries as we began creeping down the summit on the icy mountain road into Lake Tahoe Basin. The view of Lake Tahoe and the Sierras from the summit was spectacularly beautiful and awesomely scary at the same time. It was funny we could see so clearly and so far with the weather conditions being what they were. We arrived at our destination at 4:30 AM. Such a relief!

Kelly roomed with Kathleen, Susan and Debra shared the room with the twin beds, and LaRena and I moved our things into the master bedroom. It was 5:30 AM by the time everyone had settled in. We built a roaring fire. I sat down on the couch in front of the huge fireplace and promptly fell asleep in my clothes, sitting up.

We began stirring at 10:30 AM. We goofed around, and drank in the beauty of my brother's home, Lake Tahoe, the snow-covered

Sierra mountains, and the love and connectedness of the six people sharing this very different Valentine's Day celebration. We got dressed and dashed off to buy some groceries. Dinner was to be a joint effort. Everyone pitched in with their specialties. LaRena and Susan made fried chicken, filling the house with a mouth-watering fragrance. Spinach salad with Debra's special dressing, and crisp, colorful veggies by Kathleen and Kelly were added to create a really festive meal. I made dill dip for my part of the feast.

Kelly built another roaring fire. We'd gotten used to the gigantic moosehead above the fireplace and called him by his name: "Hi there, Elmer!" I went into the living room to enjoy the fire and prepare an outline of a special awareness process I wanted to lead the group through as part of our Valentine's Day celebration—a fantasy trip to our imaginations.

Debra came into the room, Kathleen and Kelly watched from another couch, and LaRena and Susan were talking in the kitchen. Debra got out the Ouija board and began playing with it. Suddenly, she stopped and stared at the floor.

I sensed something was coming up for her emotionally—maybe as a result of the Ouija board. I quickly moved to the floor directly opposite her, our crossed knees touching. I reached out and took her hands in mine and began talking, setting up a safe atmosphere for her to talk out whatever she needed to talk out.

Such sadness was coming up! Black mascara began streaming down her peaches-and-cream face. She was remembering her intense sadness as a very young child when her beloved grandfather suddenly died. She remembered being "too little" to participate, being excluded from the funeral and grieving, being "protected" by the adults from experiencing grief. It angered her and hurt, too. There was no one to talk to about it. No one to just hold her and let her know everything would be okay.

"Adults have no right to shut kids out, as if anyone could protect a child from life, or from the pain of death and loss!" Debra snapped. "It only added to the mystery of death and the fear of what no one would talk to me about. It was terrible losing my grandpa. I used to climb up and sit on his lap. I felt the security of his love for me. Somehow, life seemed safer with him around."

Debra continued viewing her life as a little girl. She was recalling a new man in her mother's life and how she had felt competitive for her mother's time and affections. She recalled feeling sad and rejected at birth, even though she had no intellectual words or clear memories to base her feelings on.

What a moving experience for me. I could sense and feel her pain as she emptied out long-buried thoughts and feelings. We wiped each other's tears as the call, "Dinner's ready," came from the kitchen.

After dinner, we lit the small candles each of us had purchased earlier in the day. I had everyone find a comfortable position on a couch or the floor. All of the group, with the exception of Kelly, had done relaxation and fantasy processes many times before.

"Just let whatever images that want to—if any—come into your mind. Watch them, like watching a movie," I explained to Kelly.

We breathed deeply and began to relax as we visualized ourselves surrounded and protected by white light. I had taken some extensive training in the past to do hypnosis, but other than helping Debra lose weight before her wedding, I did "fantasy trips" only for friends and family on special occasions.

I put on a background cassette tape and began taking them on an imaginary trip.

"Through the forest...stop and examine the tiny flowers and moss there... Note the colors and the smell... Hear the sounds of the forest... See the rays of the sunlight streaming through the trees... Listen to the sounds of a tiny brook in the distance... Up ahead is a beautiful little forest animal. He's not afraid of you as you approach him. Pet him and talk to him if you like."

Moving them through the imaginary forest and out to a sunny meadow, I suggested, "Create a thick colorful afghan on which you can lay and watch puffy white clouds play tag in the blue sky overhead. Rela-a-a-x."

To each one I gave an imaginary golden wand with a heart-shaped tip to be used for radiating warm healing rays of love and light throughout their bodies. As we journeyed, we looked for any places needing relaxation, attention, and love. Everyone looked extremely peaceful and serene as I searched each face for clues as to how the journey was going.

"Imagine just over the hillside nearby, a 'special someone' coming to visit you in this magic place," I continued. "Get a sense of feeling for that person's energy or aura coming up over the hill and into view. Now begin to see the shape of the body of this 'special person' and see if you recognize who is coming to be with you. Now visualize yourself getting up and running in beautiful slow motion through the meadow towards this 'special person.' Communicate through touch only, allowing your energy field to mingle with theirs. Now communicate through your imagination anything you would like to verbally say to and/or hear from your 'special person.'"

After waiting a couple of minutes for the communications process to be completed and any blended energies to separate again, I told them, "Your afghans are becoming 'magic carpets' that can take you alone or with your 'special person' anywhere you want to go. Choose some place that holds a magical attraction for you and fly there—now hover—rise above and circle and then fly closer to this special fantasy place. Drink in its beauty and do whatever you'd like to do while you're here. Imprint this moment in your mind and notice how it feels in your body to be in ecstasy."

I returned them via the "magic afghan carpet" to the meadow and the beautiful flowers there. "See yourself as whatever flower you choose to be and see yourself as a tiny bud. Reach down into your roots for the earth energy you need to blossom and draw it up your stem and out into your leaves and up into the flower bud itself. Feel the energy and warmth of the sun begin to feed you nourishment from above. Feel the gentle breeze and see yourself coming into full bloom, as beautiful, colorful, and radiant as you truly are."

Slowly they went from the flower back into their own bodies, back through the forest, back into this room; stretching and beginning to move their fingers and toes and preparing to open their eyes; fully refreshed, peaceful, calm, wide awake, and full of love. Everyone stood up and stretched. It had been a long fantasy trip and everyone was eager to share their adventure.

"My flowers were violet and my 'special person' was Dick, my husband," Susan shared, a smile on her face. "That's all I want to say right now." She wanted to savor the precious feeling she was experiencing.

Kelly spoke next: "I created a meadow right off the bat with trees nearby, but no real forest. The fantasy person I'd expected to see was my stuffed animal, a bear. I was surprised when a person appeared. A young boy, whose face I didn't recognize, appeared in knickers. I thought maybe I was in England. A deeper part of me knew I knew the boy well. Yet, I'm puzzled about who he might be. Could we check with the Ouija board, and 'Michael' to see if I can find out more about my mysterious new friend?"

Debra said, "I alternately visited with my husband, John, and my beloved grandfather." Tears and sadness were coming up again for her. "Sadness is okay now, though," she assured us. "I was unwilling to go into the imaginary forest," LaRena noted. We'd done this process together before, and she had always refused any part of going into a forest. "Is it the forest itself, or is it the boxed-in closed-in feelings I often fight in real life?"

Mad at herself for not going into the forest, LaRena continued, "I feel like I missed out on something. I enjoyed the rest of the trip though. One of these days, I'm going to get to the bottom of this 'forest mystery' in my life!"

Kathleen saw tiny violet flowers in her forest. She encountered a small deer but he seemed frightened as she approached and ran off. Her "special person" was Bobby, and she loved mingling energy fields with him! No words were spoken or necessary; they just touched and caressed each other. She took him with her on her magic carpet trip. It was a big fluffy cloud and they watched airplanes and identified each one as they flew by. No effort piloting a cloud! As she changed energy and visualized herself being a flower, she became a rosebush and instantly felt a sense of panic: "Where's Bobby? Oh, I'll have him be a rosebush beside me!"

The chatter about the journeys grew even more open and intimate. It was clear each had been on a very special and unique adventure. It was a perfect climax to Valentine's Day.

Kelly had really surprised everyone. She took to imaging like a duck to water! In that beautiful fourteen-year-old body resided a very mature and knowing soul. All weekend her insights and contributions were astounding. She wanted to use the Ouija board to see what she could find out about her friend in knickers.

We decided to try contacting "Michael" (the entity described in *Messages from Michael*). I told her she and I would work the board and I asked to be "guided and protected" as we tried the board. We all visually surrounded ourselves with 'white light,' asked for protection from God, Jesus, Angels, and Guides of the Light, and began.

I emphasized to Kelly several times: "Do not believe anything we might discover; only use it as a tool. Look inside yourself to *feel* if there is anything you can use and how you would use it."

LaRena got out her steno pad to take notes. We quickly discovered we could cover a lot more territory if we asked 'yes' and 'no' questions. Kelly began the questions:

Who was the boy in knickers?	HFE (?)
Past life with Kelly?	Yes
This life too?	Yes
Does she know him now?	No
Someone in future?	Yes
Child of Kelly's?	Yes
England?	No
Was image affected by "Little House on the Prairie" TV show?	Yes
How many past lives has Kelly had?	4,659

(We all laughed.)

Kelly popped out questions like an automatic Bingo machine! She "discovered" she was a mature soul who had come here determined to do a lot of growing. She needed to watch her impatience. She was indeed a powerhouse of physical energy. She asked a few random questions: no, her brother would not marry Jenny; yes, Laura Ruiz would join the Air Force soon and it would be a happy and successful choice for her. Susan would be leaving her job with Dr. Tolleth in a year or two and begin discovering her healing powers. Shirley and Kathleen would also be in for some very big changes. Kathleen would be leaving her job as secretary for Clorox and pursuing her art studies. Bobby's death had led her to begin questioning what the rest of her life was going to be about now that she was on her own. Shirley would be leaving her present job soon, too.

Kelly said we could "feel" there were other energies in the room besides ours. Who were they? "Bobby, Dick Workman, Debra's grandfather, and Kelly's grandmother, Lorraine DiMaggio," came the answers. She asked if we could communicate with Bobby directly. "Yes." I began the questioning of Bobby:

Are you aware of us?	Yes
In pain?	No
Pleased with us?	Yes
Guiding me to write?	Yes
Guiding Kathleen to her art expression?	Yes
Learned or done whatever you had been born to learn or do?	Yes
Was your death a part of that purpose?	Yes
Was premonition of death present?	Uncertain
Suffer?	No
Death a surprise (hitting Mt. Shasta)?	No
Is destiny pre-planned?	No/Yes
Comes from choice?	Yes
Frightened the moment before death?	Yes
Saw Mt. Shasta before hitting it?	Yes
We were all showing signs of exhaustion and asked if we should stop.	Yes!

We hugged each other good night and quickly headed for our snuggly flannel nighties. I chose to sleep on the couch near the fire and the dwindling candles. I loved this place and these moments of peace and serenity. It was 12:30 AM the last time I looked at the clock.

I awakened at 6:20 AM. The house was still as I opened the blinds to look at Lake Tahoe. It was fairly dark out and the street lights were forming mysterious patterns as they passed through the tall pine trees. It was such a privilege to have a spot like this for a retreat. Soon, I heard my skiers stirring. Susan, Kelly, LaRena, and Kathleen left excitedly to ski the slopes of Heavenly Valley for the day, leaving me to write and Debra to read.

I felt an urge to pamper my body with some tender loving care. I took a long hot shower and marveled at the power of water to relax, heal, stimulate, and caress a tired body. I gave myself a facial and I could feel new aliveness coming into my body as I massaged a rich body lotion into my dry, tired flesh. I loved mixing my own potions and lotions—herbs, how yummy! I blew my hair dry and rolled it into a soft casual style. I felt like a new person.

Sitting on the couch, I switched on the cassette tape Susan had asked me to listen to. It was a psychic reading she had had a couple of months ago with my "Messages from Michael" channel. I took some notes as I listened to it.

> Surround yourself with white light and create time and place to communicate with the spirit world if that is your desire. Surround yourself with mementos and begin talking out your feelings and emotions as they arise. Set the time and date ahead whenever possible to let the spirit world prepare. Let the answers come *through* you. Just write or talk whatever comes up.

The tape went on to answer some of Susan's questions.

> Yes, you and Shirley have had many lifetimes together. Your energies blend well and you're a productive team. You had a particularly happy lifetime together in England as "serving wenches" in a wealthy castle-like household. You were loved and well taken care of by the family you worked for. It pleased you to have the shiniest, most polished, spic-and-span household around.

This part of the tape amazed me because of experiences I'd had in this lifetime with Susan. She had lived with me for a time when her first marriage broke up. One weekend, we both got the notion to spring houseclean. When Susan and I both clean, a place is *clean*. We cleaned every nook and cranny with toothbrushes, toothpicks, and every other cleaning secret we knew.

We laughed all day at how happy we were to be cleaning. The next day at the office a patient asked us if we had had a nice weekend. We both chuckled as we nodded our heads affirmatively and said, "We sure did!"

We'd shared similar experiences when Dr. Tolleth was away at medical meetings. The urge to polish all the wood paneling and desks and everything in sight with lemon oil was strong. It felt so good and it always amused us to see how much joy we got out of working as a "clean-up" team. As I listened I couldn't help but smile at that part of the tape. No question in my mind, there certainly was a tie-in there.

The tape continued to relate that Susan and I had also been males in a more vague lifetime, dedicated to constructing some kind of church. An old-fashioned portrait of Susan and Dick fell out of the book of poems Susan had left for me to read. It looked just like the wedding pictures of the 1900's. The notation said: "No one ever loses in *Our* game." It felt strangely mystical and I was pleased with the thought of having lived many lives in many eras. How rich the experiences, how maturing for the soul. That must be the purpose of life.

Sitting on the sofa at Lake Tahoe, I began to feel restless and started talking out loud to Bobby. I had a strong feeling I needed to give Kathleen something to hang on to physically. I continued my thought conversation with Bobby. Yes, a gift was appropriate—a stuffed animal. Yes, Kelly had "Johnny Bear," Susan had "Priscilla, the white cat," and "John-boy," her koala bear. Yes, yes, yes—a stuffed animal for Kathleen—a belated Valentine's Day gift from Bobby, through me.

I could hardly walk to the shopping center fast enough. It was great to feel that excited energy flowing through me again. Debra said she'd walk along with me. She needed to mail her postcard to John. As we walked by the Catholic Church she said she felt like going to the 4:30 mass.

What animal would be right for Kathleen? I sensed it would prob-
ably choose itself when I saw it and it did. I had fondled a kangaroo, a teddy bear, and then I saw a beautiful little fawn with big soft brown eyes and velvety ears—that was it. All he needed was a red ribbon tied around his neck. Kathleen had chosen a fawn in her forest fantasy trip, so "Bobby Deer" it was. I went over to the greeting card rack to find the perfect card to go along with it. I found one for "Daughter": no matter what she does, with whom or where, she will always feel like a daughter to me.

Finding the card and "Bobby Deer" gave me lots of light-hearted energy. Passing a display of makeup brushes, I realized I wanted to buy a small gift for everybody. So what if it was a day late—it was the thought that counted. I found a gold-cased lipstick brush for

LaRena, a ponytail-type comb for Debra, and fluffy earmuffs for Kelly. Wine-colored combs for Susan's hair completed the gift-buying. I started the brisk walk back towards the lake. Debra was still in church, and I was "alone." Alone—I didn't feel inappropriate talking out loud to Bobby when I was alone or with Kathleen or Susan; I knew that they did it, too. As I walked alone, words and feelings began to sift to the surface.

> I don't understand—
> But I can't turn back.
> There's stagnation in limbo;
> I must hurry on
> ...to the next completion.

I looked up at the Sierras towering above me and the huge clouds floating in the blue sky. I felt like a "tiny speck" of life calling to God, the Universe, and my son for some answers about life, death, and immortality.

"I need answers, please!" I began calling and chanting a little singsong verse:

> Bobby...Bobby...
> Do you come
> If I call?
> Are you always
> Just "here"
> or maybe
> Never at all?

What a painful way to grow—inspiring and moving. If I couldn't hold the purpose of life in some larger context it would drive me insane. It seemed important to stay in contact with God, Bobby's spirit, and a bigger purpose to being alive. Otherwise, hopelessness set in. The thought that death was the end— *nothingness*—made my stomach churn.

No, I couldn't accept a universe of such precise balance and beauty as that now surrounding me without accepting God and a larger master plan that I couldn't always see or understand from my

90

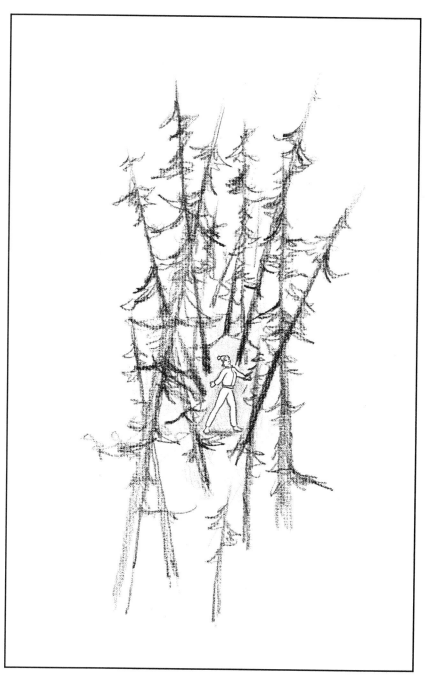

"Bobby, Bobby..."

position "down here". My thoughts started spinning me off into heady emotions.

Suddenly, I was back at the Lakeview cabin. There was no Blazer in view; I had beaten everyone home. Hurriedly, I wrapped bows around the presents I'd bought, signed the cards in red ink, and scattered my Valentine gifts on the pillows of their recipients. I sat down to await their homecoming but the wait was short.

Seconds after I'd finished, I heard my skiers trudging up the driveway. They had had a great day on the slopes of Heavenly Valley. Various degrees of tired bodies and weather-reddened faces entered the house.

Ohs and ahs came from the bedrooms. They had found their gifts! LaRena loved her lip brush. Debra thanked me for the ponytail clip as she slipped it in her hair. Susan was touched by the old-fashioned "English" greeting card with the two little maids on it and was wearing the wine-colored combs in her hair. Kelly came out and did a little song and dance with her new earmuffs on and gave me a big hug. Kathleen tenderly pressed "Bobby Deer" to her bosom. It *was* the perfect gift. She carried him around most of the evening, hugging him and releasing deep emotional sighs.

Feeling a need to be alone, I walled myself off to write in my journal. I felt that old restless feeling coming up again. I looked out the window and saw an airplane with brilliant landing lights on flying low directly over the house. Obviously we were part of the landing pattern that day. I pulled at my hair a bit and stared out at the quiet mirror images reflecting on the beautiful lake before me. Reflections of red lights from the gambling casinos across the way shone on the water and less vividly colored lights twinkled here and there around the rest of the lake. My thoughts and emotions were coming in strong again as I watched the lights. I thought about grief and decided it had these qualities:

- loss: emotional, mental and physical
- communications: misunderstood or undelivered
- goals: the unachieved in life; precious time squandered away
- agreements: unclear or broken

- fears: real or imagined
- love: all of the missed opportunities to say I love you.

Grief stirs up anger, sadness, regret, fear, and emotions. Tears of all descriptions come up for expression. And, when you're ready, love and enlightenment await your summons.

It was getting late; the weekend would soon be over. I was frustrated because my memories seemed to be erasing. The "space of Bobby" and what he looked like and felt like were disappearing. It was a feeling of panic, of time running out. Hurry, I told myself, write, write, write before you forget it all!

Kathleen came over and sat beside me and I asked her how she was feeling. "Out of touch," she replied. She shared some of the things she'd written in her journal and I found myself recapturing some of the thoughts and insights that seemed to be slipping away earlier. It felt good to capture my emotions and thoughts in written form.

We decided to call a meeting of our new club, "Bobby's Angels." With only a slight resemblance to "Charlie's Angels" of TV fame, the name fit us. The "Angels" agreed to always be on the lookout for an opportunity to do a good deed, however small. Meetings were a time to get together and share our latest contributions. We had had a meeting just before we left for the mountains. The other two members of "Bobby's Angels" were present that night, Kim and Laura Ruiz. Laura reported she had left flowers and love notes at the cemetery for Bobby and Kathy Mooney. Telling people she loved them when she felt it instead of being silent about it was the way Kim had chosen to spread love.

Here in Tahoe, the other six members had new deeds to share:

KATHLEEN: —giving away more art work and poems

SUSAN: —buying more daisies, visiting more patients in the hospital

LARENA: —lots of "I love you" teacups as gifts

DEBRA: —picked up beer cans and litter distracting from nature's beautiful snow-laden pine trees along the highway

LaRena

Debra

Kathleen

Susan

Kelly

"Bobby's Angels"

Me and "Elmer"

KELLY: —helped someone who had taken a bad fall on the
ski slopes

ME: —a backrub for a hospitalized patient, a
book to a depressed friend

We all agreed to smile more, especially at people who looked like
they really needed one. Kathleen began sketching our "thank you"
card to Mae and Robert for letting us use their cabin. It was to go
along with the popcorn popper we were going to buy them. We
laughed as Kathleen did a caricature of each one of us and then added one of "Elmer," the moosehead. He had been watching us from
his perch over the fireplace all weekend and had been voted in as
club mascot.

I awakened about 3:00 AM to the sound of voices in the kitchen.
Kathleen and Susan were popping corn in an old skillet.

"Have some popcorn, Ma," Susan said laughingly, as she passed
me the bowl of buttery golden puffs. "Neither Kathleen nor I could
sleep and we didn't want to waste our last few precious hours here."

The conversation reminisced endlessly about Bobby and Dick
and how their deaths had affected our lives. Though the deaths were
at separate places and times, we somehow all seemed woven
together through our double exposure to grief.

It would soon be time to return to the everyday world. We
weren't ready to leave the peaceful haven in Tahoe yet but at least
we were taking home some special memories. St. Valentine's Day
was a day the six of us shared with each other and those we loved
who were now of the spirit world.

It's Time to Leave

*I have been driven many times to my knees by the
overwhelming conviction that I had nowhere else to go.
My own wisdom, and that of all about me seemed
insufficient for that day.*

—Abraham Lincoln

*Sorrow forces man to take introspective inventory of himself,
wherein he may discover the cure for all of his ills and disappoint-
ments. And it introduces one to the benefits of meditation and
silence, during which unseen forces may bring aid and comfort suf-
ficient unto one's needs at a given time or experience.*

—Napoleon Hill
You Can Work Your Own Miracles

I awakened early on a dreary Sunday morning aware of
everything I had to do that day. A reminder for my 11:00 AM

97

appointment at Dr. Tolleth's house was taped to my bathroom mirror. Sundays were usually not the day for business meetings but circumstances had made this the only time I would be able to met with Vickie Doretti, who was here from Chicago, and Dr. Tolleth. The meeting agenda concerned Dr. Tolleth's taking office as National President of the Educational Foundation of the American Society of Plastic and Reconstructive Surgeons in the fall.

I looked at the calendar hanging on the back of my bathroom door. The beautiful February seascape brought back many memories of exploring California's magnificent coastline. The verse seemed in keeping with the theme of my life these past five weeks.

> The sea is a restless wanderer,
> reaching into the land,
> exploring the secret coves and caves
> along the shoreline,
> sometimes thrashing,
> sometimes caressing.

I flipped over to March. Could it really be March 1st already? I feel I'm living my life at the speed of light, watching a "Shirley Video" that's on fast forward. So much has happened, so many changes have occurred to me and the whole family. I rewound the videotape of my mind review of the last few days.

Last night Kimberly and Rick Parker had announced their engagement. Larry Jensen and I were attending the American Cancer Society's Mardi Gras Ball when the two of them, grinning ear to ear, joined us at the Concord Sheraton Inn Ballroom. Rick had surprised Kim with her engagement ring at dinner, earlier in the evening. The staff at the restaurant had delighted in assisting Rick to surprise her. Dinner was ordered from their very private, intimate upstairs dining room where a call button is used when service is desired. After the main course of Chateaubriand, their waiter suggested they have "Strawberry Flambé" for dessert. Kim agreed. Strawberries were a favorite of hers. She watched him prepare the dessert, her mouth watering at the huge red strawberries. Kim was served. There, atop the biggest, reddest strawberry of all, sat a sparkling solitaire diamond engagement ring.

"Just what every romantic girl dreams about," Kim said as she described the precious moment. The evening reminded her of the scene from the movie *Funny Girl* when suave Omar Sharif courted a starry-eyed naive Barbra Streisand in a private dining room to the tune of "You are Woman, I am Man".

It was good to see Kim laughing and smiling again. A twinkle replaced the sad look that had haunted her eyes since Bobby's death. She was grieving for Bobby, for all the children he'd never have, for dreams undreamed and unfulfilled. Bobby had so much potential. She joked it was now up to her to have the children for the family tree. I knew her heartstrings were tugging at her to settle down, marry, and start a family of her own.

Rick is a wonderful choice for a son-in-law, I thought as I admired Kim's ring and hugged the bride and groom-to-be.

Laura, too, had an announcement: she had enlisted in the Air Force. Six weeks before Bobby's death, I had had a psychic reading from my "Messages from Michael" channel. I asked about each of my children.

"Laura," the channel had said, "has chosen this lifetime to study rejection. The transition from being a carefree child spirit into a responsible adult is difficult for her. She needs to leave her present lifestyle behind. Your energy, like many parents, appears to Laura like a 'blazing sun', blinding her to her own precious flame. It is hard to see the candle light against the sun. You might send Laura away to some kind of disciplined school. By learning self-discipline, she can discover and develop her talents, improve her self-esteem, and get a handle on her energy."

"I can't see where it's financially feasible to send her away at this time," I said. "Further, Laura has blown her high school graduation by cutting classes and not completing her U.S. history requirement."

The night after the "Michael" reading, I had a vivid dream. Laura was in a blue military uniform; tears of pride and joy were streaming down her smiling face. I casually mentioned the dream to Laura as we were discussing the psychic reading. Unbeknownst to me, she spent the next month investigating each branch of the service and taking aptitude tests. She chose the Air Force. She had scored well and was absolutely ecstatic to find an opportunity to be something other than a secretary the rest of her life. Laura was not cut out to sit for long periods or do boring routine paperwork. She had too much physical energy. Toe-tapping and finger-drumming had signified her impatience even as a small child.

The Air Force position that excited her was being trained as a weather observer. She could also request overseas duty and see some of the world. Schooling for this position would start in a year, the Air Force recruiter told her. Meanwhile, she would be in the Air Force on inactive duty until the following March 1st. Laura had taken a positive step in planning her own future, and the results shone in her face and voice.

"Bobby keeps sitting on my shoulder telling me to do something with my life. I think he's proud of me right now," Laura said, a cocky smile on her upturned face.

Psychic readings may be pooh-poohed sometimes, but what I was noticing was the positive results this one had sparked. Thinking of that same "Michael" reading, I remembered when I had asked about Bobby. My hair stood up on end as I replayed the tape of the reading.

"I can't understand it," the "Michael" channel was saying, "I'm having difficulty tuning into Bobby. He's like a fading radio station— almost like he's not here at all." At the time, I hadn't thought much of that part of the reading. Now, my mind had a thousand questions: Does the soul know in advance when its lifetime on the physical plane is coming to completion? Is time of death or exit from the body predetermined or destined at some level? Is there a subconscious "knowing" of sorts?

Bobby had become very philosophical about the meaning of life just before he died. Our last evening together was a moving discussion about the purpose of being alive. He was feeling something he could not put into words and was looking forward to his "Michael" session on January 24th to add some clarity.

Bobby's airplane had had two different mechanical failures in the last few weeks prior to his death. An engine caught fire while he was flying one day. A tire blew out while he was landing another day. A mechanic friend told Kathleen about the tire blow out. Bobby had gotten out of the plane and kicked the tire and said, "I think my days are numbered."

Now, I shuddered at the whole sequence of events. Coincidental? Our lives seemed to be made up of coincidental happenings coming together. A new element of awareness that was operating in our lives was stimulating lots of questions.

"Mom, I don't exactly know what our destinies are. I only know you are a guiding ray of light for me," were the last words Bobby ever spoke to me. He had peeked back around the corner of my bedroom door as he was leaving, winking and making a thumb-to-index-finger high sign. He smiled and then was gone. The effect he was having on my life, however, was everywhere present. I'd been touched at a spot that ignited my most positive and creative energies.

Returning from my faraway thoughts to the present, I heard the kids downstairs in the kitchen. Greg's Toyota truck was fully loaded. It was time for him to leave for Davenport, Iowa. He'd been accepted into Palmer Chiropractic School, and had allowed himself several traveling days to get there before school began. Kim, Laura, and I lined up for our goodbye hugs. It was hard parting. Bobby's death had brought us even closer together as a family. We watched the little truck, loaded with Greg and all his worldly possessions, drive off and disappear into the hovering misty veil of the morning.

Oh, God, give me strength. I can't handle too many more goodbyes, I prayed. The words slipped out quietly beneath my tears. I looked into Laura's moist amber eyes and saw my thoughts reflected in her pain-filled expression.

I glanced at my watch and realized I'd better hurry if I was going to be on time for my 11:00 AM meeting. How my body and soul longed to stop the merry-go-round of life today, to get off and just do nothing for a whole day. Instead, the pace was accelerating.

A wedding: dresses to choose, color schemes, flowers, and music to plan, and invitations to send. If I chose to do anything at all today, I'd so much rather spend it daydreaming about the upcoming wedding with Kim. The wedding of my daughter had always been a great fantasy to play with.

There never seemed to be enough hours left in the day to do all the things my heart wanted to do. Two days ago, a powerful migraine headache had sent me to bed to shut out sound, sight, smell, and all my thoughts. The headache exaggerated and echoed the pain my whole body was feeling. Long ago, I had begun to relate my migraines to how smart my body really was. When I didn't listen to its needs, it finally would have to take matters into its own hands by giving me the "gift" of a migraine headache.

Stop, Shirley, stop! was the message ringing in my head. There was no arguing priorities when I had one of these headaches. Fasting from all thoughts and physical senses, shutting out everybody and everything for twenty-four hours, was the fastest, best cure. The "up" period that followed a migraine "fast" never ceased to amaze me; it induced a high state of clarity and well being. It was always great to wake up and find the pain gone; it was almost worth the price. Today the "up" period seemed to be fast-fading. What was happening to me? I felt so frustrated and restless.

I was always known as "stable Shirley." Was I becoming "unstable Shirley" now?

As I drove up the steep driveway leading to Dr. Tolleth's hilltop home I was greeted by a spectacular view. The sun was trying to break through the gray puffs of cloud overhead and I could almost make out the Sacramento River to the left. Mt. Diablo had a cloud crown around her peak. I took in several deep breaths and the glorious view.

"Come on up, Shirley-bird," Dr. Tolleth shouted down as I rang the doorbell. He introduced me to the woman I would be working closely with for the next year. Vickie Doretti was the Executive Director of the Educational Foundation of the Association of Plastic and Reconstructive Surgeons (ASPRS-EF). I would be working mostly by telephone with her and the ASPRS-EF headquarters in Chicago.

We discussed what the next year held in store for Dr. Tolleth, and for me as his administrative assistant: meeting dates, files to be set up, the task of coordinating our records with those of the Chicago office and keeping everything updated and on course. Our voices blended into the haze of data, data, and more data. Suddenly, the room started to spin. I couldn't handle any more data or smoke-filled rooms. Not today! I hastily made excuses that I wasn't feeling well and rushed to my car. I held my breath and bit my lower lip, trying to hold back a river of tears. My car seemed to be on automatic pilot; it knew the back road to Oakmont Cemetery and wanted to take me there. When I arrived, I went to the familiar "Garden of Meditation" gravesite.

I could no longer hold back the sobbing. I cried out loudly, the thoughts flying through my mind: my life's falling apart. Nothing has the same meaning anymore. So many changes, too fast. How do I integrate them all? Decisions versus choices. Mind analysis versus intuitive guidance. The deciphering of what to do does not always come that clearly or easily. Sorrow is leading me down paths I've not traveled before, diverting my attention from material things to a more spiritual point of view. I'm open to seeing things from a different perspective. How do I reassemble all my disjointed parts? I'm so confused, tired, restless, and frustrated! God, Jesus, Bobby—whoever is out there and wherever you are, *help me, help me*, I'm drowning! What should I do?

I fell to my knees on the damp carpet of grass, sobbing. Then I laid down, spread-eagled on my back, face to face with the infinity of a sky full of puffy clouds on the move. There I surrendered myself fully to the moment and let my deep sobbing run its course.

The undamming of tears seemed endless. Then, slowly, very slowly, a quiet moved in to take the place of the emotional turmoil deep within me. Then, more clearly than I have ever heard anything in my life, I heard a voice say loudly, "*It's time to leave.*" Intuitively, I trusted this voice beyond explanation. A sense of peacefulness swept through me. I *knew*, without knowing exactly how I knew, that I had received my answer. Some deeper or higher force from within me was guiding me to leave my job and old way of life. Only out of desperation had I sincerely and humbly surrendered myself to a higher power. The voice was *absolutely trustworthy*; I would stake my life on it.

Then I heard Bobby's voice: "Mom, no one knows just how many tomorrows he has left—you've paid your dues—follow your wildest dreams—you're free now—go for it, Mom!"

Tears, this time of relief and joy, once again filled my eyes. A burden had lifted. Poetic singsong began to dance in my head. I took a notebook out of my purse and began to jot it down.

FREE
I choose to be free—
to be truly free,
I must sacrifice
the need for my
old patterns

of security and safety.
Am I ready?

CHOICE
Moments of risk
for to risk
is to dance
with my higher self
in creating
a new expression
of the deepest parts of me
Am I ready?

FAITH
taking a step
at a time,
asking for Divine guidance,
not knowing
where
the path
is leading me.
Only,
that I must
follow this voice
or die of boxed-in-ness,
stuck in time,
a coffin
of my own choosing.
yes, I'm trembling,
Yes, I'm ready!

Pain, sorrow, and frustration were leading me to paths I had not been open to seeing before. I was being asked to look anew, make a course correction, and move on. Choose. Act out. Observe the feedback the universe will reflect back to me.

Actually telling Dr. Tolleth I would be leaving was another thing. He was not only my employer, he was one of my best friends. We'd been together for over fifteen years. He joked I would still be at his right hand when he retired. I remembered he'd hired me as a partner. "You handle the business end of the office and I'll do the surgery," he had offered.

I admired this man from the first moment we met. Before setting up private practice, he served humanity for a year of his life. In Africa, as a flying doctor, he flew from village to village, using his skills to handle surgical problems. Thirty-five millimeter slides captured his adventures well: lion bites, cleft lips, burns, and many other problems rarely seen Stateside. I could just picture him village-hopping. The great white doctor, "Papa Doc," flying in by the seat of his pants to perform surgical miracles and loving every moment of it!

In the fifteen-plus years since we had first set up practice, thousands of patients had touched our lives and hearts, as we had touched theirs. Dr. "T." and I were an aligned team. For me, it was a partnership and friendship *extraordinaire*. It didn't fit into any relationship category I knew of. The needs of our patients were our first priority; sometimes, to the detriment of our own personal lives and needs.

I would miss "Papa Doc." He and our patients were a *big* part of my life. Our patients' personal stories touched me; their courage inspired me. Many became "members of the family," as our lives ongoingly intertwined.

One thing about a plastic surgery practice that I absolutely loved was that whatever bad things had happened to a patient had happened before we first saw them. We got to be in on the miraculous side of medicine, and I had witnessed a full spectrum of miracles: new ears built out of seemingly nothing. A mastectomy patient's smile as breast reconstruction restored her sense of femininity and self-esteem. Faces and jaws that had gone through windshields, skillfully repaired. Hands degloved in accidents, grafted and functioning again. The long ongoing surgical treatment and emotional support of little burn victims, Scotty and Michael. Such beautiful and courageous little souls. First, they struggled to survive physically from their injuries, and then to overcome the emotional scarring.

Then there was the inner spiritual awareness and beauty of Lil. A bout with cancer had cost Lil her whole nose. When she first came to see Dr. Tolleth, a large bandage covered the hole where her nose had been. For three years, she'd gone from doctor to doctor, only to hear there was no hope that a new nose could be surgically constructed. She would need to wear a prosthesis or a bandage for the rest of her life. She prayed every morning for guidance: God, please get me through this day; and at every day's end, Thank you, God. She was a firm believer that whatever or whoever you need in your life comes to you at the right time.

She felt directed to and found Dr. Tolleth and after many hours of consultation, sketching, and planning, three years of reconstructive surgery procedures began. Susan Workman and I visited her in the hospital after the first stage of reconstruction had been done. A rolled tube of flesh from the top of her head, a pedicle flap, came down across her forehead and was attached to the middle of her face. Not exactly a beautiful nose yet, but a hairy beginning. Amazingly, Lil's attitude was one of total peace and gratitude.

"Lil, what's the secret that helps you handle all this so well?" I asked.

"This is a karmic affliction," she said, rather matter-of-factly. "I don't want to come back and do this number again, so I might as well accept it all, keep my sense of humor, and even give thanks to a higher power that I am able to handle it."

Three years later, Lil's new nose was a tribute to her inner strength and beauty and to her surgeon's artistic and surgical genius.

Dale Edison was a patient who really overcame heavy odds that he would die. He was on his way to training camp to play pro football for the San Diego Chargers when a freak fireworks accident hurled him ten feet in the air, blew off both his feet, and shattered his legs almost to the knees, along with a good part of his right hand. As I identified and labeled his patient photos, I said a silent prayer. Emergency room photos are brutally blunt in revealing the extent of injuries—in living color, yet. How could anyone have survived such an accident, I wondered. His prognosis was not good; in fact, last rites had already been administered by a priest.

Dale had an inner spark, however, a determined will to live, and his superbly conditioned athlete's body was not willing to lie down and die. The thousands of hours he'd put in preparing for a football career had given him the mental, physical, spiritual, and emotional strength to keep fighting for his life. He underwent seven surgeries in two weeks. From his hospital bed, he planned several goals. First

106

he learned to walk on his artificial legs; soon after, he was boogeying. He devised a harness for holding a drumstick in his right hand so he could resume playing in a dance band. He obtained his scuba diving certificate. He went back to school at Sacramento State University and received his Master of Science degree in counseling.

Newspapers followed Dale's recovery. Less than two months after the accident, I clipped an article and filed it in his medical chart. The interview with Dale quoted him as saying:

"I'm fortunate to have my sight and my hearing, and one thing is for sure: I still have a chance to contribute to society. This accident is one thing you can't look back on. There's no use in dwelling on it forever." Through the years he'd found many ways to contribute to society. When high school athletic programs were threatened by slashed school budgets, he inaugurated events to raise thousands of dollars to help bail out the athletic programs.

Year after year, Dale has been involved in some youth- or sports-related cause. It has never been a question of *if* he would contribute to society, but only how, when, and to whom a contribution would be made. He continues to dream up new ways to repay his community, friends, and the sports he so loves for the support they've given him to speed up his recovery. Recently he staged a Swim-a-thon during which he swan thirteen miles in an olympic-sized pool *sans* his artificial legs and the full use of one arm. I watched him in amazement. I couldn't have done it and I had full use of two arms and two legs. Some of our patients were truly an intensive, personalized, advanced course in motivation and inspiration!

Dr. Tolleth had even performed a miracle on my son, Greg. On a long-ago December 26th, my niece Kelly's birthday, I was shopping for a special gift for her. What a crazy day to shop. I had waited until after work when the after-Christmas, fifty-percent-off swarms of bargain hunters had diminished. The shops were nearly deserted at this dinner hour. Suddenly, I heard the loud-speaker at Macy's: "If Shirley Rose is shopping in the center, please report to the Personnel Department on the lower level."

When I heard "Shirley," my heart jumped! I looked around the store. I could only see about five other people still shopping. What were the odds on how many Shirleys with a last name beginning with "R" could there possibly be in the store? Maybe they mispronounced my name. My inner voice was urging me to check it out. Downstairs, I identified myself to the personnel clerks.

"I'm Shirley Ruiz. Could it be me you're paging?"

Dead silence reigned as I watched the two ladies first look to each other and then come from behind the counter to take my arm on either side. "Please sit down. There's been an accident."

Who? What? Where? My mind raced first to my husband Bob, and then to each one of my children. The ladies didn't know any of the answers. I was to call the emergency room of the local community hospital and speak to Dr. Tolleth. One of the ladies dialed the hospital number and handed me the telephone. "Chief, what's happened?" I asked in a very shaky voice.

"Shirl, it's Greg. He's had a little accident, but he'll be okay," Dr. Tolleth replied.

"How did it happen?"

"Greg was making a smoke bomb for New Year's Eve, and it exploded in his hand."

"Where is he now?"

"In X-ray. I've got him scheduled upstairs for surgery at about 8:00 PM. Take your time getting here and drive carefully. I'm going to X-ray now to check out his films."

Our conversation told me a lot about the extent of the injuries Greg had sustained. X-ray obviously meant bones were involved. Greg was in the main surgery; I'd seen a lot of pretty bad injuries repaired in the emergency room; this one must be fairly extensive. I could feel the color draining from my face.

The Macy's ladies were wonderful: one insisted on driving me in my car, while the other followed in her own car. When I arrived, my husband Bob was already there waiting for me. Soon after, Greg's father Rick Bruno arrived, too. The three of us sat quietly waiting and praying throughout the three-and-a-half hours Greg was undergoing reconstructive surgery. At 11:30 PM Dr. Tolleth came down from surgery, still in his scrub suit.

"We put Greg's hand back together better than I originally thought possible, Shirl. An angel was sitting on my shoulders as I operated—and on Greg's shoulders, too. He's doing okay now. The surgery went well. Now time will tell the tale."

The slides taken in the emergency room told their gory story. There, in living color, with a tourniquet applied to halt the blood loss, was my son's hand. Large pieces of a shattered metal shell lay beside the torn-up flesh. The skin of his fingers spiraled out like they'd been laid open by a whirling can opener. A chunk of his palm was missing entirely, tendons and nerves had been shattered and severed.

Time had told the tale, all right. Focused determination led Greg through months of slow, repetitive strength-building hand exercises. Greg was applying for entrance into the Naval and Air Force Academies and he *had* to regain full use of his hand in order to be accepted. When the notification finally arrived, Greg was one of Vice President Spiro Agnew's choices for the Naval Academy, but after much inner debate, Greg chose to accept Congressman Jerome Waldie's Air Force Academy appointment. Dr. Tolleth and the angels had worked their miracles, and Greg had done his part, too. He had regained a one-hundred-percent functioning hand.

Now I was planning to leave all this. I owed so much to Dr. Tolleth and I'd miss working with Dr. Ransdell, Susan Workman, Robin Burchett, my daughter Kim, and all of our wonderful patients. Leave? Yes, it was time to leave a whole way of life and circle of friends. It had been a distinct privilege to have interacted with and received so much from so many powerful experiences for the past fifteen years, but it was now time to move on, even though I couldn't yet see clearly exactly what I was moving on to.

How could I tell anyone else about the voice, this force that was magnetically pulling me in a new direction? Well, whether or not I could explain it, sometime in the next several months, before Dr. Tolleth would take over the presidency of the ASPRS Educational Foundation, I would leave. I trusted that the voice would guide me in the "how" and "when" when the time was right. What lay ahead of me in the future was nowhere in my present line of vision. The only thing I could still hang onto was my *unshakable faith* in the voice.

Mother's Day

How strange it was to be driving to the cemetery to visit my son on Mother's Day. Fate had played strange tricks and things seemed ridiculously wired up—backwards.

"Bobby, you're supposed to be bringing me flowers today, not the other way around," I told him, arranging the colorful spring bouquet of daisies, mums, daffodils, and carnations in the vase on his grave. I got the clippers from the trunk of my car and trimmed and manicured the grass overgrowing the tiny, white temporary grave marker. Deep breaths of cool crisp air stimulated my memory and feelings.

Last week, Laura had had some minor surgery. While waiting for her in the waiting room, a mother with three little boys came in. She had her hands full. The boys were close in age. It reminded me of my own sons some twenty-two years ago. Greg was the firstborn; Steven came along twenty months later; and Bobby was born three days before Steve's first birthday. I felt empathy for the mother sitting across from me. The two oldest boys went off to surgery leaving the youngest one rocking quietly in a rocker. He was staring at me. Our eyes met and locked in an intense moment of soul-essence connection. It was so special and beautiful that it momentarily took my breath away, triggering a whole series of feelings. Love and gratitude were playing a balancing game with longing and sadness.

Here at the cemetery, as I thought about the hospital scene, a tidal wave of tears and hopelessness began to engulf me.

> The grandchildren that might have been—
> The dreams gone undreamt—

Looking around me, I saw a lot of grown children bringing flowers to their mothers today. I let my tears flow as I felt my loss and the sense of loss others around me were feeling. A funny thought flitted by: if I caught all my tears in a crystal bowl, how long it would take to cry a gallon?

I wanted to hang onto my sadness and I started talking to Bobby out loud, "Talking seems like the only physical connection I still have with you, Bobby. There's a lot of agreement, though, in the books and people I'm seeking out, that you're around in a spirit form now. Still, I'm sad. I guess my sadness is because I haven't learned to recognize you in your lighter form yet. I long for physical ways to communicate with you directly. Please send me a physical sign that you're still around me.

"You've been away before—school at Embry Riddle Aeronautical University in Florida; sailing the seas and living in Japan while in the Navy; and then to San Diego, California. But you came back before and we could always pick up the phone to say, 'Hi, I love you,' when we wanted to connect.

"I miss you, Bobby! Is there a telephone number in heaven I can call? A c/o God P.O. box number, maybe? I want to send you a care package of love and poems and pumpkin pie."

> ALONE AGAIN
> Bobby,
> I've felt
> *alone* before,
> And
> I grew faster

than ever
had I previously.
Now, *aloneness*
shows its face
again.
It hurts
to see
me growing
so fast—
because you are
gone
from my physical world.
My love for you
is like
God's "carrot on a stick,"
calling and leading me
up the mountain
of spiritual awareness.
An almost urgent acceleration
of life experiences.
I'm feeling my feelings
spontaneously and fully,
moment by moment.
God, I sense your nearness
—and I feel Bobby's, too.
I know
I'm not really *alone*.
Please give me
strength and direction
to make some
sense and use
out of all this,
and—
my life!

Returning from Oakmont Cemetery, a red rose in a crystal and brass vase awaited me. A card in Kimberly's handwriting was propped up in front of it:

Happy Mother's Day! This one is from Bobby; he didn't want you to think he had forgotten you today.

Ask and it shall be given to you.

—Matthew 7:7

ASSET

He who knows others is learned.
He who knows himself is wise.

—Lao-tsu

Grief is similar to experiencing a very long, dark, unending winter. Then one day you awaken to a moment of joy simply because the sun has come out to play in a clear cobalt-blue sky. A delicate, golden butterfly flutters near and lights on a spectacular orange zinnia. In a nearby tree, a bird warbles his love song; the breezes carry it along until it reaches your appreciative ear. A feeling of gratitude sweeps through your body.

It was spring in full bloom; a season for new growth and dreams. It was also a busy and exciting time to take a week's vacation and assist Larry Jensen in putting on another ASSET training.

Larry and I had chosen Pajaro Dunes, California, as the place where we would hold our first ASSET training in August of 1980, and we had decided to do it here again. My first meeting with Larry Jensen had been at a "singles" luau. George Nelson had invited me to attend as his guest. Though George and I arrived together, we went our separate ways once there. After all, this was a "singles" event, and my very first experience with one of these popular groups.

Over in a far corner of the room, I spotted a good-looking man with an impeccable hairstyle. Every hair on his silvered head was in place. I wondered if it ever got messed up, as I asked the lady next to me who he was. "Larry Jensen," came the reply. He was one of the founders of Lifespring, a higher-consciousness training program. Later that evening, we were formally introduced to one another. Larry handed me his business card which bore the information: Larry Jensen, M.B.A., Ph.D.

I next heard from Larry a whole year later when he called and asked me to lunch. "Love to, but I'm leaving for the dream-of-a-lifetime vacation tomorrow. Visiting the Orient at last!" I said excitedly. I told him the approximate date when I would be returning to California. Larry sounded a bit disappointed I'd be away so long and set up a lunch date for the first day after my return.

During lunch, we found we shared many interests: dining, dancing, warm sunny beaches, and best of all, we were both extremely interested in the Human Potential Movement and ways to contribute to the well-being of others as well as ourselves. Lunch ran into dinner, another lunch, another dinner, for almost a week. While having dinner one evening, Larry told me about a dream he had to create the ASSET training (Awareness, Sensitivity and Spiritual Enlightenment Training).

As Larry shared more and more of the details of his dream, I felt excited. I almost visualized it myself. It was to be a tailor-made highly individualized psychological and spiritual growth experience that would support each participant to achieve his or her highest potential. Logistically, the training would need to be restricted to a maximum of twenty people at a time. Ideally, it would be a seven-day live-in session held at a hotel or retreat center.

115

"What do you think?" Larry asked.

I couldn't remember when I was more excited about another person's dream and told him so; thus, a new partnership was born. I was to set up, create, and handle the logistics and paperwork for the training and be Larry's assistant trainer at the sessions. I'd need to learn how to run the video feedback camera, too. Larry was ready to move his dream from the inspiration stage into physical reality.

"Pick a place, pick a date, and we'll do a training!" Larry said. I loved the challenge of organizing and pulling things together. Imagine—he had asked me to be his assistant!

Looking for the "place" was easy. While attending a bridal shower that weekend, I overheard someone mention Pajaro Dunes. I "knew" this was the perfect place and my intuition proved to be correct. Larry and I checked out the facilities at this community of beautiful private beach homes by the sea. It was perfect. Now a dream of mine was also about to come true. In a seminar once, I had described what my "ideal" job might look like: working with people in a loving vocation—on the beach. At the time, I couldn't imagine doing anything that wonderful and wrote it off as a pipedream. Now it was about to become a reality.

We rented three private homes on the beach. The first one was a large multi-bedroomed house where the participants would sleep and have their meals. The second house was in a eucalyptus grove and had a large living room that seemed custom-made for us to use as a "training room." The third house we rented was a condo unit to be used as quarters for the trainer and assistant. I chose Emelie Dumpit-Watson to handle all the food arrangements. She had an interest in preparing attractive and nutritious foods, and at one time had even toyed with the idea of opening a health food restaurant. Emelie was open to the challenge and said she'd give it her best shot.

Planning and talking about the intellectual concepts of what the training would be about and actually doing the ASSET training itself were two different things. I couldn't even begin to imagine the impact the training, and those people attracted to it, would have on my life.

On day one of the first ASSET training, I became a "Jill-of-all-trades"—welcoming committee, den mother, video camerawoman, setup lady, and cleanup lady, as well as an extra set of hands, eyes, and ears for Larry's unique work. I loved it! Becoming accustomed to living in the surprise and spontaneity of the moment was part of working with Larry. As we began the first training, Larry pulled up an extra chair, pointed to it, and told me to sit down.

"What for?" I asked.

"You need to actually *do* the training in order to fully experience its value," Larry said. So I got to wear both hats—to participate as well as perform my other functions.

Nine of us began the first seven-day adventure. By the end of the training, we had become a tight-knit family. Our awareness and sensitivity grew and unfolded in leaps and bounds, day by day. Pajaro Dunes, a long private strip of sandy beach located on the California coastline just north of the Monterey-Carmel area, was a gorgeous place to begin and end each day.

During the process of the training, I experienced some revelations about my life and some decisions I had made at the early age of eighteen months that were still affecting how I lived my life today. At that age, I had had a bad fall, smashing my nose and knocking my front teeth up behind the broken bones of my nose and face. At an appropriate emotional stress point while recalling the incident, Larry asked me to lie down on a bed of foam cushions in the middle of the room. There, he proceeded to regress my memory back in time to the very incident where he suspected I had made some early-life decisions of which I should now be aware.

I floated back in time under Larry's direction. I was suddenly seeing and feeling the drama of eighteen-month-old Shirley in a San Francisco hospital, struggling to breathe. My lips were cut, dry, and very swollen. No air could pass through my broken nose. Pressure bandages covered my eyes to keep down the swelling. I couldn't see and I couldn't breathe. My arms were strapped down to the bed in restraints to keep me from ripping off the bandages. I kept calling out for my Mommy and Daddy to rescue me, but no one came. Unbeknownst to eighteen-month-old me, my parents *had* come— and gone. They were upset at the sight of me in so much distress and had been told not to talk to me. When I heard their voices I started to cry, which only intensified my struggle to breathe. Against their better judgment, they chose to stay away from the hospital until I could be discharged to come home, two weeks later.

There on the pillows of the Pajaro Dunes training room, I vividly relived the feelings and thoughts of a vulnerable, hurting, and seemingly deserted eighteen-month-old Shirley. I discovered I'd made up some conflicting decisions and beliefs about life out of that incident that would, in turn, play themselves out in the ongoing script of my life:

1. People leave me when I need them most—I will never "need" anybody again. I can take care of myself!

2. I will always be there in moments of trauma and pain when others need me. Nobody should have to go through those times by themselves.

Larry again guided me through the same incident with grown-up Shirley's awareness to look at my belief structures more appropriately. The lights went on about several areas of my life and my feelings about being left. I had set myself up to give but had blocked myself from much receiving. It was no wonder that I often found myself burnt out, an empty cup with nothing more to give. It had been a heavy evening for me, but uncovering my feelings and re-experiencing them from a more constructive perspective had left me feeling lighter than I'd felt in a long time. I could feel in my whole body that I'd freed myself from something.

Later, on the fifth day of the training, the whole group went to the beach for a special meditation. It was my birthday. The golden sun was sinking into the white-capped deep blue of the Pacific Ocean. What a spectacular sight! For my birthday present, Katharine Parker dedicated a Sunset Silhouette Dance to me. She was magnificent. Her lithe body almost flew as it arched, spun, leapt, and melded itself with nature's glorious stage. She was part seagull, part dolphin, part ballerina, and part gymnast. The rest of us hugged, shoulder to shoulder, feeling privileged to watch this professional dancer in a peak performance.

When we returned to the main house for a dinner break, a huge banner saying "Happy Birthday, Shirley" hung from the rafters along with balloons and streams of colored paper. Larry's daughter and the cook had been busy. The smell of a roasting turkey filled the house, adding to the festivities. A round of "Happy Birthday" was sung as

Sunset Birthday Dance

I opened a gift from the group. It was a Steve Halpern cassette tape I'd enjoyed listening to earlier in the day. My Pajaro Dunes "family" brought me gifts they had chosen and gathered from nature: a deserted bird's nest, in it a hollowed egg saying "I Love You"; a perfect sand dollar; a piece of driftwood; and tiny seashells. The group was teaching me quickly how to receive without delay.

By the end of day seven, the rest of the group had experienced major psychological and emotional breakthroughs, too. We saw in each other new expressions of joy, aliveness, and love. We'd been witness to a "miracle" or two. Each person enriched the whole group as they unfolded themselves into higher spiritual awareness. It had been a nurturing and enlightening seven days. All of us were anxious to return to our loved ones and the everyday world; we knew we would view everything through "new" eyes of awareness.

The second ASSET training had amongst its participants the familiar face of my eldest son, Greg. I looked at the circle of stoic faces as the training began; another unique "family" to love and support. This training, Larry gave me the opportunity to create my own early-morning exercise periods using our mini-trampolines and some processes on the beach to open up everyone's sensitivity levels. It was a great way to start each day.

During the training, Greg, too, got to look at some of the patterns of his life. On the sixth morning, the last day for doing individualized processes, Greg surrendered his "got-it-all-together" stance and found himself being regressed back to a time when he might have set up a block to experiencing happy, satisfying relationships.

When Larry is in his trainer role, his personality almost disappears and he becomes a clear channel for higher consciousness and intuitive guidance. He jumped on the opportunity to assist Greg in making a breakthrough.

In the back of the room, I could hardly contain myself as Larry began the regression. Sitting on my director's stool behind the video camera, I could see and feel my son's pain, and I also felt the joy of knowing he was about to break through something that was blocking him psychologically. The issue was brought up when Greg had a confrontation with a young lady in the training. He was very angry, and Larry used this anger as a tool to regress him back to a specific incident.

Greg went back to a scene I'd uncovered during my 6-Day training two years earlier. At the time, I was looking for whatever had come between Greg and me that was diminishing our ability to lovingly communicate. In our separate regressions, we both recalled the same scene.

In the recalled incident, eight-year-old Greg had overheard his stepfather Bob and I in a heated discussion about how I allowed my children, Greg particularly, to walk into my bedroom unannounced whenever they felt like talking to me. I told Bob I could understand his feelings and I could also understand my children's. Their father Rick and I had raised them during their early years with a lot of openness. Rarely did we lock doors or require a formal invitation for the kids to feel free to come pounce on our bed for hugs and a chat. Bob had a different point of view.

I realized that if this second marriage was to survive, I was going to have to learn to do a dance on the high wires to maintain the delicate balance between being a good wife and being a good mother. I compromised myself and chose to subtly cut off some of my accessibility to my children. "Busyness" was my name for this change; it was an easy-to-do game plan, because the boys were young, Kimberly was a toddler, and Laura was newborn.

I really *was* busy, and this put up an effective, invisible curtain between us. From Greg's point of view, he only knew he didn't feel very close to me anymore. No matter how or what he tried, things between us felt different. The warm affection that used to flow spontaneously now felt stifled and restricted. Consciously, the incident had long ago been buried and forgotten, but the effects of it in Greg's life could now be more clearly seen.

From the age of eight, Greg kept trying to figure out what he had done to change things between us, and what he now had to do to have them be the same again. Thus, he followed a path of achieving and achieving, hoping to find what he had to do to be number one with me again. As Larry uncovered all the feelings and thoughts of eight-year-old Greg, life-shaping decisions he had made out of this incident emerged and were looked at with new awareness and in a more beneficial way. My heart was both pained and joyful as I relived the scene with Greg in his regression—pained for the twenty years of closeness it had cost us and joyful that the block had been discovered and cleared.

After the regression Greg rejoined the circle of his ASSET family. Larry began talking about the hidden incidents in all our lives that greatly influence how we operate today.

"They are not good or bad in themselves," he said. "However, how we perceive them and decisions and beliefs we make out of them could create present-day blocks to our awareness and aliveness. There is always another side to the same story, a different perception of the same event. We always *choose* how we perceive anything that happens to us," Larry went on. "You've all been in on Greg's perception of this incident. You now have a really rare privilege—the opportunity to hear another perception of the same story. Greg's mother is sitting in the back of the room, and I'd like her to come to the front and share what went on from her point of view."

Larry caught me by surprise with his invitation. I blew my teary nose and described my "moment of choice" and how it had affected my life. The whole process had been invaluable for everyone. We got to see clearly how we each choose how we perceive everything that happens to us in our lives. Perhaps with this new awareness, we'd see our lives and the people in them with new eyes.

The third ASSET training took place in late January of 1981. I was part of it in spirit, love, and prayers only. The search for Bobby on Mt. Shasta was taking place the day the training began. Greg was scheduled to do the cooking for this newest training group, and Laura planned to attend as a participant. Under the circumstances, all three of us were absent from the Pajaro Dunes scene. ASSET graduates from the two previous trainings quickly volunteered to fill in for Greg and I when they heard about Bobby. Larry kept in touch with the happenings on Bobby, and on the sixth day told the group about Bobby's death. That evening the newest members of the ASSET family took a break, went to the beach, and dedicated a sunset meditation to Bobby's spirit.

The March ASSET brought nine more participants, including LaRena, to the Pajaro Dunes training room. LaRena was anxious to gain more insight on the boxed-in feelings of anger she sometimes felt. She also wanted to get to the bottom of "not wanting to go into forests" in her meditations. By now, I had witnessed enough processes to know that there was a great chance this would all come up in the training room for her. Sure enough, during one early-morning session it happened. Her present-day anger led her right into a red-hot regression session which revealed the long-forgotten anger of an adventurous child forbidden to go play in a nearby forest the grownups had labeled as very dangerous. She now understood her reluctance to go into "forests". LaRena's normally green flashing eyes looked beautifully peaceful and blue on ASSET graduation day.

Now it was May, and I wondered what lay ahead this time? Three of my closest family members were enrolled in this one: Laura, Kathleen, and Debra Maines Cotter. Deb had always called me "Ma II" over the many years we had known each other. Kathleen, my daughter-in-law, was open and searching. Bobby's death had left her a widow at the tender age of twenty-five. They had been a big part of each other's lives for almost ten years. Where was the rest of her life going to lead now that she was alone?

Laura was here to break through her frustration with repeating patterns in her life and to look at the deep feelings of rejection she'd had as long as she could remember.

Several people were flying in from the Los Angeles area to take the training. We rented an extra beach house to hold them all. What a beautiful one it was—right on the beach, and the large dining room/living room area had a huge fireplace and picture windows that looked out to the ever-changing Pacific Ocean.

As the participants gathered together, the training began. In the middle of the third day, something Larry said to Laura pushed her "hot" button. On the lunch break, Laura stomped out of the training room towards the ocean. She flung her ASSET notebook down into the sand dunes and disappeared out of sight. I crossed my fingers. I knew she was at a point where it would be tempting to run away from her anger and leave, even though she'd originally agreed to stay until the training was complete. I said a silent prayer that she'd see her own life patterns and choose to stay and delve into what this recurring anger and running away were all about.

The afternoon session started. No one had seen Laura during the lunch hour. We began without her. Several minutes later, the sliding glass door opened, and Laura quietly slipped into the room. Larry gave her the opportunity to acknowledge she was late and ask the group for permission to rejoin them. She said she'd been walking on the beach for two hours, watching an internal battle going on deep inside her. The angry part of her wanted to quit the training and leave without a word to anyone, but another part of her, now growing stronger day by day, was tired of running. It wanted her to stay and get to the core of all her frustrated, angry feelings.

"Laura, I don't think it's so much anger at all. I think under that anger is a lot of pain and sadness," a lady sitting next to Laura said, starting things off. With that remark, Laura doubled up, hugging her stomach, and started to cry. Emotional upsets had always seemed to show up as a bout with stomach pains for Laura, even as a colicky newborn.

Larry arranged the pillows on the floor in the center of the group and invited Laura to pursue the roots of her pain in a regression process. Laura quickly agreed and laid down among a group of loving supporters. The lights were dimmed and the regression began. Larry asked Laura to describe the pain she was feeling. Using it as a tool, he had her drift back in time to the last time she could remember experiencing the same intense pain. "At my brother Bobby's funeral," Laura replied.

Gently, Larry proceeded to explore the many past incidents of pain. She recalled being a pre-teen and overhearing the neighbor boys and one of her brothers say, "Poor Laura, she'll never have a pretty figure like Kim. Too bad for Laura."

The pain struck again as she recalled the scene. Then she went even further back in time...further back...further back she drifted. Laura sobbed and doubled up; the pain was stronger than ever now. Larry told her to *be* her awareness and see what was going on outside the pain.

"Where are you now, Laura?" he asked.

Suddenly Laura was peaceful as she described being warm and feeling like she was floating. "I'm in my Mommie's tummy. I like it here. I feel very safe and peaceful. I'd like to stay here."

Just as suddenly, Laura was in intense pain again.

"I'm being pushed and squashed now. I'm stuck somewhere and it hurts." There was a long silent pause before she continued, "Now, I'm being propelled somewhere. It's bright and strange. Ouch! Someone slapped me on the butt. I don't like it here at all. Where's my Mommie?"

Laura continued to recall the details of her birth. It was strange to hear my own child describing her birth so accurately. She had deep awarenesses and feelings as a newborn infant, though not the language or ability to express it.

"They put me in a plastic box and cut me off from my Mommie. Somebody says I'm not very pretty. I'm purple and have big hands. My hair is thick, black, and straight and my nose is all flat. Nobody wants me!"

Skillfully, Larry explored all the dark corners of her mind and then took nineteen-year-old Laura's awareness back into the birth situation to look at her rejection beliefs and decisions she had made at birth. At the end of the process, her new ASSET family made a cradle with their arms, picked her up, and rocked her as they sang "Rock-a-bye Laura" to the tune of "Rock-a-bye Baby." They told her how beautiful and loved she was, stroking her blonde hair and kissing away her tears. "Baby Laura" now had a new nurturing "birth" experience to remember.

It was an incredible privilege to watch a process like this, particularly when it was my own child involved. I could only wish that each of my children and every child in the world could have an opportunity like this to free themselves from early childhood traumas. I'd seen phenomenal benefits many times over in the lives of people who had undergone similar regressions.

I knew what was coming next: Larry called me to the trainer's chair in front of the room to tell the other side of this story. I stopped first to give my "baby" a long, loving hug. Taking in a deep breath, I began.

"My pregnancy with Laura was a surprise. She was conceived in spite of birth control devices and was due thirteen months after the birth of her sister, Kimberly. Overdue and anxious to deliver, I decided to take castor oil to speed the process. The only way I could keep the awful-tasting stuff down was to blend it with concentrated orange juice in my blender and quickly swallow it. Labor began immediately but progressed slowly. After a few hours, it stopped entirely. The labor room nurse checked me and said I had '...a ways to go.' She would check with the doctor and see what they could give me to induce labor again. In moments, she was back with a bottle of nose spray.

"'Nose spray to induce labor?' I asked. She instructed me to inhale deeply as she sprayed my nostrils. As she left the labor room, I experienced a long hard labor pain and told my husband Bob to '...get the nurse quick! The baby's coming!' Bob looked a bit puzzled and went to call the nurse.

"'Relax, Mrs. Ruiz, I just checked you and you're not ready to deliver yet,' the nurse instructed.

"I insisted I was! Reluctantly, she checked me and said, 'Oh, my God!' as she tore off her glove and ordered Bob to go to the father's waiting room.

"In the delivery room, all nine pounds of Laura burst into the world. She had poor circulation and was immediately put into an incubator. She looked awfully big to be in that tiny plastic box. Early the next morning, I was taken into surgery to repair the delivery damage and have some exploratory procedures done. Physically, Laura and I were separated for the first ten days of her little life. I could only view her through the nursery window. I longed to hold my little daughter, but surgical patients did not have 'rooming-in' privileges in the surgical wing. Rules were rules.'"

Another interesting thing revealed itself in all this. Since infancy, every time Laura tried to drink orange juice, she got violent stomach spasms to the point of vomiting it up—projectile style. Hmmm... that was certainly food for thought. Was this severe "allergy" also directly connected to the birth trauma?

As the training went on, others in the group were making breakthroughs of their own. What a privilege to be a part of this process. It filled me with new insights and compassion for the human experience of life. My love for humanity was intensified and growing in leaps and bounds with each new awareness.

Late on the fifth day, after a short break, there was an opportunity for anyone in the group to share what was going on with them. One man said he had "seen" his guides on the break. He hadn't "seen" them in months. He sensed something very spiritual was going on here today.

"There is a beautiful and mysterious-looking halo out over the ocean right now. I saw it as I walked along the beach during the break," he continued.

I had heard about "guides," but if I had any, I'd certainly never "seen" them. Still, I sensed they existed and wanted to know more. One of my jobs each day was to let Larry know the exact time of sunset. Weather permitting, we'd all go to the beach to meditate and practice special breathing techniques. Then, we had a free period to spend as we chose. Today, everyone seemed to be sensing something different in the air and wanted to adjourn to the beach right away. Larry agreed. It was fast nearing time for the 8:14 PM sunset. He told the group to bundle up in their warm sweaters and jackets and head for the beach.

I lagged behind to blow out the candles, straighten up a bit and lock up the training room. The path to the beach was a wooden walk-way between several houses. As I approached the stairs leading down to the beach, I stopped in my tracks and took in a deep breath. The seaside panorama of Monterey to my left and Santa Cruz to the right was spectacular. It was almost sunset and a warm golden luminous light shone through soft gray fluffy clouds. A halo was on the water in front of us.

From my high vantage point on the stairs, I could see the line of my ASSET "children" stretching across the beach, holding hands and gazing silently into the water. Larry must have given them a signal to break off and do whatever they wanted to do individually while the sun prepared to set for the day. I could pick out Laura and Kathleen very clearly.

Suddenly, Kathleen and Laura darted off in opposite directions. Kathleen ran towards the south while Laura skirted the waters northward. At the very same instant in time, both of them dropped to their knees. The halo expanded its rays of light in both directions and encompassed them both. Immediately, I became aware that the light of the halo had encircled me, too, as well as everyone in front of me on the beach. I *felt* Bobby's presence intensely. My mind started wildly questioning what was happening to us.

"Bobby, are you here?" I asked.

A plane appeared out of nowhere directly overhead, blinking bright lights, and it tipped its wings, like it was waving. The plane disappeared in an instant, as quickly as it had appeared. On the beach I could see some of our group taking off their shoes, rolling up their pantlegs and walking knee-deep in what I thought was a

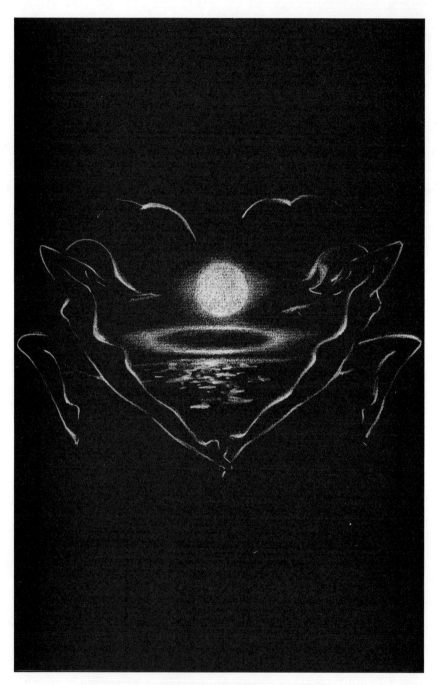

Halo on the Water

cold, but now very gentle, surf. Deeply touched, I dabbed at the tears running down my cheeks and headed back to open up the training room. What had happened? Had the others been aware of anything out of the ordinary?

One by one, the participants returned. I looked at each of their faces and saw that something had happened to everyone. Kathleen came in first and then Laura; they had both been crying. Larry opened the time for sharing. Someone requested that the large candle from the kitchen be placed in the center of the circle of chairs. Several people movingly described their experience of the halo and how they let Kathleen and Laura run off by themselves, sensing something important was happening to each of them that they needed to fully experience alone.

Kathleen said she felt an urge to run and then, just as suddenly, felt the urge to drop to her knees. She felt strangely warmed, like a big hug from Bobby, as the shimmering "light" embraced her in its arms.

Laura was crying as she echoed some of the same sensations. First she had felt a need to run. She stopped as the "light" reached out and enfolded her in its brilliance. Looking upwards, she could see millions of firefly-like bits of energy. In her words, it was like "...little stars of light, twinkling, turning, and spinning. At that moment, a plane flew above me and flashed its lights. The ocean water washed up around my ankles. It was so warm. I fell to the wet sand in a kneeling position, as though obeying some invisible command. With my eyes closed, I asked, 'Is it you, Bobby, is it you?' I opened my eyes and saw the pattern in the sand my hands had made when I'd fallen. It was a big Y! I bawled like a baby. I didn't wonder anymore; I *knew*!"

Up on the wooden stairway, I had participated on two levels. I was included in the same encirclement of the wondrous "light," and, from my higher vantage point, I had also observed the whole miracle.

Everyone agreed that something exquisitely beautiful had happened to all of us. The ocean, moments before, had been rough and icy cold. Now, it was miraculously warm and inviting. The "witnesses" bathed in its soft gentle surf, and drank in the last rays of sunset. It was a spontaneous mystical experience of *agape*, divine love.

129

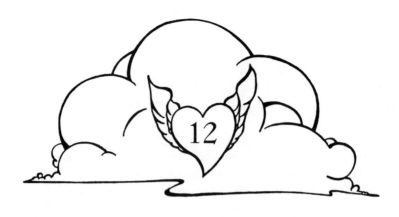

Janessa Bobbi

Kathleen and I drove to the San Francisco airport to meet the flight bringing son Steve and his wife Darsie to visit. A very special young lady was accompanying them on this trip—Janessa Bobbi, my five-and-a-half-week-old granddaughter. My parents arrived at the airport at about the same time as Kim and her fiance Rick Parker. What a welcoming party!

We had a few minutes left before the scheduled arrival of Flight 53, so I left the family and went looking for a flower shop. As a young pilot walked by, my heart did a double-take and I turned to look again. Bobby? No.

Oh, God, I thought. I was so hoping that a miracle had happened. He so looked like my son; he even had the same walk, hair, and smile. I was vividly reminded of Bobby in his pilot's uniform.

"Mom, you just wait. When I'm a pilot, you'll be able to fly anytime you want, anywhere!" I could hear Bobby saying to me.

Bobby and I had had some memorable times together in the air: a late-evening flight, with me playing tourist, viewing the fascinating nightlight layout of San Diego; a Sunday morning flight to Half

Moon Bay on the California coast; practicing "touch and gos" at Buchanan Air Field in Concord; and a flight along the coast of the blue Pacific Ocean where at the precise moment of sunset, the Golden Gate Bridge came into view. The whole sky was afire with gold, orange, and scarlet as the sunset spread its fingers of fiery light over the western horizon. Twinkling lights outlined the silhouettes of the skyscrapers of San Francisco. Across the Golden Gate, towards Sausalito, multi-colored sailboats were heading home as a full, butterscotch-yellow moon began to rise over the Bay Bridge on the eastern horizon. It was a priceless, timeless moment of reverence, wonder, and ecstasy.

Now for my son—my pilot—his dreams and my dreams hadn't come true. Or had they really, perhaps way beyond our wildest dreams? If the human soul truly chooses to be born into a particular physical body, at a particular time and place, to add some learning by taking a few specialized classes, how would Bobby's life look?

Bobby had wanted to be a pilot since the day he picked up his first airplane toy. He felt an inner calling to fly even as a small child. On the very day he was old enough, he soloed. Thereafter, he quickly obtained his private pilot's license, his instrument rating, and then his multi-engine, instructor, and commercial licenses. Consistently, he set a goal, reached it, and set a new one. He found his special love at age fifteen—dated, loved, and married his Kathleen. They thoroughly enjoyed playing their guitars, flying, and doing their art work together. He had loving relationships with every member of the family, and his fastidious pilot skills were respected by those he flew with.

Who am I to judge that his "schooling" here on planet Earth was not complete in twenty-five years? He had set and attained his goals and was surrounded by love. Sometimes people are still searching for that level of satisfaction no matter how many years they've punched in on their earth timeclock.

I purchased a flower for Darsie and began walking back to the gate where the flight would arrive. My faraway thoughts were quickly brought back to the present as I heard Kim and Kathleen excitedly shouting, "There's their plane!"

My heartbeat accelerated. Grandchildren are supposed to be a joy. How will I really feel deep inside when I hold this first grandchild of the family tree? I truly didn't know.

131

Janessa Bobbi and her Granny

I stood on tip-toes and strained through the crowd of deplaning people to catch the first glimpse.

"There's Steve, and there's Darsie!" I couldn't miss Darsie's gorgeous red hair. In Steve's arms was a yellow bundle. He walked straight towards me, said "Hi, Mom!" and placed little Janessa Bobbi in my arms. Feelings of absolute ecstasy flooded through my body as I peeled back the soft yellow receiving blanket and viewed the tiny package of perfection. Flashbulbs started flashing, forever capturing my broad smile and my gentle tears of pure joy. God taketh—God giveth!

The following Monday at the office, I was wondering how my leaving was going to finally come about—and when. The voice within me had been silent on that matter. I had told my bosses in March I'd be leaving by the end of October and nothing more had come of it for the past four months. It wasn't brought up again. Maybe they thought I was only reacting to the stress of the moment when I said it and had changed my mind. Even I began wondering how it was going to unfold.

I thought about putting an ad in the paper so I could start interviewing for my replacement. Every time I thought about it, it felt like the voice inside said, "Ugh." Was it my imagination? Surely, I must do something soon. Could it be I was just avoiding what looked like a chore—long hours of interviewing appointments? There would be plenty of applicants, that was for sure. In my opinion, I had the very best job a person could land in my field.

I dashed over to Mt. Diablo Medical Center Hospital to grab a quick lunch before afternoon office hours started. My peach yogurt was almost gone when I saw an old familiar face coming towards me. It was Mary Costello, a patient from out of the past. She looked radiantly gorgeous as we exchanged updates on what we each had been doing. She had been in Yountville for awhile and was in the process of moving back to the Bay Area.

"Keep me in mind if you hear of any doctor's offices needing someone like me," she said, as we hugged good-bye. As I looked at her, a halo of flashbulb-type lights appeared to light up the space around her upper body and "light bulbs" started flashing in my head, too. Could it be this simple? Is Mary the one I have been waiting for? Just like that?

I could hardly keep my mind on the payroll checks I was writing, I was so excited. What do I do now? Tell Dr. Tolleth and Dr. Ransdell? Interview Mary on my own first?

That evening, after the last patient had left, I went into Dr. Tolleth's office. "I think I've found the perfect person to replace me," I said excitedly, as I told him about my meeting with Mary. Dr. Tolleth blinked like he didn't believe what he was hearing. Had he thought I had changed my mind about leaving? Possibly.

"Well, go ahead and interview her and let me know what you think," he answered in a monotone.

A telephone call to Mary set up a lunch meeting for us the next day. I *knew* she was the best person for the job and our meeting had been divinely arranged. A great sense of relief came over me, as the process of finding a replacement was a crucial one, much like finding a loving surrogate mother to take over the rearing of my precious children.

Mary had the experience and the smarts to carry off the big job she and Dr. Tolleth would be handling as he took over the Presidency of the ASPRS Educational Foundation. It also appeared she had the one other *crucial* quality I was looking for: someone with "people love"—a loving patient-oriented point of view. The practice had been built from day one with healthy doses of compassion and love as part of the post-op care. I thanked my "little voice" for urging me to be patient. Mary interviewed with both her new bosses, and we set a date for her to begin training for my job.

Meanwhile, in the evenings, little Janessa Bobbi often found herself cuddling up with her Granny. It had been a long time since I had changed a diaper or fed a baby. My, how things have changed in twenty years! Diapers were now disposable and so were the liners in Janessa's baby bottle. But one thing hadn't changed: an infant responding to someone who loved her dearly. When Janessa would start a fussing period, I'd take the cover off my trampoline and the two of us would gently bounce to soft music as we looked over the lights of Walnut Creek. One morning at 5:00 AM, we watched a big orange moon sink and set into the Lafayette-Oakland hills. Such fun it was being a grandparent. I could fully enjoy her and then hand her back to her parents when it was time for me to get on with my life. I knew I was going to love being a granny!

Kim and I planned a baby shower for Darsie. A rare treat, the honoree, Janessa, was present to model all the darling baby clothes. It was a joyous way to see many friends I hadn't seen since Bobby's funeral. Now, we could share a lighter, happier time.

We made a trip to San Francisco to see Janessa's great-grand-mother Mary and great-great-grandmother Cleo. What a privilege to have pictures of five generations in a family photo album. I was grateful Kim had thought to bring her camera along. Times like these shouldn't slip by without being recorded.

Sneaky little Kimberly had planned a surprise birthday party for me at the Concord Pavilion. I thought I was just going to see a show, but when I arrived, lo and behold, balloons were everywhere and a picnic was spread on the lawn. By the time Donna Summer came on stage, we were rocking on the grass. It was hard to watch Donna and sit still. I opened presents during the intermission, and Kathleen saved a special one for last. I opened it and wept. It was a framed sketch of a twin-engined airplane cruising above the clouds. The corner of the picture identified the plane as an Aztec "F," the date as 7-3-77, and the artist's signature was "Bobby." How precious and priceless a gift.

The night before the kids were leaving for home, my Pittsburg High School reunion was held. I almost cancelled going so I could spend one last evening with my granddaughter and her parents. As things worked out, Steve and Darsie had some other relatives they wanted to see, so I had a free evening after all. Kathryn Davi-Billeci and I decided to go together without male escorts. Taking a date along might rob us of the opportunity to visit with old classmates all evening.

All through the reunion the subject of Bobby's death came up. Harry and Barbara Dillon came up and we gave each other big hugs. The death of a child somehow makes parents instant kin. A classmate, Jack Becker, said he was sorry to hear about Bobby's death. How was I pulling myself back together so well? He didn't think he could have handled it if it had happened to him. Two months later, fate dealt Jack and Dora Becker new roles. Their oldest son, Michael Becker, was killed in an automobile accident. Bobby's voice seemed to echo in my ears as I heard about Michael's death: "Mom, no one knows just how many tomorrows he has left. Go for your wildest dreams, *now!*"

The next morning I fed Janesa her last bottle before the trip to the San Francisco airport. It would be hard to let her go. She'd be so far away from me, growing in leaps and bound between the times I'd get to spend with her. I kissed her goodbye gently.

"God bless and keep you, little Janessa Bobbi, till Granny sees you again." I watched the plane take off, keeping my eyes glued on it until the tiny speck in the sky had disappeared from view.

Another "goodbye" had been said.

Ouch! It hurts.

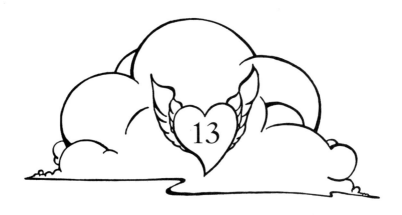

The Birthday Picnic

Tomorrow would be September 8th, Bobby's twenty-sixth birthday. What in the world should I do? Forget about it? Pretend that it doesn't matter anymore? Buy Bobby a present? He certainly couldn't use any of the usual gifts; shirts, airplane books, and shaving lotions were no longer appropriate. Flowers? I did that regularly anyway. Maybe I could just stay busy and let the day pass with no particular significance given to it? I knew myself better—that wouldn't work either.

I called Kathleen to see if she was going to go to the cemetery. "Yes!" she replied. As we talked, the inspiration came to have a "birthday picnic" for Bobby up at the Oakmont Cemetery. The idea sprang out of nowhere into a teamwork plan. Kathleen would bake a cake. Susan Workman and Kim wanted to come, too. Laura said she would meet us there.

At noon on September 8th, we arrived and descended on our favorite area of green grass loaded down with bags of goodies. As if following some well-orchestrated script, we spread out blankets and began talking out loud to Bobby, laughing as if we *knew* he was with us, though not in a form we could physically see. We devoured the Kentucky Fried Chicken and coleslaw after saying grace and giving additional thanks to the "Colonel."

A cemetery cart with two young men in it cruised by now and then. They slowed down as if in disbelief at what they were seeing. Joy, dancing, and celebration in a cemetery? Kathleen uncovered the cake she'd baked and began lighting the candles. Impossible task. The wind on this grassy hill seemed to play laughingly with the match flames. This would never do! "Wind! Stop it!" we commanded jokingly. The wind obeyed instantly. Kathleen quickly lit all the candles. We joined hands and sang "Happy Birthday," thrilled at how "powerful" we were to be able to call to the wind and have it answer immediately with stillness. At the very instant we finished the last note of "Happy Birthday," the wind again stirred. It unleashed the breath it had been holding, blowing out all the candles in one swooping whoosh. We looked at each other in disbelief, our bodies sprouting giant goosebumps. Then, two of the candles relit themselves as if by magic. They reminded me of the "trick" candles I had once bought in a specialty shop. The candles we were looking at, however, were just ordinary birthday candles. These unexplained incidents were becoming increasingly commonplace in our lives.

I handed Kim, Laura, Susan, and Kathleen each a little "Bobby" present. It was a cassette tape of Richard Harris' musical interpretation of "The Prophet." This particular interpretation of Kahlil Gibran's classic was done with a hair-raising intonation and orchestration. I looked up at the sky as I listened. Each time I played the tape, I heard something new or understood the message with new clarity and awareness. It opened my mind to higher thoughts.

The clouds were moving very fast across the sky. Everything was moving very fast. Relationships, money, family—the direction of my life!

"Happy Birthday, Bobby. You sure are a catalyst for people to get on with their lives! Your death has been an earthquake, shaking everything to its deepest levels. Where's it all leading?"

As we were packing our things to leave, the two young men we'd seen passing by earlier stopped their cart. They told us what a joy we were to watch. They could feel our love as they heard us singing

138

"Happy Birthday." They never saw much dancing and laughing around here. They felt touched and inspired. I remembered an est aphorism:

If God told you
exactly what it was you were to do,
you would be happy doing it
no matter what it was.
What you're doing is
what God wants you to do.
Be happy!

Was there a key to life hidden somewhere in all this? Should I follow my heart, my feelings, and my intuition in what would make me happiest in the moment in any circumstance? And in moments of exuberant joyousness, is this vibration picked up by those around me so they become more joyous, too? To help create a happier, more harmonious world would it only take finding the things that make me the happiest, most harmonious me I could be?

Oh, Shirley, your philosophical wandering and questioning never stops these days, I mumbled to myself. This balance between functioning in the philosophy-oriented spiritually awakened world that was calling me and functioning in a physical body in a physical world was a delicate and ever-changing dance movement. One asked that I become a joyous, loving, and receptive spirit; the other demanded that bills be paid and the laundry be done. Was I leading a double life, or what?

Following my intuition was vastly different from figuring things out in my mind. I was trusting this inner guidance to lead me more and more each day, developing a willingness to "go with the flow." An unshakable faith that I was being guided by a force within and bigger than any "me" I'd previously known was also developing. Without that faith, I might have stopped everything I was doing more than once, frozen in fear or, at the very least, in limbo. Change was now an accepted part of my everyday life. One blink, and the course of my life had shifted again.

Coming back to the party, I hugged the girls and thanked them for coming to Bobby's party. It was a perfect way to express the love we all felt for him and wanted him to receive today.

Back at the office, the physical side of life was calling loudly. Twelve surgeries needed scheduling and payroll checks had to be written. Ah, yes! There was also that full clothes hamper awaiting me at home tonight, too.

Saturday morning arrived, bringing with it all that had to be done to finalize Kim and Rick's wedding reception plans. The wedding invitations were ready for addressing. The photographer had taken a beautiful outdoor shot of the two of them by a big oak tree, sunlight streaming in the background. This photo formed the center of the engraved wedding invitations.

The size-four beaded wedding dress was ready to be fitted to Kim's tiny waist. Rust-colored satiny-silk gowns for the four bridesmaids also awaited fitting. Two hundred and fifty sets of golden wedding rings, tied in pairs with satin, sat atop the apricot-colored netting housing white Jordan almonds. China, crystal, and silver patterns, as well as Kim's color preferences, were registered at the leading department stores. Honeymoon reservations in Hawaii had been confirmed by Rick's travel agent. We'd have to put our heads together to find a way to let Kim know what kind of clothing to pack without giving away the "top secret" honeymoon destination. I was also tying up the last week of loose ends before Mary Costello took over my job with Dr. Tolleth and Dr. Ransdell.

Taking the hot-roller curlers out of my hair, I looked up to see Kim's reflection joining mine in my bathroom mirror. One look at her face told me something was very wrong. She had obviously been crying hard.

"Mom, I can't go through with the wedding," Kim said tearfully. "I thought maybe I was having a bad case of the pre-wedding jitters, but it's more than that. My little voice has been saying 'no, don't go through with this' for some time now. I tried to ignore it for awhile, but I just can't anymore. Rick and I broke off our engagement last night. I just don't like the person I've become lately. Rick deserves better. After Bobby's death, I wanted to be married and have a family more than anything. Maybe my grief made me jump into a relationship. I don't know. I only know that to jump into marriage, the way that I feel now, would be a bigger mistake. I'm sorry Mom, for all the trouble and expense I've caused you." Kim had hardly stopped talking long enough to take a breath. I took her shaking body in my arms and held her tightly.

"Honey, I'm so proud of you," I said. "It takes guts to follow your inner voice. That seems to be the big lesson we're each learning in our own way. You've got a lot of courage, this near your wedding date, to call it all off. It would have seemed easier to get swept up in the pageantry of planning a big formal wedding and just quietly bury your feelings and follow through with the 'I dos.' The expense is cheap compared to the price of marrying before you're ready to make that kind of a commitment. Somehow it's all for the best. Rick and you have grown a lot in these past months. You opened his heart to give and receive love, and his love for you warmed you during a heavy time of loss. Love shared is never love wasted."

*　　*　　*

The timing of everything had come together with amazing precision. It was a great time to be leaving the medical profession; I had reached the peak of my career in the field. Dr. Tolleth was about to reach a peak in his career, too. He'd soon be installed as President of the Educational Foundation of the American Society of Plastic and Reconstructive Surgeons. It'd been almost sixteen years now since I first went to work for Dr. Tolleth. The cherry on the cake of our professional lives together for me was a trip to the National Convention in New York to witness his moment of achievement.

Attending a national convention in the "Big Apple" was exciting; it was my first visit to "New York, New York." There were wonderful side benefits, too. A ride through Central Park in a horse-drawn carriage, Broadway shows, shopping excursions, and cuisine adventures to write home about. I almost felt guilty because I was having such a great time. Mary Costello and I were sharing a room. She was spending most of her time in meeting rooms, while my responsibilities lessened each day, leaving me more time for play.

The Presidential Ball was a beautifully orchestrated formal affair. As Hale Tolleth made his acceptance speech, I was moved by deep feelings of pride, gratitude, and love for this wonderful man who had been a part of my life for so long. It was a fitting climax to the work we had done together to be sharing this moment with him.

On the way home from the New York ASPRS Convention, I flew into Phoenix, Arizona. The Association of Plastic Surgery

Assistants (APSA) Convention was being held in Scottsdale. I had been National President of the organization the year before. This time, I could just relax and enjoy the seminars and reunions with many long-time friends. What a crazy contrast! From New York, the city that never sleeps, to the gorgeous stillness of a spectacular Arizona sunset; from taxi rides through the garment district of New York to a covered wagon ride into the desert for the biggest steak cookout I'd ever seen; from elegant ballroom gowns to jeans and boots—the variety of experiences in such a short span of time was rich and exciting.

I had come in on the tail end of the Arizona convention and time to head for home came too soon. Back home, lugging suitcases stuffed with New York and Arizona goodies, I had a good case of jet lag and two very tired feet. The girls in our medical building gave me a "going away" dinner and the gift of a 35 mm camera to record some of the adventures ahead. Sixteen years in this setting was fast coming to an end.

Dr. Tolleth and Dr. Ransdell honored me with a farewell dinner party in Dr. Ransdell's beautiful hilltop home. We celebrated the years we had all worked as a team, a team of service and love. After dinner I was presented with a tree laden with familiar green leaves— money! Dr. Tolleth's "farewell to Shirley" speech raised a big lump of emotion in my throat. The realization that I had really severed the "cord" impacted me.

I was now *free*. To do *what*? *Where* was it I was in such a hurry to go?

"Please, God, I followed You this far, please don't leave me now!" I whispered silently as I thanked everyone for being such a wonderful part of my life.

No looking back now, Shirley, I lectured myself. You've already chosen. Now's the time to focus forward. Do tightrope walkers ever look down while they're walking the narrow highwire?

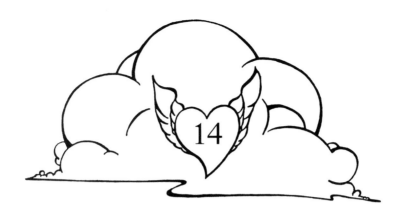

The A*L*L Game

Ask, and it shall be given to you;
Seek, and you shall find;
Knock, and it shall be opened to you.
For every one who asks receives...

—Matthew 7:7-8

I was asking, I was seeking, and I was a-knockin'. At 5:30 PM, I completed my sixteen-year career with Dr. Hale Tolleth. At 6:30 PM, I was about to begin a week-long intensive workshop to learn to work with the A*L*L Game, meditation, and dreams, as well as develop my counseling skills. Was there a pattern here—jumping headlong into the next thing without stopping long enough in between even to take a deep breath? That particular pattern had been repeating itself in my life for as long as I could remember.

That part of me that kept urging me on to the next thing clearly had nudged me the first time I played the A*L*L Game earlier in the month. I was fascinated by its unique and dynamic gameboard journey into unlimited creative self-discovery. Our trained A*L*L Discovery Game Guide was the creator of the game, Christi Ana Davidsunn. Lawyer, mystic, lecturer, management consultant, and crisis counselor, Christi Ana had been leading spiritual and personal transformational groups since 1970. She had become interested in metaphysics and comparative religions when she was accepted into the University of Virginia Law School, one of the most prestigious in the country. By the time she became a Juris Doctor in Law, she was no longer interested in saving the world with her intellect.

"The heart is the only road to real transformation," was how Christi Ana put it. She plunged headlong into the study of the workings of the mind and emotional nature of the human species. She was attracted to the process of self-growth and all that the subject encompassed. She worked for the Association for Research and Enlightenment in Virginia Beach, Virginia. She familiarized herself with the psychic readings of Edgar Cayce, the man hailed as the "Sleeping Prophet." She had been meditating and studying her dream life for many years and began to receive intuitive information from a universal source in her meditations. It was through this process that she received the idea for a self-growth tool in the form of a game.

The colorful A*L*L Discovery gameboard was circular, consisting of seven life-paths which provided a fascinating journey through seven major facets of life experiences. Each path had its own characteristic theme. Playing the game through these seven themes provided a remarkable overview of oneself, highlighting important current issues.

Christi Ana reminded us often that all seven paths must be equally balanced for the whole wheel (the gameboard) to turn smoothly. I felt that that was true of real life, too.

Security was the theme of the first path; it's color was red. Where do you look for your true security? Family, success, sex, religion, money, education, or expanded consciousness were some of the places people looked.

Pleasure was the path on which you learn about the best point for you on the continuum from denial of pleasure to overindulgence. Only as you come to love and accept yourself can you allow the right quantity and quality of pleasure and happiness. On this orange path you could also learn to integrate your masculine and feminine aspects.

Energy was the path associated with your ability to implement your goals and discover some of the ways you hinder that ability. When energy is not working, you feel at a dead end. It was the home of "fight or flight," determination or passivity, enthusiasm or anxiety. The color yellow highlighted this path.

Relationship was the path which examined your ability to reach out to others and your ability to allow people and loving relationships into your life. The relationship path was green.

Willingness was the path for exploring your flexibility, creativity, intuition, and connection with the inner self. When this path was blocked, you were not able to clearly receive the impulses, inspiration, and the creative spark. When this path functioned well, you were clearer about what is and needs to be going on. You could flow with life. This path color was blue.

Mind was an indigo-colored path closely connected to patterns, memories, and belief systems and to the gathering, analyzing, and storing of data. The mind is a lens through which we perceive everything—mental, emotional, physical, and spiritual. Belief systems are often set when we are young. We react to the world through those patterns as though they were a groove in the brain, a habit. It is important to become aware of these patterns so that reactions are not automatic. Forgiveness was the key to the release of inappropriate habit patterns.

Oneness was the violet path and it dealt with abundance, unlimited creativity, and the interrelatedness and unity of all humanity. This path had much mystery and awe because it spoke of the vastness of the universe. It implied that there is a basic orderliness to the cosmos. Oneness was access to anything; it gave you anything you were willing to receive.

Tailored to each person individually, the game had an uncanny ability to mirror whatever was going on at that moment in each player's life. The journey through the paths was done in a loving, supportive small-group setting where new insights were gained that improved the quality of daily living for each participant. It was through Christi Ana and the game that I was first introduced to the principle of synchronicity. I looked it up in the dictionary, but the term wasn't there. It was C.G. Jung's concept of "meaningful coincidence" operating in a person's life. Synchronicity was a new word in my life, but the principle itself was no stranger. As I looked at my life, particularly since Bobby's death, evidence of synchronicity was present everywhere.

The first time I played the A*L*L Game I wanted to know more about this marvelous loving tool. That night in bed, I could feel the excitement still surging through my body. Early the next morning, I called Christi Ana Davidsunn to see what it would take to bring her up from Los Angeles to do an A*L*L Game Intensive in the Bay Area. Christi Ana explored my intentions and interest. After much discussion, she said her schedule was full except for a possible seven-day period beginning the evening of October 30th. If we started at 6:30 PM that Friday, we could get the whole training in. Talk about the "dance of timing": I would be leaving my job with Dr. Tolleth and Dr. Ransdell an hour earlier.

I began checking amongst my friends to see who else would be interested and available to do the training with me. On the first evening of the training, five very special friends showed up at the Walnut Creek apartment where the A*L*L Discovery journey would begin. The apartment belonged to Bill Orlich, who graciously allowed us to use his home as our home away from home for the next seven days and nights. Six of us were to participate.

After Christi Ana led us through orientation and a guided reverie to discover our purpose for being here, we began to familiarize ourselves with the dynamics of the game by playing it. Right from the start, the game began calling our attention to any part of our lives we needed to look at more closely. It highlighted important current issues for each one of us, some deep, some much lighter. One of the things I loved best about the game was that each participant could play the game at whatever depth and level he chose to play it. You could explore what you chose to explore or just skip over the gameboard to your next move.

On Saturday, October 31st, Suzie drew and read a game card from the energy path. It said "I have a tremendous amount of ability, radiance, and creativity that I am sitting on." She was instructed to discuss how she felt about the card she had drawn. The A*L*L Game cards made a statement on one side of the card and directed an appropriate activity on the other side. Suzie was directed to express and release more of her ability, radiance, and creativity through dance and/or a drawing.

Halloween

As she read the card out loud she giggled and then asked if Bill had any grocery bags in his apartment. I got up and looked in his pantry; he had plenty. Suzie handed each one of us, including Christi Ana, a bag. Because it was Halloween everybody had to create a Halloween mask out of a brown bag.

Out came scissors, multi-colored felt pens, and crayons. It was nearing time for our lunch break and part of the deal, Suzie told us, was that we'd have to wear our masks when we went to lunch. A half-hour later, six bodies with paper bag mask heads danced and skipped their way through the green grass pathways of a nearby park, across a major four-lane road, and into a deli.

There's power in numbers, or whatever, but as we put on our bag masks, a sense of joyful craziness engulfed us. As we skipped and walked, we made curtsies or bowed from the waist, singing out, "Happy, happy Halloween!" Observing the responses we were getting from passers-by was a ball. A few people tried to look "cool" and ignored us entirely; they busied themselves looking anywhere but at us. But most people caught on to the spirit of what we were doing. By the time we got to the main drag, car horns were honking and people were waving and whistling and shouting "Happy Halloween" back at us. They were connecting with the "kid" inside of them, too, loving an excuse to be spontaneously silly and joyful. It was as if in having the brown bag to hide our "real" identity, we'd given ourselves full permission to be outrageously joyous and playful. It felt so good and freeing to our spirits. Enlightenment feels like this? Right on!

We began formulating "dream incubation" questions and recording our dreams. I couldn't believe it—not only was I remembering my dreams, but I was recalling them in vivid detail. Normally, I didn't remember my dreams when I awakened. They most often slipped away like vapors in the early morning dawn.

Christi Ana invited us to share our dreams with the group each morning. LaRena was looking at the issue of closed-in anger and the forest again. Suzie was dreaming of a pond in her childhood where she used to go as a child, but the pond wasn't safe anymore; a shark kept showing up in it instead of minnows. "What message is this recurring dream trying to give me?" she asked.

Jody and Georgia were having profound philosophical dreams. They were both of Jewish heritage, yet in their dreams Jesus was showing up a lot and talking to them. One night they were discussing the subject, wondering about the significance of it all. The sky "answered" them with a series of spectacular, flaming shooting stars streaking across the sky. We were all experiencing inexplicable mystical phenomena. I was feeling something stirring and calling me, like a far-off voice I could only sometimes tune in to. I had dreamt a "baby" had been left in a stroller in a huge stadium. I knew the baby had been left for me to nurture and take into the stadium arena.

One day on our lunch break, Suzie was showing us a beautiful brass Tibetan bowl she had brought with her. She cupped it in one hand and hit it with the heel of her other hand. As the Tibetan bowl vibrated its sound through the whole room, I began choking up with intense emotion and chills. Christi Ana intuitively sensed something important was going on and asked me to sit down and close my eyes. She nodded to Suzie to continue striking the bowl now and then.

"What are you feeling, Shirley?" Christi Ana began.

"Intense sadness," I answered.

"What are you seeing?"

After a long silence, "A clear vision" (visions were *not* an everyday occurrence with me) "of a little village surrounded by very high mountains." I shivered as chills ran through every cell of my body. "*D*éja vu of some kind."

"Why are you sad?"

"It's time for me to leave."

"Where are you going?"

"I'm not sure. I just know I *must* go. I must begin the climb up the mountain."

"Why are you going?"

"I don't know. Something's calling me there. I don't know. But I *must* answer the call."

"Describe what's happening to you now."

"I'm climbing and climbing. The village behind me is getting smaller and smaller. It's just a small speck in the distance. I'm very *cold* now. I'm stopping near a cave."

"What's happening?"

"Nothing... I'm just sitting... and sitting... and sitting ...silently ...nothing ...nothing."

For what seemed like a long period of time, nothing was happening. Then, the vibration of the Tibetan bowl again filled the room.

"I am filling up with a sensation of golden warmth and luminous, brilliant white light is flooding every cell of my body."

"What's happening now?"

"I'm not sure. Whatever I came up to the mountain to get, I think I got. It's time for me to go back down the mountain to the village."

"How much time has passed?"

"I have no idea. Feels like a *very* long time. I can see a long white beard in front of me and long hair is by my side. I don't remember seeing them as I climbed up the mountain. It feels like a very, very long time."

Though I was seeing the "vision" in my mind, my present-day body was actually experiencing the golden warmth and luminous, brilliant white light running through it as the experience took place in my mind's eye. It was a sensation like none I had ever experienced before. If that was a taste of what heaven was like, I wanted *more*!

I opened my eyes to question Christi Ana about this vision. It appeared to be a vivid past-life recall of a life as a monk or priest near Tibet. The meditative experience was of blending with the divine light of God. I was breathless. What did it all mean? I didn't know what to make of "past-life information," if anything, although it did fascinate me. Christi Ana spoke about life and things being revealed to us when it is the most appropriate time for us to know or recall something.

"It must be important for you to be aware of this information now," she said. At that instant the lights in the whole house quivered and trembled with a unique vibratory rate for several seconds with "no apparent cause."

"You just received confirmation on that!" Christi Ana said.

My friend LaRena had tears in her eyes as I looked at her. She had seen the very same village when she closed her eyes. We compared notes and the descriptions matched perfectly. She was sad because she was left behind in the village when I started my climb up the mountain. Truth is stranger than fiction, though neither of us fully understood what was going on. I was quickly learning to just "tuck away" or "hold" pieces of information or experiences

I didn't undertand. In the puzzle or tapestry of life's plan, I knew I would find the "pieces" fitting in when the time was right.

On the lighter side, while playing the game I drew an assignment to write a card for the oneness path. My instructions were to write a statement that showed a strength.

My sense of oneness and wholeness is complete when interacting with this caring, sharing, and nurturing group of people, I wrote.

The second part of my instructions was to devise a related action, preferably including a physical activity.

I wrote: While each member takes a turn in the center, the group will sidle with no verbal communication. Sidle (my definition, not Webster's): to move in a circular group hug by making little shuffling movements of the feet—bare feet—with humming and *om*ing accompaniment preferred. "Sidling" was an instant hit! It brought laughter that neared hysterics and raised the energy level of all who participated.

We were realizing that the A*L*L Discovery Game could be played at any level of participation. It could be played like Monopoly, moving your "piece" around the board and drawing cards that told you what to do. Or, it could be used as a tool to look at some of the things going on in your life and to gain more insight and support in improving the quality of daily living. I noticed that when players wrote down their purpose for playing the game after coming out of a closed-eye meditation, inevitably, the game would reflect that very issue. Synchronicity, "meaningful coincidence," popped up everywhere. Someone would be looking at a broken relationship and the game would deal them cards about relationships and group hugs and lots of "love tokens." A person unhappy in their present job would draw cards and moves dealing with their self-expression and creative talents.

Synchronicity: once we were in tune with the word and its concept, we noticed it operating in everyday life, at many levels. We were sharing personal incidences of synchronicity with the group when I suddenly recalled one very clear instance of it. Bob Ruiz and I had been married twelve years, but we had never had a formal honeymoon or vacationed alone together. Raising and supporting kids and fixing up our home took a lot of time, money, and energy. I had children from my first marriage, so did Bob, and we had two daughters. His, hers, and ours; though, in reality, they were all "ours" to raise and love! We had put our needs last, always resorting to the familiar "someday." After twelve years of this, Dr. Tolleth gifted us with a belated honeymoon. I had been working very long hours to organize and move us into new and larger office quarters. Dr. Tolleth told me he had sent a check to a local travel agency in my name.

"Shirley-bird, if I give you money for all the time you've put in, you will spend it to pay the orthodontist's bill or buy something for the house or the kids. I want you to have a real vacation, so the money's sitting at the travel agency, and it's nonrefundable, so start planning!" he told me.

What a gift! I loved it. I couldn't even feel guilty spending the money so frivolously, on Hawaii. It was wonderful boarding the big United 747 together, alone with Bob at last. It was worth the twelve-year wait. No kids (bless them), no yard work (somebody else could knock the walnuts off the trees this year), no household chores (I trusted the house would still be in one piece when we returned), and no 9:00 to 5:00 schedules.

A "Beachcomber Holiday" was the tour we chose, four islands in thirteen days. No schedules? Well, vacation schedules don't feel like everyday working schedules.

"Would Mr. and Mrs. Robert Ruiz please identify themselves," a stewardess's voice broke into the intercom system about an hour after we'd been in flight. I was shocked to hear our names.

"Oh, God! Something couldn't have happened to one of the kids already!" I waved my hand. A tan, strikingly beautiful stewardess came over to us and handed us a bottle of champagne, two orchid leis and a note. It was from my sister Virginia and her friend Arlene Di Mercurio. "Have a fabulous honeymoon!" was the message printed on the United stationery.

We were flying high already, even without champagne. We had chosen to reverse the usual itinerary and begin our holiday in Hilo, Hawaii. Hawaii felt like a second home to me the moment I set foot on her soil. I loved the warm balmy breeze that kissed my face with an "aloha" welcome, soon followed by our tour guide encircling our necks with orchid leis. Bob was in seventh heaven looking at pictures of some of the golf courses he would be playing.

As we were escorted to our spacious room at the Orchid Isle Hotel, the bellboy set down our bags and asked us if there was anything else he could do for us. The breeze was blowing across our room from the lanai and music floated on the breeze.

"No thanks, we've got everything we need," Bob said as he handed the bellboy a tip. The door to our room closed, and as if on cue, a very familiar melody mingled its magical notes with the warm, tropical breeze coming from the lanai—"My Funny Valentine." That had been my favorite song before being involved with Bob, and it had been his, too. It had became *our* song when we said our wedding vows on St. Valentine's Day twelve years earlier. We stopped talking and just held each other as tears of wide-eyed disbelief and joy splashed our beaming faces. That song was one we sang to each other every year on our anniversary, as it was partly responsible for the search for other things we had in common that led to our marriage. Talk about meaningful coincidences—here we were on a "belated" honeymoon, thousands of miles from home in Hilo, Hawaii, and "My Funny Valentine" came sailing into the room, in October, yet!

Some incidences of synchronicity were as obvious as that, and could make your hair stand on end. Many others, I noticed, were much more subtle. I needed to be open, sensitive, and alert to catch them.

In its subtler forms, synchronicity seems to be a tool used by God to confirm, lead, or connect me with people or things I had asked for or were of value for me to know in the moment. I loved the essence of synchronicity and started tuning myself acutely to its distinguishing characteristics. I reminded myself a little of my teen literary heroine, Nancy Drew. She loved solving mysteries, clue by clue, mystery by mystery. I had followed her adventures through volume after volume: *The Secret of the Old Clock*, *The Clue in the Diary*, and *The Clue of the Broken Locket*, along with another twenty or so similar titles, had helped me pass many a summer vacation. Or maybe my life was more like the fairy tale, "Hansel and Gretel." Only, it was God leaving the breadcrumb clues for me to follow through synchronicity incidents. What did it matter if the birds had eaten all the breadcrumbs behind me? One can never go backwards in life; forward is the only way to go!

Talking about "breadcrumb" clues to follow, it seemed God used whatever means were most readily available to clue me in and guide me. He had lots of means and there were some I was much more open and receptive to. Since beginning the A*L*L Game Intensive, a new one had been added. I was now paying more attention to my dreams, particularly when I used a pad beside my nightstand to write down a "dream incubation" question. I was catching on to the verse "Ask, and it shall be given to you." If God made me with a free will, He also needed to wait and watch patiently as I stumbled through life until I learned to *ask* Him for guidance. He'd never impose on the free will He'd given me without an invitation.

Unfortunately, it was only in moments of *great* stress and need that I ever thought to ask, such as the occasion of Bobby's death. Then, I had surrendered myself totally out of not knowing what else to do. In that moment of sincere, humble, and deeply-felt prayer, I had *asked* to be assisted and had *opened up* the channels for God to guide and inspire me. Throughout the whole period of time surrounding Bobby's plane crash, I was aware that an incredible source of energy and love had entered my life. I wanted never to lose touch with that divine energy. Chatting with God about my everyday decisions and joys had become part of my daily life—asking for guidance and waiting for the answer. It often came in a synchronistic event. But, it *always* came, in one form or another, when I was open to receive it.

On the last day of the A*L*L Intensive, I awakened early and immediately captured my dream on paper. It was the first time I had what could be called a "billboard" dream. There, on the dream billboard, a picture or statement would be left for me. Now when a message arrives in "billboard" form, it usually catches your attention, even if the meaning is not immediately decipherable. The message on the "billboard" of my dreams was: "You have connected with divine forces." Beside the statement was a picture of my hand in a group handshake with the group from the A*L*L Game Intensive. I pondered the dream a bit and had an urge to make a "gift" list for our closing ceremony.

The little jade old-man-of-wisdom in my jewelry box now symbolized my Tibetan past-life recall and I wanted to give it in gratitude to Christi Ana. I gift-wrapped five little spray bottles of French mineral water and tucked a bigger one in my purse. The little ones were gifts for each of the girls . The closing ceremony was complete with candles and incense. The atomizer of mineral water was symbolic of a baptismal blessing. As the mist of clear Alpine spring water was sprayed over each one of us, Suzie got a case of hysterical giggles. Later, she told us that when she heard the swishing noise of the spray, she had visualized the insect killer on a TV commercial and couldn't stop laughing. She lovingly apologized for breaking up the sacredness of the blessing. Suzie's spiritual vision could always clearly see the sacredness of life, and, in the same moment, you could always count on her to find its hilarity.

It had been a spiritually intense intensive. Christi Ana remarked that she had not had one quite like this before. We had felt and/or seen the presence of Jesus, Babaji, St. Germain, and Mother Mary. Considering the different ethnic backgrounds represented in the six of us, this was quite a guest list attending our seven-day retreat. I found myself talking aloud or mumbling under my breath with God and the masters a lot. Funny, I used to think that people who did that belonged locked up in mental institutions. Now, I was wondering if maybe some of the people we locked up were really the sane ones. I supposed that would be dependent upon whom one was talking to, and who was answering.

The six of us left Bill Orlich a thank-you note. He had graciously gotten "lost" for seven days and he stayed away until we hung out the "all clear" ribbon on his door each night. Many nights, that was very near the hour of midnight. We nicknamed our group the "NOVA" chapter of the A*L*L Discovery Game after a *nova*, a star that increases in brightness thousands of times its original intensity. Something spiritually powerful had been stirred within each of us. For me, a channel for higher inspiration had been opened and somehow I had "crossed over" some kind of "bridge" in my life since 5:30 PM, Friday, October 30th. I no longer desired or was capable of returning to my former way of life. I have never felt so much love and inner peace, I thought as I went to sleep that night.

The next morning, a vivid dream stuck in my thoughts. I wrote it down. The dream was about a lot of men running around a room. They had computer-machine insides; no heart. I had been in the dream as the observer, watching their activity. My pen began writing; automatic writing. The words appeared on paper without my being conscious of my thought processes thinking them first. It was as if I had momentarily become a steno machine for a message coming to me from outside of myself. When I finished writing, I read:

> You have always held the male and trainer images to be the persons of higher intelligence and awareness, sometimes without even questioning it. At this point in your life, you need to validate *yourself* as the person with higher awareness, more and more. Then, the frustration will recede from your life and inner peace will come. You must now *follow your inner guidance only* and let loose of needing agreement from outside sources. Trainings and trainers are useful tools when climbing the spiritual mountain, but you need to notice when it's time to put your trust and faith in a higher source. On the spiritual mountain, there comes a time for every soul to realize that he has transcended some of the physical-world growth steps and entered into a plane where higher spiritual law reigns supreme. There, the gift is freedom. Old rules need to be looked at *anew* and checked out with your inner guidance for their appropriateness in the moment. More and more of the old will drop away as you trust yourself and your spiritual guidance. Enjoy your journey and *go with the flow*!

The message and its timing were perfect. I had a lunch date with Larry Jensen shortly after we finished the November ASSET to discuss my further participation with him in the ASSET training. As an independent A*L*L Game Guide, I did not seem to fit into being a part of Larry's organization any longer. In the training room, Larry was an open channel for intuitive wisdom, and we worked harmoniously. Outside of the training room, we had some very basic and conflicting differences about how to live a spiritually enlightened way of life.

A moment of choice was again at hand. I remembered the message I had received about trusting my intuition and the gift of freedom. It was time to leave another "partner." Like ships, our paths had crossed long enough for us to enrich each other's lives with an exchange of gifts and love. It was getting a bit easier to say "goodbye" and simply be grateful for the incredibly rich cargo each passing ship shared with me on the seas of life.

Transitions

> *What the caterpillar*
> *calls the end of the world*
> *the master calls a butterfly.*
>
> —*Richard Bach*, **Illusions**

The view from Oakmont Memorial Park was spectacular today—there was a powdered frosting of snow on nearby Mt. Diablo, and the green Oakmont lawns were all dressed up in their holiday best, polka-dotted with pots of red poinsettias and miniature ornament-laden Christmas trees. The wintry wind was crisp and chilling. A blue down jacket warmed my body as my face met with the wind head-on. A tear on my cheek turned into an icy droplet. I felt it was time for some walking and talking.

"You started this, God. Where do I go from here?" I queried.

I put on the earphones of my Sony Walkman cassette player. They almost felt good. A little small for earmuffs, but they protected my eardrums from some of the achy coldness they were feeling. Walking and talking and listening to Richard Harris's taped version of *The Prophet* were a now-familiar part of a wonderful healing ritual. Every time I listened to the tape, I would hear new meaning in the messages. Tears of sadness, once shed, always left me room for more joy and inspiration. Thoughts would float on the breeze and into my head effortlessly. There they'd play in my mind for a moment before moving on in their merry chase through the ethers. I pulled my steno pad and rainbow-colored pen from my purse and tried to capture some of their playful philosophy.

> Sometimes I feel like a piece of driftwood—
> tossed, weathered and seasoned by powerful forces.
> Sanding and smoothing rough edges,
> the forces of the Universe tirelessly toil
> and polish me until
> they begin to reveal
> the golden patina
> of my Higher Self.

> Sometimes it feels mystical and sacred.
> Other times, it's more like the hundredth run
> of a bad "B" movie!
> If I can just view my life as "playing the role"
> I've chosen for myself in this particular movie,
> I can find my sense of humor,
> laugh with myself and—
> go for the Academy Award!

> It's only when I play my role from the viewpoint
> of "victim of the Universe"
> that nothing makes any
> sense.

Walking through the "Garden of Meditation," I talked out loud to the spirits of those buried on this beautiful hill. Sometimes I cried as I read the grave markers, hungering for a clue or sense of the essence expressed during the lifetime of each person. Many were impersonal—a name and a couple of dates. Sometimes, there'd be a direct hit to my heart.

Like Debbie's—a mountain and an airplane adorned her marker. Another plane crash? Bless you, Debbie.

Howard—I could really feel the effect his death had on those left behind. Engraved on his was: Superb Meteor, whose blazing spark burns a glowing trail. Howard sounded like someone I would have loved to meet.

In all my walks, one marker in particular had a great impact. It told the whole story of a young soul's struggle to "fit in"—the saga of an adolescent trying to mold himself to fit the pictures society expected of him. It was poignant and to the point, obviously written by the two loving parents who had been gifted with this young soul. A motorcycle on the marker finished saying what the words did not.

GARY

Dear Friends,

The Spirit has burst the bonds of temperance, tolerance, moderation and those other graces demanded by earthly society. It shook itself free in a moment of exuberance while still restricted by the confinement of our human vestment the body. This Spirit came to us on May 30, 1955, bound even then by a condition which manifested itself as asthma. It struggled, it endured and eventually controlled that condition only to enter another nearly overwhelming restriction, adolescence. Adolescence, that period of turmoil during which the 'person' must mold itself to fit the picture of social position and there spend a controlled existence following the rules of contemporary conduct. The Spirit attempted to conform but could not. It flew the narrow path dictated by statute. It tried, it tested and it deviated, swerving, at times violently, from this course. In the process it touched countless others. Some flew with it as birds fly in migration, together and with a common destination but alone in this flight of survival. Freedom came October 24, 1978. We cry, we console, we smile, we reminisce. We feel an acute sense of loss though we should not.

We called our Spirit Gary.

Love,
Don and Gloria

Dabbing my eyes with a piece of crumpled-up kleenex, I walked on.

"Hi, Abe, Merry Christmas!" I called. Some of the names had become old friends as I made my circular walk.

Returning to my car, I took out a candle and a plastic sheet to protect my quilt from soaking up the dewdrops on the lawn. The candle had a tall glass chimney to discourage the wind from playing its little game of "pouff-pouff and you're out." A book chosen randomly from the stack on my nightstand turned out to be Elisabeth Kubler-Ross's *Death, the Final Stage of Growth*. I was familiar with the concepts and her work with the terminally ill. She rated very highly in my book of present-day humanitarians. My eyes focused in on the words I had highlighted with my yellow marking pen:

For those who seek to understand it,
death is a highly creative force.
The highest spiritual values of life
can originate from the thought and study of death.

—Elisabeth Kubler-Ross,
Death, the Final Stage of Growth

I stared at the words, letting their meaning sink in deeply. The truth in the statement echoed something I could feel ringing true in my heart. Person after person flashed across my mind. Each one's death had taught me a different aspect of dealing with the loss of a loved one. I called them back into my mind and pondered the circumstances surrounding my memories of each one.

Nono: My great-grandfather died at the age of ninety-five. At the time I was just a child living on my grandparents' ranch. I don't recall any sadness. Death seemed like a very natural conclusion to living. I was impressed that he still had all his own teeth in his mouth except one that had been pulled by mistake. He died with the one that had been bothering him still in his mouth.

Theresa: I had gone through high school with Theresa Capeto. She was very beautiful and had been blessed with the alto voice of an angel. We had had a lot of fun in our senior year putting on makeup and going to elementary schools to perform our duet number, "The Wedding of the Painted Doll." I was feeding my toddler Greg lunch when I heard of her death. Theresa had just given birth to a son and had died of a blood clot shortly afterwards. I cried as I watched Greg playing with some blocks. She would never be around to enjoy her new son the way I was enjoying mine. And somewhere, a son would grow up without ever knowing the loving goodnight kisses of the mother that had given birth to him. It didn't seem fair.

The radio serenaded me with the haunting and appropriate opening line of "Stranger in Paradise." I had a vision of Theresa in a white, billowy chiffon gown, adorned with golden braided belts and jewelry, going some place it wasn't time for me to know about yet. To this day, the song "Stranger in Paradise" still fills me with the same mystical vision of Theresa entering "Paradise."

Frank Bruno: Frank was my father-in-law. I remembered the look on my husband Rick's face as he came home from work to tell me about his dad's death. I was in my ninth month of pregnancy with Bobby, my third child. I told Rick his dad had died. He was surprised I already knew. So was I. I couldn't explain the feeling in my body or how I just "knew" Frank had died.

Victoria: I was working as a lab receptionist for Kaiser Hospitals. My three boys were little "stair-step" toddlers. It didn't appear a daughter was in my future. I had always wanted one, particularly around Easter, when adorable little Easter outfits dressed every department store window in town. A precious little blonde girl came in to have some lab tests done. Without thinking, I said, "She looks like she got the worst end of that fight!"

Eighteen-month-old Victoria had big purple bruises on her beautiful little face and all over her arms and legs. Her mother looked me in the eye and quietly said, "She has leukemia."

My mouth hung open in surprise, not knowing what to say next. Week after week, Victoria returned to the lab in the little round Kaiser outpatient clinic building. We became friends. Victoria began to trust me and would let me hold her as Peg, the lab technician, drew still another sample of blood. Victoria was hanging on to her little life by threads, when a neighbor's child inadvertently exposed her to the measles. Measles might not be very serious for most children, but for Victoria, it was life-threatening. She was immediately hospitalized.

Victoria's pediatrician was also my sons' pediatrician, and we had become good friends. Lab tests had been run and Victoria's and my blood were compatible.

Her doctor called me, "Victoria needs a direct blood transfusion, as soon as possible. Can you meet me in Pediatrics in a half hour?"

I arrived at the appointed time and found Victoria hadn't waited. She had died fifteen minutes earlier. I wept. It felt like I had lost a child of my own and I began questioning the "fairness" and sense of it all.

Pee Wee: Little Edward Ruiz III, my nephew, was as close to an angel as I could imagine as I kissed the tiny body, swathed in white, that lay in the casket. Surely that is the role God called him to. A "crib death" is what they called it. I remember the telephone call saying my sister-in-law Martie was rushing to the hospital with him. Nothing made sense. Pee Wee was a husky little baby; I was sure somebody was exaggerating.

Bob Ruiz and I rushed over to Martie and Ed Ruiz's house to stay with their toddler daughter Kellie until her parents returned from the hospital. The looks on their faces as they walked in the door preceded the verbal message that Pee Wee had been pronounced dead on arrival.

Martie, Ed, and Kellie Ruiz moved in with us for the next month until their new house was ready. Going back to the house where Pee Wee had died was much too painful as Martie relived the nightmare of finding her baby son dead every time she went into the infant's room. It was unbearably cruel to keep looking at the empty crib that reminded her that her son was gone.

At the funeral, I sat beside Martie holding her hand. I felt deeply the pain this mother was going through as we drove away from the tiny casket still in view and now being lowered into its final resting place in the San Bruno cemetery. I had five little ones of my own and couldn't even imagine what the pain would be like to lose one of them. Why Pee Wee?

Grandma "GG": The lessons in death didn't get any easier. My paternal grandmother, the one who had raised me for six of my most impressionable early years, was dying of breast cancer at the age of seventy-six. She had been my role model for many years after my parents divorced and my dad went off to fight in World War II. She was a "pioneer-type" woman, this Edvidge Ferrero; short in stature but gigantic in love, everyday survival, "know-how", and faith in God. There wasn't a chore on the ranch she didn't know how to do. She'd rise before the sun and still be going long after it had set. When she was in her early twenties, a panel of five doctors agreed she had very little time left to live. Her heart was weak and about to give out, but she was *not about to die!* She left her Catholic upbringing and started studying Christian Science — Science of the Mind. She credited it often and always for the fact that she outlived all five of the doctors that had predicted she would be lucky if she lived another six months.

Now, some fifty years later, it was painful to watch someone I loved so much die such a long drawn-out horrible death. The pain was excruciating. Because of her firm religious beliefs, she never even took an aspirin. I watched her wither away, go deaf and blind, and finally die. She had stuck to her own unique commitment to God with her last dying breath. It drove me further away from Him. How could God be just and allow someone who spent an hour or more a day in solitary prayer die like that?

Years earlier, she had had all her teeth pulled for dentures. She took no anesthesia of any kind, using only the power of her mind to handle the pain. Her dentist couldn't believe it. He had never heard of or seen anything like it in his life. He refused to charge her for his services, saying it had been a privilege to witness the power of her mind.

When Grandma "GG" died I experienced guilt and very mixed-up feelings about God. Watching her die such a long painful death was more than I could bear at times. I felt guilty that I wasn't strong enough to endure my own pain and be with her at the end. That old standby, "busyness," had been my excuse to the world. No excuse was big enough for me to forgive myself for not being with her when she needed me most. Grandma "GG" planted the seeds of the belief that I had the power to do anything I put my mind to. She was a living example of commitment, persistence, and faith.

Dr. "S": He was a brilliant man, a devoted humanitarian, and my employer and good friend. A self-inflicted bullet claimed his life. The Tuesday night before his death, I was standing by the kitchen sink at my stepmother Teresa and Dad's house. I put both hands to my head and held them there.

"Are you getting a migraine?" Teresa asked. "No, but there's a strange, staticy kind of nonstop buzzing noise. It feels like my head is being used as a short-wave set and nothing is coming in but a loud static sound. It feels like somebody's short-circuiting my brain!"

The next morning I awakened abruptly in the middle of making a long blood-curdling scream. The bedside clock said it was a couple of minutes past 6:00 AM. My husband Bob Ruiz sat up beside me as all five of our sleepy-eyed children came running into our bedroom to see what had happened to me. I was hugging my painful solar plexus area. Six pairs of now very wide-awake eyes were staring at me, waiting for an explanation.

"I feel like I've just been shot," were the words that came out of my mouth. I apologized for scaring everybody and told them to go back to bed. A restlessness I couldn't explain was flowing through every part of my body.

"Might as well go to work early," I thought. The scream had pumped so much adrenalin through me I couldn't have gone back to sleep if I'd wanted to. Within the hour came a phone call from the emergency room of a local hospital—Dr. "S" was dead. I couldn't believe what I was hearing or the uncanny "coincidence" of my awakening at or near the exact moment of his death. It haunted me but there wasn't much time to dwell on it. I had to get to the office. Patients would soon be streaming in. How was I going to tell them what had happened?

At the office, there was a hum of activity as physician friends stopped by and a police officer came in to question me. I was in shock and still couldn't believe what had happened. As I looked over at my desk, an envelope caught my eye. It was a letter from Dr. "S," dated the evening before. The time was neatly typed under the date.

It was exactly the same time that I had begun experiencing the buzz-ing sound in my head the previous evening.

"If anything should happen to me..." the note said. He asked me to handle a few details for him. I did.

His parents flew to California for the funeral and begged me to give them one good reason why this had happened. I couldn't find one and my heart bled with theirs. His young children would proba-bly never understand it either. Maybe someday I would be able to tell them how very much he loved and worried about them. I helped with the details of selling the practice and picking up loose ends. Several doctors called me after the funeral and offered me a job. I debated about what I should do next.

A friend called to tell me about a plastic surgeon, the first one in our area, who would be hiring a medical assistant for his new prac-tice soon.

"Maybe I'll try a new specialty field of medicine once I pull myself back together," I said out loud as I pondered what the future held for me.

Dr. "S" brought in a new aspect of death for me to look at. What is the "straw" that pushes a soul over the edge? My "little voice" had told me to stay and chat with him the night before he died. But there were a husband and five little kids waiting for me to come home, and I had been working extra long hours as it was, debugging the new computer billing service we were installing. I "chose" to go home and spend a rare evening with my family instead of staying at the office to see if I could "feel out" what was troubling my boss. Now, it was too late. Would it have made a difference? Lots of not-easily-answered questions danced through my head. What was the "fine line" that makes life worth living or not? I allowed my thoughts to accumulate in the back of my mind for further observation at a quieter time.

Grandma "C": Grandma Cordano was my stepmother Teresa's mother, and I *was* able to rise above my own emotions and be with this ninety-year-old grandmother when she breathed her last breath. It was a Sunday evening when the convalescent home called. My dad and Teresa were out of town and I was the next of kin to be called in an emergency.

Grandma "C" was breathing laboriously. The doctor thought her time was running out. I remembered my beloved Grandma "GG" death—no one should die alone. At the convalescent hospital, I sat beside Grandma "C's" bed and held her hand. She was comatose and every breath took a lot of effort. Sitting there beside her, her labored breathing became my labored breathing. I synchronized my breath with hers, without really realizing I was doing it. For nine hours we suffered together. Just before dawn she took her last breath. I'd seen it in the movies, but never in real life. An inner battle was going on inside of me as I kissed her forehead and left her deathbed.

Part of me was happy it was over and that her suffering had come to an end, but a bigger part of me was sad. Even if you are unconscious, every second of life is a precious one, and Grandma Cordano's hourglass had just run out of sand.

Walt: This time it was my husband's friend who used the gun. Terminally ill with cancer, Walt couldn't bear to watch his kids suffer through a long drawn-out bedside vigil while he fought a losing battle with the big "C." Walt's friends avoided being around him whenever possible. They didn't know what to say and it was very uncomfortable to pretend that everything was okay.

How sad, I thought, this is probably the time when a man most needs friends and this is the time when they seem to be disappearing from the scene fastest.

I remembered Grandma "GG's" long bout with cancer and how painful it had been for me to watch her. There and then, I made up my mind to learn all I could about helping the terminally ill. For several weeks, once a week at 7:00 AM, I reported to Mt. Diablo Medical Center for the two-hour Elizabeth Kubler-Ross class on "Death and Dying" before going to work for the day. The class deeply affected how I dealt with death and dying thereafter.

Nancy: Nancy was a patient of ours and was in the last stages of her cancer illness. She appreciated my hospital visits. I simply allowed her to talk out her feelings about death and an afterlife. It was too difficult a subject for members of her family to hear her talk about, but she needed to and I had the privilege of hearing her innermost thoughts.

An unspoken thank you went through my head. Thank you, Elisabeth Kubler-Ross. Thank you for the insights and inspiration of your work with people who are making the transition we call dying.

Dee Dee: DoDo and I had been friends for over twenty-five years when she introduced her sister Dee Dee to me. Dee Dee and I were like old friends the first day we were introduced. She was thinking of making some changes in her lifestyle and when she attended an est Guest Seminar with me, she quickly enrolled in the next training. After completing the training, she called me to say how "free at last" she felt. She was grateful I had introduced her to it. One week later, Dee Dee died in a blazing fire in her home. Were the words "free at last" an omen of some kind?

Jewell: Blonde and beautifully courageous, Jewell had lost both breasts to cancer and her husband to the process of not being able to deal with and handle her "deformity." She was a very depressed woman, feeling bewildered and rejected. After all, it was she who had lost the breasts. Her husband had only to look or not look at her body. He chose not to.

After her divorce, fate guided Jewell into a very special and precious relationship with a man who was all she had ever really wanted. Her young son loved his new stepfather, too. As Jewell chatted with me on her deathbed, her only concern was what would happen to her son. Her wonderful husband was a black man, and maybe family and society were not yet ready for a black man to raise a blonde son.

"Where there's a will, there's a way," I said hugging her good-bye.

I was sitting at her funeral looking at the casket when two figures started a hand-in-hand walk down the aisle to say their last goodbyes to Jewell. They wore matching gray satin "Corvette" jackets. One figure was over six feet tall and black. The other was shy of four feet and very blonde. Nothing could have broken the tight handgrip they had between them. I cried and smiled at the same time, knowing Jewell was watching this scene from somewhere and it was filling her heart with love and joy.

The soul knows no color boundaries, of this I was sure. We humans still housed in physical bodies had a lot to learn in that respect.

168

Grandpa ''GG'':   The other half of the team who had given me love and six glorious years of growing up in the arms of nature on a ranch died at the age of ninety-one on St. Patrick's Day. Hardworking and a man of enormous physical strength, he'd taught me well the value of a hard day's work and clean living. Near his death, he told me and my daughters Kimberly and Laura something that would stick with us for the rest of our lives. "Live your life *now*. I waited too long to go to Europe and do all the things I always wanted to do. My money isn't doing me any good here in my convalescent hospital wheelchair."

Kim and Laura remembered his words well, also. The small inheritance check they each received was spent on an airplane ticket for their first trip to Hawaii. I didn't cry much at Grandpa "GG's" funeral. Funny how I had always equated the depth of my love for someone with how much I cried when they left. Not so. I loved my grandfather with all my heart and there was little sadness. Instead, my heart was filled with pride as I listened to this successful self-made man's eulogy. His story was a part of my heritage and roots. I felt privileged to have lived on the ranch with him. He taught me about "being the best you can be" and baseball.

Rose: Rose had been a patient and my friend for several years since her first bout with an opponent named cancer. Near the end, Rose was in the hospital across the street from our office. I longed to do something for her. Remembering how good a loving massage felt when I was sick, I began visiting Rose. Lunch hours became massage time for Rosie. What Rose taught me besides courage was that one can never underestimate the power of the human touch to bring a little sunshine into a sick person's day. A little tender loving care goes a long way and is a priceless gift that is always available for giving. Never miss an opportunity to share love. For many years now, her wonderful husband Frank has sent me a box of See's Chocolates every Christmas; his quiet way of saying, "Thank you for caring".

David Gonzales: Another nephew laid to rest. When David Gonzales died in a train accident, I went to his funeral solo. Bob Ruiz and I had been divorced by now. A piece of legal paper may divorce you from a husband, but not from a family you've loved and cared about for twenty years. My heart ached as I looked at the pained faces of Manuel and Cathy Gonzales: they had lost their only son.

Really, God, I thought, if You do exist, I understand Your ways less every time a young person like David dies, in the prime of life.

A member of the family mentioned that David had had a premonition that his time was up. This sent the mechanism of my mind into a questioning mode: How, how, how? Why, why, why?

Dick Workman: He taught me to look beyond the exterior personality and facade and get a glimpse of what lies in a person's heart, where the treasure is hidden.

Dick and I connected and developed a feeling of trust as human beings. Once that was established, our friendship allowed us to explore each other's intellect and philosophical natures. It was challenging and fun. Dick had a sharp wit and the mind of a master chess player. He set up "games" to test out his strategies and stimulate his mind. He loved the challenge of "going for it" and winning. He died as he lived, going full speed ahead. His motorboat accident on Lake Berryessa called upon me in another fashion: to capture the essence of this highly charged man by writing his eulogy. In doing so, seeds were planted that would sprout at the time of Bobby's death.

Looking back, I could see how these sixteen different aspects of death experiences had each played their own part in shaping the course of my life.

Bobby's death had also profoundly altered my path. This was clarified for me in a channeled reading with Christi Ana Davidsunn. Georgia Kahn was present, serving as the conductor of the reading, asking questions of the universal source from which Christi Ana received her information. Georgia meticulously set the session up by asking that the divine energy give me information that was beneficial, practical, and inspirational in my life. Christi Ana cleared her mind and went into a deep meditative state where answers to my questions not normally available to the five senses were available to her. I was told only useful information would be given me from the universal pool of knowledge (sometimes referred to as the Akashic Records).

The ninety-minute reading was taped for my future use. It contained many bits of wisdom for me. I did not need to believe in anything, particularly reincarnation, to receive the value of this information, but just to be open to whatever my heart told me was important for me to know.

According to the reading, my recent recall of a past life as a monk in an area near Tibet had been revealed to me at this time to re-anchor my spiritual strengths. That lifetime had advanced the spiritual growth of my soul. It was a solitary style of life where empathy was not developed. I had set up "themes of distress" this lifetime to more fully develop the quality of empathy in working with others. It was now time for me to bring the two lines of experiences, spirituality and empathy, together and share with people from that combination of awareness. It was an opportunity to serve others, "sharing, enlightening, and enlovening". Finding my "niche", assisting others, would lead me to joyfulness.

"Joy is an essential basic expression and essence of the nature of God," I was told.

It was suggested I use the percentage—both quality and quantity—of joy in my life as a "joy barometer" on which to measure how much God energy I was allowing to flow through me.

"Joy, love, and serenity are very intertwined. Different aspects of the same diamond. Joy is the one most easy to notice. A good cue for Shirley to look at."

There was advice on assisting my body in serving me well. I needed more water in my life, internally and externally. Whirlpools, saunas, steambaths, and lots of water internally would help avoid "karmic hitches" in my body. There were some potential health difficulties that could be avoided if I cared for my body wisely.

"An ounce of prevention will be worth a pound of cure." Frequent massages would be very wise, especially to the feet. Ummm—I liked that suggestion! A simplified diet would be supportive. Lots of fresh fruits, vegetables, and grains. Fresh flowers in my environment were also recommended.

When Georgia asked the source for other lifetimes influencing this one, it was revealed that the six people in the ALL Intensive had all been alive together in the lifetime of Jesus. This was why his influence came in so strongly all through the training. It was not appropriate for me to know all the roles we had playd, and it was not yet time for Georgia to know what her role had been, either. It would be more important to her later. All of us had grown a lot since that time and we were very comfortable being back together again. The information coming through Christi Ana revealed that I had been a matriarchal type, a wife of some sort, and a member of the Essenes. Having many children, I was developing protective maternal qualities, keeping my "brood of chicks" in good order. Supportive of Jesus, I had hosted some of His disciples. Abilities to organize, pay attention to rituals, and hostess qualities were enhanced by this lifetime.

Other meaningful lifetimes in Israel, China, and Egypt, as well as one of a hard, harsh, and brusque female in a New Mexico-type desert, were revealed. Some of my current "distress themes" came out of the desert lifetime. One really bad lifetime had included LaRena Maines. It was not important for us to know the details; only that it had brought us closer together in times of trouble.

When Georgia asked about Bobby and the significance of Mt. Shasta, several pieces of information were given us.

"Robert left because he was complete," the channel said. "He chose to experience this lifetime, though short, as it was valuable for him to experience love and a depth of connection with those people close to him. The main thing calling him out now was that he has a role to fulfill in the next century and he needs a younger body. He will be coming in with a whole group of souls working on similar things. More tools, talents, and abilities will be made available to him. They weren't needed in this lifetime. A loving and well-developed soul, Robert has a light-heartedness about him. He feels good and complete about his Earth life. Leaving via Mt. Shasta is not just a comment on his present life, but more of a comment on the metaphysical and spiritual significance his next life will involve. He is very 'Earth-oriented' right now and is excited about his present helping and guiding role. That's why many people are feeling special towards him."

It was suggested I go to Mt. Shasta several times. It would help release any sadness and attune me to the joyfulness of Robert now. Also, I'd meet a couple of interesting people there that would fit into my future outreach plans. It was emphasized that I had the guiding influence of Robert and there was much, much more spiritual

172

guidance available to me. I was being "nudged" to meditate deeply to anchor in the more broadly developed spiritual beings of the Christ-consciousnes.

"Acknowledge them or it limits their being able to work with her," the channel said. "The reasons for her not accepting her full potential simply *don't exist* anymore. It is *freedom* time!"

Before obtaining my reading I had read and signed a form that stated:

> The Source of the information in your psychic reading is beyond our normally accepted sources of knowledge. Therefore, this information is necessarily to be regarded as experimental in nature. Results from its use cannot be guaranteed as there are unknown factors involved. Since psychic readings are on the frontier of human con- sciousness, there is no way to be certain of the validity of information gained in the altered state of consciousness in which these readings are obtained.

Now, sitting here on the lawn at Oakmont, I pondered it all. "Believe" in the information and, reincarnation or not, the informa- tion given to me was still very valid for me to look at. It certainly made a lot more sense of "how" and "why" people leave their physical bodies through the process called death. It also released me from judging the value of another's life. If each soul only brought in the tools needed for the particular lesson or quality they were developing, it would only be possible to see a soul's total storehouse of talents and virtues and his evolving progress from a higher spiritual vantage point. From there, only God and each person's higher self could view the lessons, choices, and reasons for "death" in its true perspective. Thus, it would be quite arrogant for one human being down here on earth to judge another, *ever*!

Through having a higher spiritual awareness from which to view life, it would be possible to totally release our loved ones to their highest good, leaving the individual destiny of their souls to God, and thus being at peace with what is. The other choice was to see physical death as the end of existence and life as holding little or no purpose or meaning. No thanks!

173

My niece, Kelly Ferrero, and I had recently discussed some of the aspects of physical death. Bringing flowers to Bobby's grave one day, we sat and talked to each other and to Bobby.

"My Mom and Dad want to be cremated and have their ashes scattered to the winds when they die. It makes me sort of sad to think I won't have any special place like this to bring flowers to or sit at to think," Kelly confided.

I encouraged her to let her parents know her feelings. I'm sure they felt that having "no place" to take flowers to would release her from any "duty" to periodically come to a cemetery and feel sad.

The conversation with young Kelly emphasized to me not the right or wrong of any particular funeral arrangement, but rather the importance of fully communicating feelings in an open, supportive, and loving environment.

Hmmm, I thought, were funerals more for the deceased or truly more for the completion of the grieving process and a ritual for those left behind?

Looking just east of Bobby's grave site, I noticed someone setting down a beautiful Christmas tree, complete with red ornaments and candy canes. Its silver tinsel sparkled as it got caught up by a gust of wind. I looked at my watch and found it hard to believe I'd been sitting here thinking for almost two hours! Time to scurry home. Kim had tickets for us to see Dorothy Hamill in the "Nutcracker Suite on Ice" later tonight at the Oakland Coliseum. Ah, a night of fantasy.

Right now, though, I needed to hightail it and buy the groceries for our annual Christmas Eve Open House, the evening when we opened our hearts and home for friends and family to come join us for as long as they wanted. It was always a full house and often a stranger with nowhere to go would find himself in our midst, warming himself before the roaring fire with a glass of spicy hot apple cider.

Christmas Day dinner would be a family affair at Mae and Robert's house and an opportunity to finally relax and unwind, drinking in the warmth and camaraderie of this special day.

One of the parts of Christmas Day I looked forward to most was my participation in the "Holiday Project." Each year, groups of smiling volunteers went caroling together at the local hospitals and convalescent homes. Dressed in our most colorful holiday clothing, we sang our hearts out, visiting each and every person and giving them a small gift. This year, we had chosen a convalescent hospital to share our love, joy, and abundance with. Some of the beautiful elderly folks had forgotten what the holidays were all about. Strains of the familiar melodies of Christmas often brought tears and smiles of remembrance. I particularly remembered a lady named Helen.

We had been caroling in and out of convalescent home rooms, up and down each and every hallway. In the corner of one of the hallways was parked a wheelchair with a high-chair-type tray across it. In it was a lady with her head face-down on the tray. She hadn't moved a muscle since we first arrived. Stopping behind her wheelchair, I wondered what, if anything, I could do for her.

A nurse's aide said, "That's Helen. Don't bother with her; she can't see or hear you. She's been like that for a long time".

Something inside me deeply responded to that remark. I remembered when I had been in a coma, unconscious to those around me, but *very* conscious within myself of everything that was going on around me. Only thing was, my physical body couldn't react and communicate with anyone else in the normal fashion.

After asking for permission to wheel Helen's chair up the hall, the head nurse allowed me to join the rest of the carolers when they came by. Meanwhile, I thought, it was highly possible Helen was aware of our presence, though physically unresponsive. I joined in singing the carols I could hear echoing from the rest of our group, and rubbed the back of Helen's bent neck. Her hands and face were very dry and cool to the touch. I reached for the small bottle of moisturizer cream in my purse. Gently, I kept massaging the soft silky lotion into Helen's face, and then into her hands, singsonging, "Wake up, Helen, it's Christmas!"

After about ten minutes, a lone tear found its way out of her eye and trickled slowly across her face. She had heard! Spurred on by the acknowledgment of the tear, I kept massaging and rooting for Helen to wake up and open her Christmas present. Then, with all the energy her frail little body could muster, Helen jerkingly lifted her head, struggling against its weight to stay upright. Her eyes rolled back, then opened. She was crying and so was I! By now, the rest of the carolers had surrounded us; all had been aware of Helen's

plight when we had arrived. Everyone was cheering for her as I opened the little Christmas gift. It was a pair of fluffy yellow bootie stock-
ings.

"Do you want me to put them on for you, Helen?" I asked. She
shook her head negatively and waved her shaky hands wildly in front
of my face. Of course, it was Helen's hands that were so cold. She
smiled as I put one of the yellow shortie socks on each of her hands.
We started down the hall with Helen's wheelchair in lead position.
As we caroled, Helen led us with her yellow-mittened hands. This
was her moment to be choir director and "star of the show" and she
was loving every single moment of it!

"Reach out and touch someone" had a new meaning for all of
us who had witnessed the "Miracle of Helen." Through Helen, the
message "never underestimate your ability to reach another human
being, even though they may appear to be in an unconscious state,"
was clearly being received. The "Miracle of Helen" was the greatest
gift Christmas could ever have given us.

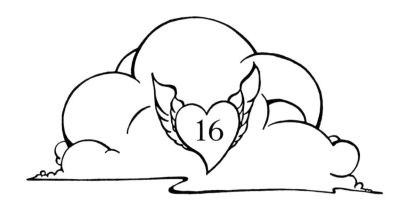

16

Teachers, Travels, and Tools

Know thyself.

—Socrates

*There are no unnatural or supernatural
phenomena, only very large gaps in our
knowledge of what is natural... We should
strive to fill those gaps of ignorance.*

*—Edgar D. Mitchell, Apollo 14
Astronaut and Founder, Institute of Noetic Sciences*

QUESTION: how can you tell the guru in the black robe
from the guru in the white robe?

ANSWER: the guru in the black robe
keeps you wondering
whether it is safe for you to go off into the
sunset
without him.

the guru in the white robe
smiles serenely
as you bid each other farewell,
having taught you to become
your own guru.

—Rusty Berkus, *Life is a Gift*

The only thing turning me on right now was my enthusiasm for a journey called Seeking Truth. Pension-and-profit funds, tax refunds, and cashed-in insurance policies provided some money and the time to study and "listen to the needs and longings of my heart." At times life felt like a mystery story; other times, more like Hansel and Gretel. "Clues of synchronicity" led me to "travels", many, many "teachers", and a collection of wonderful "tools" along the way.

More and more, I was trusting the part of me that says "stay awhile, observe and listen, there is value here for you". I was also responding more quickly when it said "it's time to move on *now*. You only came here to make a connection with a particular person, place, or thing and it's time to say goodbye again, now". Goodbyes were coming more often these days; some were easier than others to move through. Usually, I felt some feelings of sadness or pain. As I moved on to other things, though, I discovered sadness would soon dissipate, making room for new circles of wonderful, loving friends to form. They too, were seekers on the path, searching for the deeper meaning of life. We were all teachers and we were all students, exchanging our gifts of learning wherever and whenever the opportunity arose.

A friend told me about a new group I might be interested in joining, The MasterMind Alliance Group. It was being formed to study the books and principles of famed author Napoleon Hill. As the organizational meeting led by Rick Gettle finished up, I felt a "tap" on my shoulder. A beautiful lady with frosted blond hair introduced herself to me as Carolyn "Gail" Ortega.

"I knew, when you came in this room, it was no accident that we meet," she went on to say.

Life was full of wonderful surprises and Carolyn was one of them. We were "sisters" instantly—a *déja vu* feeling. We joined the new Napoleon Hill study group and took the full eighteen-week course studying his teachings.

At the end of the course, four of us agreed to teach the next semester of the class on a rotating basis. One of our students handed us a card that said, "You teach what you most need to learn."

We teachers laughed and heartily agreed as we spent hours listening to Napoleon Hill cassette tapes, reading his books, and gathering materials for each of the specific class lectures we had been assigned to teach.

Two of my favorites topics, "The Power of Enthusiasm" and "21 Traits of a Pleasing Personality," were assigned for me to study and prepare a class on. We four newly appointed teachers rose to the occasion, past our stage-fright, and made up for any lack of expertise with a lot of enthusiasm. Our classes became a fun learning experience for us as well as our students.

One day after class, Carolyn handed me a book and said, "I know I'm supposed to give you this book." I took the book, *Golden Moments with the Ascended Masters*, wondering what "gift" the book was bringing me.

Home in my bedroom, I sat in the cushioned net swing hanging from the ceiling near the picture window. It was one of my favorite spots in the whole house. Soft music from the radio filled the room while I admired the beautiful sunny view of the green Walnut Creek hills. What message was this book bringing me? Where should I start? At the beginning? No, I decided to open it to a page randomly and see what I got.

Closing my eyes for a moment, I asked for guidance silently, took a deep breath, and opened the book. I had turned to page 151. My eyes caught the name General David Eisenhower, Ex-President of the United States of America. I was a bit puzzled as to the meaning of the page I had turned to. Then my eyes dropped to the next line of purplish-blue type to read "Chapter 49".

> A trip was made [it began] today (February 13, 1976) to
> Mt. Shasta City, a four hour drive in intermittent rain.
> Upon our arrival it was dark and cloudy so the mountain
> was not seen, but we did feel the vibrations from being in
> its proximity.

My heart pounded with excitement as I read the whole chapter about the beautiful, majestic spiritual mountain. That's interesting, I thought, they use the word *majestic*—the first descriptive word that came to me when I was writing Bobby's eulogy.

At the end of the short chapter, I continued on to the next chapter. "Today, February 14th, is St. Valentine's Day," I read. By then I knew that synchronicity was right on target, whatever the meaning. My whole body was covered with goosebumps as I read about my favorite day of the year. It talked of Twin Flames, Divine Complements, Holy Matrimony, and a passage from the Holy Scriptures:

> Be ye not unequally yoked together with unbelievers.

Hmmm, more food for thought. Wherever this book came from, it had some great messages.

I quickly read on for more messages from the masters. One was from the sage of wit and wisdom, Confucius; "The Gift of Ultimate Love" was from Jesus the Christ; "Compassion for All of Nature's Children" was a message from St. Francis of Assisi; and there were also messages from many others including the Prophet Joseph Smith, St. Germain, and the Angels Gabriel and Moroni.

The book contained 108 chapters about Freedom, Love, Wisdom, Brotherhood, and Oneness. Some of the messages were from the Forefathers of our United States and how they were led and inspired from within to lead this country to be "the land of the free."

Could we people of the United States fulfill our destiny to lead the world into the new age of peace? The new age coming in was "The Golden Age" long ago prophesied. A speeded-up planetary vibration was ushering in this new age; it was a critical time when each of us could choose the spiritual path for creating this "heaven on earth."

Entranced and fascinated by what I was reading, my own thoughts were being stimulated to question why we now hold spiritual matters separate from those of state. No prayers are allowed to be said in our schools these days but our forefathers must have known something. Our dollar bill has a pyramid on it with the all-seeing "third eye" at the top. What moved them? What source had they tapped into for strength and guidance? It had to be the same one I felt sourced and guided by—God, Universal Force, or whatever name we or our religions chose to give it, the same one available to *all* mankind, regardless of color, nationality, or creed!!

I opened my wallet and pulled out a dollar bill, a ten-dollar bill, a quarter, and a Kennedy half-dollar. They each had the same words on them: "In God We Trust." It was obvious that the forefathers of our great nation who wrote the Declaration of Independence and the Constitution of the United States which declared "all men equal" had to be tapping into the power of God to inspire and lead them. The clues were everywhere for anyone who cared enough to look. How foolish it seems for us now to want to separate ourselves, *state*, from the supreme guidance of God that had guided and sourced us in the first place to the freedom we now enjoy.

I picked up the phone and called Carolyn to thank her for sharing the Ascended Masters book with me and to verbalize some of the insights it had stirred.

"I have another book for you," my new walking-encyclopedia friend answered. Carolyn had an extensive library, covering a broad spectrum of subjects. And it was the ones on metaphysical and spiritual topics that excited me the most. If Carolyn didn't have the book I was looking for, I probably didn't need it or else it was one of the few she hadn't heard of—yet.

The following week, she brought me *A Spiritual Bouquet from the Ascended Lady Masters*. I opened right to the index pages and started looking for messages or symbols of the red rose and the pansy. Recently, in another "billboard" dream, the two flowers had appeared on the billboard—a long-stemmed lush red rose and a long-stemmed velvety maroon pansy with a face of gold at its center.

Checking the index, I opened first to the red rose chapter. The red rose represented love and the evolvement of the soul. It was the flower of Lady Meta. I was unfamiliar with Lady Meta, but very familiar with the message of love coming from her.

181

I could hardly wait to hunt up the "pansy." The pansy was the flower of Amelia Earhart, who left the Earth domain while flying an airplane. It told the story of how Amelia Earhart loved the glorious feeling of freedom and happiness she experienced whenever she was flying. Flying had struck a cord "somewhere deep within her and she knew she was *born to fly*." It described her last flight when high stormy winds got her and her airplane into serious trouble.

Tears ran down my cheeks as I read about Amelia and thought about Bobby. Not anything to make of it, but the synchronicity, a meaningful coincidence for me, was leading me to search on.

Carolyn called again as I sat pondering all the thoughts I was thinking and the emotions I was feeling. She had found another book on the symbolism of flowers and wanted to read me more about the pansy. The pansy was symbolic of the "bridge" between the third (physical) and fourth (spiritual) dimensions of life. What that all meant at this moment in my life, I didn't know. But I was feeling a strong urge to go to Grass Valley, California, and try to locate the authors of the "Ascended Masters" books and see if I might possibly spend a little time with them.

There were more questions running around in my head and more answers to seek. And so my ongoing search and recorded journey to many "Teachers, Travels, and Tools" began.

TRAVEL:

Grass Valley

The urge to go to Grass Valley and meet the authors of *Golden Moments with the Ascended Masters* was strong as I called Carolyn Ortega and Robin Blanc. It would be nice to have their company while hunting up the whereabouts of White Dove and Samuel George Partridge. The information inside the cover of the book *A Spiritual Bouquet from the Ascended Lady Masters* mentioned a "Universal Mother Mary's Garden" which I hoped would not be too hard to find.

Arriving in Grass Valley, we realized we hadn't called ahead and wondered if we needed an appointment. We stopped at a nearby pay phone and Robin called.

White Dove answered and said, "Yes, you need an appointment. We're not open to the public. I have company right now, but as you've come all this way, perhaps I can see you briefly around 5 PM." Robin discovered in talking with White Dove that her husband, Samuel, had very recently passed away. She was not feeling up to par since his death.

We followed the directions given us to get to "Universal Mother Mary's Garden". We weren't sure what to expect when we arrived and knocked on the door. White Dove answered the door. With that name, I thought she might be an Indian lady, but she was not. White Dove looked tired as she invited us in. After we talked awhile, her sparkle and vitality seemed to be returning, and she absolutely glowed as she began talking about her wonderful husband and invited us into Samuel George Partridge's study.

Carolyn was "in heaven" amongst all of Sam's books and papers, and began looking through one of his books while sitting behind his desk. Robin was sitting to my left. I sat cross-legged in the middle of the library floor talking to White Dove, who was standing in the doorway nearby. A strange expression must have been on my face as Carolyn looked at me.

"What's going on?" she asked.

"I really don't know," I replied. "I'm feeling sort of...strange, *real strange!*"

"What does 'strange' feel like?" asked White Dove.

"Feels like I've got a wet hand that's plugged into an electrical outlet." I couldn't believe what was happening. The pulsating energy circulating throughout my whole body was powerful and I soon felt like I was sitting on the electrical socket! My ears started ringing and I could hear the sound of my pounding heartbeat at the same time.

"I think Sam's here in the room with us, White Dove." I listened to my own words in disbelief as they exited my mouth, as though I hadn't really said them. White Dove nodded and agreed she felt his presence. She suggested I make myself open to receive a message from him as Carolyn handed me a piece of paper and a pen.

When we had arrived at "Universal Mother Mary's Garden" earlier, I had felt extremely peaceful. Now, moments later, I felt "plugged-in," literally. Slowly, I cleared my mind and began to write down just the thoughts that were coming to me. I could barely handle the energy pouring through me. Whatever was happening, it was not a normal feeling and it was scaring me.

Running to the garden outside, I sat down on the steps that led to the little pyramid meditation house to see what would happen next. I reread what I had originally written down: "White Dove is in danger—must not be left alone tonight." Just then, a black cat making weird noises darted out of the rosebushes, startling me. It must be time to go back in the house. Things were getting spooky.

Back in the house, I was reluctant to give the message to White Dove. Normally, I'm a very positive-minded person and this did *not* feel like a positive message.

"Let me see what's on the paper, Shirley." Carolyn asked. As she read the message aloud, White Dove announced she felt very tired and was going to the back bedroom to take a nap and pray for clarity and guidance about this message.

Two hours later, White Dove rejoined us. She confirmed my message was from her husband Sam, and asked us to spend the night with her. She advised me to always protect myself when channeling by visualizing being protected and surrounded by white light and asking to channel *only* the highest spiritual messages.

Robin, Carolyn, and I chose to sleep in the living room: it was a spontaneous pajama party. "There's strength in group power," Robin joked. We laughed as we gathered and lit every candle we could find and made a "barricade" of Celaya Winkler paintings all around us. Portraits of Jesus, St. Germain, saints, angels, and other Ascended Masters surrounded our new sleeping quarters. One thing for sure, we were in the best of company.

The next morning White Dove was in good spirits as we left and offered an invitation to come back soon. Robin and I had each bought a few books and Carolyn, whom we had aptly nicknamed "The Keeper of the Universal Records," lugged out two very heavy boxes of written treasures she had purchased from White Dove. We left, promising to return soon.

*   *   *

We did return soon, this time accompanied by Janice Hamby and Maureen Mitchell. What a great time we had, singing while Maureen played White Dove's piano. Later in the evening, Maureen began playing "blues" tunes and asked me to sing along. We "grooved" instantly and half-joking, half-knowingly, without knowing how we knew, felt like we had done this "gig" before— probably in New Orleans when we were both black musicians.

The "past-life" stuff kept coming up, but I didn't know what to believe or disbelieve about reincarnation. It sure threw some interesting light upon the accumulation and development of our talents.

It explained the wonder of Mozart, who was a genius at the age of five. Where do genius and master talents come from, I wondered.

The next morning we drove to a piece of property White Dove and Sam owned out on Wolf Mountain, seventeen miles southwest of Grass Valley. White Dove told us of a magnetic connection this land had with Mt. Shasta as we wandered around the almost-deserted area. A nearby Fire Ranger's Station was the only visual connection with civilization.

Maureen and Janice went exploring and discovered an open-ceilinged "arena" with what appeared to be astrological symbols painted at intervals around the walls of the circular cement building. Charcoaled bits of wood and ashes gave evidence of someone's recent visit.

Curiously, we started exploring the grounds below our newly-found "temple". Maureen felt like we were standing on an old Indian Burial ground. Feelings of great sadness crept over me as she said it. Images of a young Indian girl in labor, watching some kind of massacre while hiding for her life, started flashing across my mind. I could see a whole village being destroyed...murder...fire! The handsome blonde-haired face of a man in uniform flashed by—the father of the child the young Indian maiden was carrying?

Maureen was also feeling a personal tie to what I was seeing in my mind and feeling in my body. The sadness I was feeling increased as I rubbed my swollen abdomen, sensing that I was the Indian maiden who had just given birth to a stillborn infant.

The sun was setting fast and darkness would soon be upon us as we scurried back up the dirt path to our car. We had done a little blessing ceremony near the "mounds" of dirt and rock.

Part of me was excited about the things that were happening and the possible past-life recalls I was experiencing. The other part of me pooh-poohed such things and wanted to hurry away from Wolf Mountain fast and retreat to the nearest Kentucky Fried Chicken outlet and get into some "normal" civilization-type conversation.

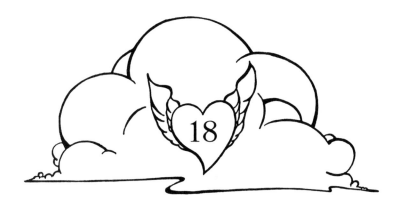

TEACHER:

Nana

Nana, my beautiful and spirited eighty-eight year-old maternal grandmother, was a wonderful role model while I was growing up. Elegantly well-groomed, she always stood erect, proud of her 5'8" height. As a child, I loved exploring her handbag where I always found Wrigley's Doublemint gum and other "goodies." On teenage birthdays, there was many a trip to San Francisco and a shopping spree for a new coat or outfit. Having spent a good part of my childhood on a ranch, long-awaited and rare shopping trips to the "City by the Bay" boggled my mind and eyes.

The next-to-the-last time I saw Nana she was in a hospital. The nurses wouldn't allow her to have her false teeth in her mouth except at mealtimes, and she was strapped in a wheelchair. My spunky Grandmother was ticked off and said so, *loudly*. There was no way she could or cared to hide the frustration she was feeling.

"Damned old body won't work anymore!" she hissed as she

struggled to get loose from the restraining straps that imprisoned her in the wheelchair. In anger at her failing physical body, she threw her teeth on the floor. Since then, they were kept in a labeled container and taken out only for mealtimes. This infuriated Nana when I came to visit. Pride in her personal appearance was still very evident, and she felt stripped of her dignity being seen toothless by visitors.

Even being angry, however, was better than the "nothingness" state. The last time I saw her she had been moved to a convalescent home, and a state of "absolute nothingness" was written across her face. When I said "Hi, Nana", it was as if her body was there, but the real Nana had checked out for awhile. I touched her and spoke to her again. Tears welled up in her eyes—a sparkle and recognition came into them. "Shirley!" She was "back in her body" again and so glad to see me!

Shortly thereafter, a phone call came from my Mom. "Nana died at 5:15 this morning."

Nana wanted no funeral, no memorial, just cremation and a scattering of her ashes. When my Mom heard that the normal arrangement for scattering ashes was for it to be done at sea, she cringed.

"Must be some place where we can legally scatter them on land," Mom said.

A call to my brother Robert resulted in arrangements being made for Nana's remains to be taken to Robert's ranch in Modesto and scattered in the almond orchard there.

Two weeks after Nana's death, the mortuary called. I signed the formal papers releasing her ashes for private disposition and picked up the little white box. At home, I sat "Nana" on my mirrored dressing table and "talked" to her on several occasions before driving her to my brother's in Orinda.

Robert carried Nana around in the back seat of his Mercedes and also "talked" to the Grandmother he had never had the opportunity to know very well. On Memorial Day, Robert and his young son, Robert Jr., held a private memorial service as the two of them scattered Nana's ashes. Surely the almond orchard will blossom more beautifully than ever now.

Nana's death was an important lesson to me in how crucial it is to maintain the dignity of life until the actual moment of death. Like birth, death is a difficult process and those facing the end of their lives need the love and support of family and friends to make the transition. No matter how much the body has deteriorated, the spirit *does* remain intact; the individual *does* respond to your presence; your love and caring will definitely be felt and appreciated.

TEACHER/TOOL

Intensive Journal® Workshop

The Intensive Journal® process thus becomes
a self-adjusting compass by which each
person finds the direction and meaning
of his or her own life.

—Ira Progoff

I'd been leading the A*L*L Game for over four months. As
an A*L*L Game Guide, it became evident that synchronicity (meaningful coincidence) was in operation in each game. It further became
obvious that if synchronicity was operating in each game (a microcosm
of life), it must also be operating in everyday life (a macrocosm of
life). If this theory had any credibility, it ought to be observable

and I ought to be alert to it, what it might mean, or where it might lead.

One morning I was heading to Palo Alto to do an A*L*L Game presentation at the San Andreas Health Council. The evening before as I shuffled through a stack of magazine clippings, one in particular caught my eye. It was an article clipped from an old *Psychology Today* and told about Ira Progoff's Intensive Journal® Workshop. Across the article in bold red lettering, I had written "Find out where to go to take this!"

As I finished my A*L*L Game demonstration and was walking towards the front door, I stopped to glance over the huge bulletin board. It was covered with flyers and business cards on health-related subjects. My eyes scanned flyers and notices of every size and color and came to rest on one announcing the San Andreas Health Council's presentation of Ira Progoff's Intensive Journal® Workshop. I signed up on the spot.

Synchronicity and I had begun a journey together. Sensitive to its principles, I wanted to test and experiment with how effortlessly and spontaneously it might lead me or to confirm my "next step".

It was an exciting experiment. How far "divine guidance through synchronicity" would go and how long it would continue were still unknowns. All I could do was ride the "crest of guidance and energy" as far as it would take me. Life seemed so much easier when I rode in the "flow".

On the second day of the workshop, the introduction to this book wrote itself. From then on, with all my considerations about writing a book expressed, the book had room to begin taking a definite shape and form. I also signed up for the Progoff Meditation Workshop to be given at the Jesuit Retreat House in Palo Alto over the upcoming Memorial Day weekend.

The Journal® Workbook, with specifically-guided journeys into each of its indexed sections, became a precision instrument I used to explore many areas of my life. As I did so, I could see the "tapestry" of Shirley's life begin to weave and paint its own unique patterns and pictures. In one of the "dialoguing" sections, I talked intimately with my body. My "body" hilariously nailed me when I said I wanted to support its well-being.

"Oh yeah, what was that sweet roll and coffee you fed
me for breakfast all about?"

I dialogued with persons important in my life. Bobby told me it
was difficult for him to "reach" me now. I trusted messages I received
from other spiritual beings, but always doubted them when I'd sense
the message was from Bobby. Bobby chided me gently in our
dialogue. He said he always needed "props" to get my attention.
Zapping electrical sources, making them tremble, and guiding
airplanes to fly low overhead usually were effective in directing my
attention to the thoughts I was receiving. The registered, numbered
Intensive Journal® Workbook I received at the beginning of the
course became a treasure house where I could discover the shape,
colors, and textures woven through the tapestry of my life. As I
journeyed through the different sections, definite themes, currents,
and flows in my life emerged. I had never seen it all quite so clearly
connected before. Events and decisions, made early on in life,
shaped my character and potential destiny. *Everything* led to making
me the person I am today.

The dialogue section with "society" revealed some interesting
insights. In it, I talked with "society" about "religion" and "prejudice" from the point of view of an eight-year-old Shirley forming very
definite opinions about the world she lived in.

Religion: I was raised in many different homes and foster
homes. Each had a different religion for me to look at. How do I
chose the "right" one? By the guidance of the person who introduced me to it? *All* religions seem to say love is the essence of God and
their way is the "right" way to God. It seemed to me that religions
only separate people and make them righteous about their own
beliefs and points of view. It looked like too small a game for the real
God and me to play.

"I think I'll just hang back a bit and watch, if you don't mind
God," I wrote. "At least, until I can find a path to reach you that
unites people and excludes no one. Religions *can* separate."

Prejudice: Memories of being a naive, smiley-faced, and very
inquisitive child of eight continued to float by. One day in early

December of 1941, while I was hand-cranking an old ice cream machine at my Uncle Bartie and Aunt Anne's home in Lincoln, California, a radio blared out, "Pearl Harbor has been attacked and the United States of America has declared war on Japan."

The adults around me were moaning loudly and in a state of near panic. What did "war" mean, I wondered.

As that small child, I shortly discovered that war meant my Japanese playmate, Tamiko Kaneko, and her family were suddenly whisked away from the ranch community where I lived with my grandparents. They were taken to a concentration-like detention camp. Sweet, artistic little Tamiko and her family dangerous to our security? How absolutely ridiculous!

My own day to taste the bitter fruits of prejudice was soon to come, as well. My Italian surname Ferrero made me "different" now. Overnight I went from being a sunny little "Pollyanna" with a lot of friends to an outcast, teased and taunted by playmates that now called me a "dago" and a "wop." What in the world were they? Why didn't anybody want to play with me anymore?

I didn't understand how a war in some far-off place could change the way my friends saw me.

Prejudice separates.

At the end of another section of dialoguing, I found the words

Divorce separates.

Another section noted that

Death separates.

In a section called "Wisdom Figures", I dialogued with God directly, telling Him about inner conflicts and separations from Him and religions that I had long had going on in the back of my mind. Part of me had tried to talk to Him through Jesus and there was also a part of me, even at a young age, that was very attracted to Buddha and Eastern philosophies. Now there was a part of me saying I could talk to God directly. When asking God about the path I should pursue, I received the following answer:

> Separation only exists on the physical plane. There is no separation with the Masters and those who truly abide with me. There is only oneness. Follow your heart and diminish separation in your own life until there is only the harmony and love of oneness.

Love unites.

On Memorial Day weekend, during the next part of the available Progoff workshop series, I took the Process Meditation Workshop. The setting for the weekend was the beautiful, peaceful Jesuit Retreat House nestled high in the wooded hills overlooking Los Altos and Palo Alto, California.

In the course of the day, we were shown how to make a seven-syllabled mantra that was personally meaningful. We then meditated on it. Mine was "Airplane crashing—mountaintop."

Slowly, I deeply relaxed and let the mantra repeat itself silently in my mind. Clear *vividly-colored* images began flashing in my mind's eye like a 35mm slide show:

- a reddish-gold "sun-ball" rising over a darkened mountain.
- a long-haired bearded man in a flowing off-white robe standing on a mountain, staff in hand.
- an indigo-blue midnight sky and Mt. Shasta glistening with snow, with a luminous "spirit light" arising from its crown.
- a monk in a yellowish robe entering a secret chamber in a jagged mountainside.
- Bobby's smiling face, winking and making a thumb-to-index finger "high sign".
- a billboard upon which was a long-stemmed red rose and a long-stemmed maroon and gold pansy. (I'd seen this vision in a dream once before.)
- a smiling madonna figure holding a newborn child.

- a mountain with the silhouette of a seagull soaring against the rising sun.
- a cobra snake swaying as it uncoiled itself with its head fully hooded.
- the wreckage of an airplane—papers strewn all over; Bobby with a jagged head wound.
- a crystal triangle hanging in the sun, reflecting rainbow colors.
- a wide golden thunderbolt tearing across a darkened sky.

As I came out of the meditation and began writing what I'd seen, I thought, what a *great* show! Wonder what channel I'd plugged into. As I reread what I had seen, I was feeling a *lot* of emotion—and *love*.

The second day of the Intensive was Memorial Day. I got up very early. It was an hour-and-a-half drive or more from my house in Walnut Creek to the Jesuit Retreat House in Los Altos. I wanted to take some flowers to Bobby at Oakmont Memorial Park. It was before sunrise and very dark as my friend Bill Orlich and I hiked around, past the locked gates and up the long winding road to the "Garden of Meditation," flowers and flashlights in hand. As I arranged the flowers near Bobby's grave, I turned to see a reddish-golden sun rising and sending its first rays of the day over the darkened silhouette of Mt. Diablo.

It was breathtaking and it was the *exact* scene I'd seen the evening before in my mantra meditation. Synchronicity—!! Confirmation chills ran up and down my spine for several seconds.

Very different than merely writing in a diary, Progoff's process of journal writing provided me with an on-going tool and self-generating contact and interaction with the deepest parts of my personality and spirituality.

On the way home, I stopped at the Jesuit Book Shop and picked up a copy of *Jung, Synchronicity, and Human Destiny* by Ira Progoff. Late that evening, I began reading it and couldn't put it down. I felt incredibly "turned-on" by Progoff's discussion of C.G. Jung's concepts. I couldn't believe that I was actually intellectually grasping and agreeing with his information. Before the A*L*L Game and my own growing personal awareness of synchronicity, any discussion of a word by that name and the theory behind it would probably have put me to sleep very quickly. Now, I felt like Nancy Drew again, hot on the trail of solving another mystery.

One other "meaningful" incident quickly followed when I returned from the workshop. My daughter Laura called from West Germany. She had felt homesick on Memorial Day and her thoughts had been with me all day, she said. As she lay down to sleep (her time in Europe was nine hours ahead of California time), she kept concentrating on being home. The next thing she knew, she felt she was riding in the back seat of my car. It was sunset, she said, and we were crossing the San Francisco-Oakland Bay Bridge. A man whose face she couldn't see was driving my car. Also, I was wearing a rust-colored dress and jacket. When she "awoke," she wasn't homesick anymore. Shades from the *Wizard of Oz* and "click your heels three times Dorothy/Laura, and you're home!"

The strangest thing about it was that a man (Bill Orlich) *was* driving "Valentyne" home from the Jesuit Retreat House. At sunset, as Laura had described, we *were* crossing the San Francisco-Oakland Bay Bridge. I remembered thinking about Laura a lot as I admired the sun setting across the way, sinking slowly behind the Golden Gate Bridge. Laura had even somehow "seen" exactly what I was wearing that day, a rust-colored dress and jacket. The hair on my arms was standing straight up as I hung up the phone after talking with Laura. Some things were beyond explanation, that was for sure!

Washington D.C.

Doest thou love life?
Then do not squander time,
for that's the stuff life is made of.

—*Benjamin Franklin*

Mom's brain tumor had been diagnosed and prognosed. Big "C" had come again to do battle with her. Her doctors said that radiation treatments had bought her a little more time. Maybe they had but the quality of her time left was in question. She was weak and the nausea she was experiencing made her wonder if she had chosen the best thing under the circumstances. Loss of all her hair hadn't helped her morale, either.

She knew I was planning a trip back to Washington, D.C., to see son, Steve, his wife, Darsie, and my now one-year old granddaughter,

Janessa Bobbi. Would Mom's doctors possibly give her permission to accompany me?

"Yes," was the answer. "Whatever brings her a little happiness at this point is all that counts."

United Airlines was great. They had a wheelchair waiting for us when we arrived at the San Francisco airport. Mom, however, was determined to walk down the ramp to the plane on her own power. She was going to see her grandchildren and didn't want them to know how sick she really was. Stubborn lady—but I had to admire her courage.

The trip, from being a spontaneous idea of a solo trip for me, was fast turning into a grand family reunion. Son Gregory was driving down from New York City to meet me at Steve's. I decided to keep Mom under wraps and surprise both the boys. Once the idea of a "surprise visit" was shared, it proved contagious. Kim booked herself on the same flight as Mom and I. The next day Laura called. She had just finished Weather School at Chanute Air Force Base in Illinois and had some leave time coming. What fun it would be to fly in and join us in surprising everybody. Bobby's wife Kathleen "just happened" to call from Pasadena, California, where she was now an art student at the Art School Center there. The spirit of all being together again excited us as Kathleen called back to confirm her flight from Los Angeles to D.C. We hadn't been together as a family since Bobby's funeral.

The carefully orchestrated and timed "surprise" took place when we deplaned and I distracted Steve at the Washington, D.C., baggage claim area. Mom walked out from where we had hidden her and tapped Steve on the shoulder. He turned around and was caught totally off guard.

"Grams, where did you come from?" he asked as he hugged her tightly.

On cue, Kim, Kathleen, and Laura came up from behind, tapping Steve on his other shoulder and folding him in a huge group hug. Everybody was laughing and crying at the same time. We hadn't seen Laura in almost six months and it had been even longer since Kathleen had left for art school.

Greg and his girlfriend, Emily, would be arriving in town early the next morning. It would be great fun to pull the same surprise tactics on him when he met us at our motel. Mom, Kim, Laura, and Kathleen hid in our motel bathroom as I answered the door to greet Greg and Emily. Steve talked to Greg to distract him while I maneuvered him with a hug to have his back facing the bathroom door. Mom came out first, and Greg picked her up off the floor with a big bear hug. Next came Kim, then Laura. Kathleen was the last one to tap him on the shoulder.

"Mom, who else have you got hiding in that bathroom? How did you guys pull this all together?" Greg, true to form, was trying to figure out all the mechanics of everybody getting time off at the same time. He suddenly remembered his girlfriend and said, "Everybody, this is my Emmy."

Mom seemed to get a new surge of energy from being the center of attention and having weathered the five-hour flight much better than anyone could have expected.

Darsie came to our hotel room with Janessa Bobbi. "Nessa" felt a bit overwhelmed seeing so many strange and excited new faces all at once so a baby-sitter was found for her. Mom wanted to bed down and recharge her energy after dinner. The rest of us wanted to go out for a night on the town. We made the rounds, ending up dancing at Bronco Billy's in Georgetown. Spirits lightened as we danced the night away.

The next morning after breakfast, Mom wanted to go sightseeing while she still had some strength. The day was hot and humid as we headed for Arlington Cemetery to see John F. Kennedy's Eternal Flame gravesite. It was a moving experience and I felt saddened by the loss of such a great man. After a couple of hours of sightseeing, Mom started to show signs of pooping-out. Greg and Steve put her in the car and said they'd meet us at the Lincoln Memorial. Somehow I didn't want to miss walking on my own two feet along this historical walk down from Arlington Cemetery, across the Potomac River to the Lincoln Memorial. Kimberly, Kathleen, Laura, and I were marching when we were caught in a sudden downpour. We were soaked to the skin in a minute flat, but it didn't dampen our spirits a bit. Laura called off cadence: "sound off— sound off," as we joined in, laughingly welcoming the rain as we skipped through the puddles. It was a wonderful way to cool off hot, sticky bodies.

Halfway across the Potomac Bridge, I stopped to soak in the reality of where I was standing. To my left was Arlington Cemetery and the Lincoln Memorial was to my right. Leaning against the bridge railing, I stared out into the choppy waters of the Potomac. I was overwhelmed at having just walked the same cobblestone road where a horse-drawn caisson had carried the body of John Fitzgerald Kennedy on that November day so long ago. In a split second of time, I experienced a moment of timelessness. Somehow my mind floated beyond the barriers of time and space and I could feel to the roots of my soul, the uncompromising level of commitment and integrity the forefathers of our great country had felt. Their courage to follow their guidance built us a country founded on the principles of equality and freedom for all men. The gratitude I felt filled my heart with a silent prayer of thanksgiving as tears rolled down my cheeks. They were willing to die for the freedom I so often took for granted. The freedom to be, do, have, and go as I chose. No one but me could put limits on what I or anyone could become in this land of the free. History used to be just a subject stuck somewhere in a tenth-grade school book. Now, it was the very essence of our great heritage, and it occupied an elevated spot in my heart.

The following afternoon we went to the Smithsonian Space Center. Airplanes were everywhere. Sadness kept creeping up on me, and several times I went off by myself to cry, blow my nose, take a deep breath, and then rejoin the family. I didn't fool anybody. We were all having similar thoughts. Bobby would sure enjoy being here with us, and maybe he was, in spirit.

Hours and days passed too soon and it was time to go to Dulles International Airport for our return trips home. It was unspoken, but obvious by now that Mom wouldn't be here the next time we had a family reunion. Smiling, we loaded our cameras and recorded the precious moments and last photographs of Mom. We soaked up each hug. They'd have to last for quite a while.

TRAVEL

Mt. Shasta '82

A crescent moon hung in the night sky
as if it were God's index finger
beckoning us to the mystical Shasta.

—Journey to High Places

I knew one day I would journey back to Mt. Shasta. There
never was a question of if; only of when. One day, I randomly opened
the book, *Golden Moments with the Ascended Masters*. My eyes fell on
the line, "They are held in the 9th month and on the 9th day." That
was it—the place where I'd spend Bobby's birthday on September
8th and stay over for "the 9th day" of the "9th month."

Excited, I began phoning eight very special friends who in the
past had expressed an interest in going to Mt. Shasta with me whenever

I felt the inner calling to return there. To my absolute joy and surprise, all eight friends said yes and manipulated their busy working schedules to be free for the Mt. Shasta trip.

At 11:00 PM on September 7th, Carolyn Ortega, Janice Hamby, Maureen Mitchell, Robin Blanc, and I loaded two cars with gear. Billy Liles, Georgia Kahn, Jody Friedman, and Guy Heckenlively would drive up on the following day.

Carolyn drove her car and I drove Valentyne as we headed for Interstate Highway 5. The five of us arrived in the sleepy town of Redding at 2:30 in the morning and pulled into a restaurant for something to eat. Originally, we had planned to find a motel in Redding and continue on to the mountain early the next morning, but by the time we had finished our snacks, we were too excited to sleep, and chose to continue on up to the Mt. Shasta area.

A crescent moon hung in the night sky as if it were God's index finger beckoning us to the mystical Shasta. Stars appeared magnified, like brilliant diamonds, sparkling their twinkling messages on a sky of dark blue velvet. We could "feel" the presence of Mt. Shasta even before she came into actual view. Suddenly, as we rounded a curve of the highway, the mountain came into full view and awed us with her magnificence. Shadows were dancing everywhere on Everitt Memorial Highway as we wound around the base of the mountain and began our ascent.

We drove as high up on the mountain as we could go by car to one of the lower parking lots. Carolyn and I aligned our cars as close together as we could possibly get them. Our side-view mirrors were touching. We weren't "afraid" really, but we had made an agreement to stay together at all times, especially while it was still dark.

The sound of the cassette tape, "Oxygene," filled the night air from our rolled-down car windows. We parked facing the Eastern sky to await the birth of the new day from our cozy reclining seats.

Slowly, the sky was being painted with soft rays of pastel light. Silhouettes of the nearby mountains came alive as a golden ball of light rose over them, chasing away the remaining shadows of night.

We got out of our cars and stretched. Carolyn lit the candle she had and strains of "Happy Birthday, Dear Bobby" echoed across the mountain. My emotions were in high gear as I blew out the candle for Bobby. I felt so close to him this morning, as did the others.

Though they had not known Bobby in his physical form, they all felt they knew him well in spirit. His life and his death had uniquely touched their hearts and souls, too.

"Whew, guys, it's time for breakfast and a little shut-eye," Robin said.

We'd only had a few winks of sleep and tiredness was beginning to show up in the form of yawns and chilled bodies. We needed to find a comfy motel and rest awhile. Jody, Guy, Georgia, and Billy would be arriving later. Tomorrow, the 9th day of the 9th month, would be time enough to climb and explore some of the higher elevations of Mt. Shasta.

After resting for a few hours, we awakened anxious to explore the city of Mt. Shasta. As we got out of our parked cars we realized we were parked in front of the Golden Bough Bookstore. In it we discovered shelves full of holistic health, metaphysical, and spiritual book treasures—the very kind I most hungered for. As my eye scanned the shelves, an orange-colored volume stood out. I took it down from the shelf and read the title, *The Brotherhood of Mt. Shasta*. Yes, I was ready to devour and appropriately digest any information I could discover about this spiritual mountain named Shasta.

"Are you here on vacation?" asked the owner of the store, who introduced herself as Dorothy.

"Well, sort of," I replied. "We're really here to celebrate my son's birthday."

"Is he with you today?" Dorothy queried.

I hesitated a moment before replying. "My son died in an airplane crash on Mt. Shasta a year ago January."

"I remember the accident well," Dorothy continued. "Gladys, a friend of mine, was on Police Department duty when the call about the crash came through on the radio. She told me about it, and my son David was one of the first volunteers to go out on skis to search." Boy, did my ears perk up!

Between bits of conversation, Carolyn had been accumulating a huge stack of books to buy. I wasn't doing badly in that department either. I wanted to know everything I could about this mountain, and the experience called death, and what the soul's journey after death might be like. Dorothy cautiously asked me if I felt Bobby's presence here with us in the bookstore. I assured her that was an okay subject with me. In fact, I hungered for spiritually-aware people to share those kinds of feelings and knowledge with me.

"Yes," I replied "I do feel Bobby around me at times. I want to be in communication with him so badly I sometimes wonder if I make all of this up."

Dorothy smiled knowingly. "I feel he's here now and there is a lot of blue energy about him. I associate that particular energy vibration with Christ and those that are now working on the mountain with Him."

I had no idea what "blue energy" was about. One thing I did know: there was an inner peace inside me as we left the bookstore.

*   *   *

The five of us enjoyed the varied menu at Michael's Restaurant and shared from each other's plates. We returned to our motel to soak in the inviting outdoor hot tub.

Later in the evening, we assigned ourselves a sleeping spot and each cuddled up with a metaphysical book. We were a nucleus of like-minded souls. A loving, warm camaraderie of spiritual seekers, each in turn punctuating the silence with "listen to this" and finally succumbing to the lure of the sandman, books still in hand.

Carolyn's glasses were still on her nose the next morning as we awakened and took turns showering. We dressed in layered clothing, as some Shasta old-timers had advised us to do. The *Mt. Shasta Climbers Guide* said, "The mountain makes its own weather which can change within minutes." We wanted to be prepared for whatever the mountain had in store for us.

The five of us arrived at the lower Ski Bowl parking lot, quickly followed by the arrival of the rest of our group: Jody, Guy, Georgia, and Billy. After a warm round of greetings and hugs, we set out hiking, looking for the perfect spot for a group meditation.

We gathered beside a small stream of icy water trickling over rocks and shrubby pine trees. The sound of the stream rushing down the mountainside sounded like something from a cassette meditation tape—playful, soothing, refreshing, and peaceful—perfect!

Billy and Guy gathered wood and we built a small fire in a safe clearing of rocks. Candles were lit and we formed a circle. Guy began leading us through the "Rainbow Bridge" group meditation, a powerful soul link-up meditation suggested for groups of nine or more. We had done it as a group the previous week when we met to lay out the final plans for coming to Mt. Shasta.

It was a moving experience to be doing it on Mt. Shasta at an 8,000-foot elevation in the early morning splendor of a new day. The fresh, crisp mountain air pinkened our noses and cheeks as we sang out another round of "Happy Birthday, Dear Bobby." Somehow, through Bobby, we had all chosen to be together this marvelous day.

Splashing our faces, we laughed as we drank from the stream of melting snow. Carefully, we extinguished and buried our small campfire remains and started off in various pursuits. As a group, we had chosen to go in whatever direction we each felt led to go. Guy, Georgia, and Billy headed up the mountain toward the radio antenna and quickly disappeared out of sight. Robin, Maureen, Janice, and Carolyn could be heard laughing as they climbed some rocky ledges east of where we had started.

My heart wanted to fly me to the site of Bobby's crashed plane. It was somewhere around the Whitney Glacier Headwall, from the information we could gather. From where I stood on the mountain, Whitney Headwall was not a safe destination for unskilled, novice climbers without appropriate preparedness and climbing gear.

Jody and I turned and began climbing towards snow-covered slopes to our right, south of Mt. Shasta herself. The sun was blazing brightly in the cobalt blue sky. Soft white clouds formed around the top of the mountain, crowning her with a heavenly halo of white fluff.

We peeled off some of our layered clothing so we could absorb more of the sun's warm, tanning rays. As we wandered, we came across a patch of the most incredibly beautiful flowers. I'd never seen any like them before. They looked like strands of white velvet with burgundy and violet centers. When I closely examined their incredible beauty and intricacy, it left no doubt in my mind that there really was a God.

Below us lay a most magnificent view of the Master Creator's works. Multi-green hues painted the mountain ranges. The valleys were dotted with an occasional blue, blue lake here and there, mirror-like, reflecting all of nature in its most splendiferous dress.

Talk about "Mountain High"! It seemed natural to be here breathing in the essence that we were immersed in.

Higher and higher on the mountain Jody and I climbed until she pointed out a rock that looked like a great place to stop and be still for a while. We made ourselves comfortable, sitting back-to-back, and noted we were sitting in a direct line between Mt. Shasta and Mt. Lassen. We talked a bit, then simultaneously went into a quiet meditative state.

After a short while, we stretched and broke into a run toward a patch of snow just above us. We were thirsty and the snow tasted so good. I threw a snowball and Jody returned fire. Here and there were icy patches to shoe-ski down.

The sun was telling us it was time to start hiking back down the mountain. We needed plenty of time to find and reunite with the other members of our party. Earlier in the day, we had heard voices occasionally. It had been absolutely quiet for some time now.

"Robin...Maureen...Carolyn...Janice...Georgia...Guy...Billy... Where are you?" we began singing out.

In the distance, I caught sight of a green jacket. "Here come Robin and the girls."

Soon a lavender-sweatered figure came into view. It was Georgia. Guy was right behind her. As we all came together, we began questioning who had seen Billy last, where, and when.

"The last I saw of him, he was heading straight for the summit!" Georgia said. We waited and said silent prayers for his welfare as our eyes continuously scanned the white glacier slopes leading to the summit. He would be just a small speck if he had really gone that high.

One, two, three, all together we shouted, "Billllllllyyyyyyyyy...!" We called him in unison several times. Suddenly, way off in the distance, we spotted a small figure—Billy. As he approached us, not only did he look "okay", he looked vibrantly alive and radiantly joyful. He had climbed to the top of the Redbanks and skied and slid all the way down the ice fields on his tennis shoes, and finally, on the seat of his pants. He was exuberant and his torn-up tennis shoes and jeans validated the ski-trip that Billy said was an absolutely exhilarating experience.

Had there been a "ski patrol" on the mountain, I'm sure they would have had a word or two of caution and advice to offer. Billy's way might not have been the safest and sanest way to descend a mountain.

Arm-in-arm, shoulder-to-shoulder, we laughed and sang our way back to the Ski Bowl parking lot. We each shared a bit of our adventures of the day. The outer part of our journey was physically exciting, challenging, and full of the surprises of nature's beauty.

At a spiritual level, something indescribable had happened to all nine of us. We'd been given a "gift" of inner peace and the spiritual experience defied being captured in words of the physical dimension. "It's so quiet," Maureen said, "it appears there's nothing much happening at Mt. Shasta...HA!!"

TOOLS:

Guides on My Journey

Meditation

My first experience with "sitting still" was an open-eyed, quiet time at The 6-Day training. I was intrigued by meditation but it struck me as something weird only people in caves in India did.

Anticipation of silent times at The 6-Day training sent a terror running through me; it was obviously something my EGO (Easing God Out) mind definitely did not approve of. It *knew* its days of being in charge of my reality were numbered as it tried all the tricks it could to interrupt my silence. But the intuitive part of me was growing stronger day by day and refused to go unheard. The "little voice within" kept giving me attractive reminders about the benefits of meditation and slowly I began trying different techniques.

After meeting Georgia Kahn at one of our ASSET trainings, I asked her to formally instruct me in the Transcendental Meditation (TM) technique. The ritual Georgia created for my first TM session was both sacred and beautiful. I entered into a deep meditative state quickly as the mantra I'd been repeating took me down a tunnel of consciousness and then faded out of my mind. I experienced a sense of great peace, a feeling that I was hovering above the reality I physically lived in. It surprised me when a feeling of *déja vu* swept over me; I *knew* I'd meditated this deeply before.

After my first TM experience, meditating was no longer a weird thing to do. It brought me a sense of tranquility that pervaded my whole day. Using affirmations after meditating was a powerful magnet to draw to me the things I wanted in life. But I could handle things going smoothly only so long before my old nemesis, "busyness", popped up to distract me from my meditation routine. I wondered if there was a "saboteur" part of me that really didn't want me to "win" at the game of life. Still, throughout all the gaps of "busyness", a very patient call from within would urge me to begin meditating again.

Dreams

A "dream" steno book was usually close beside my nightstand, though I didn't use it often. I did jot down the date and dream when it was clear, vibrantly colored, or if it left me with a feeling of *knowing* when I awakened and recalled it. I had a dream about buying a ticket to freedom after selling my house because freedom was clearly more important than owning a house. Had I heeded it, this dream could have instigated my putting the house up for sale six months earlier than I actually did, at a time when the market was more favorable.

When I was a small child, I had three recurring dreams that etched themselves in my mind. I can still remember them to this day—as vividly and clearly as when I first dreamed them. One was about smelling the hair on my body burning, and it was always restimulated when I watched my grandmother singe the hair off a freshly-plucked chicken she was preparing for dinner.

The second dream I often had was of walking through the cold darkened tunnel of an arena and out into the sunlight to come face to face with a lion. We would both stop in our tracks and just stare at one another in exaggerated silence. That's as far as the dream ever went.

The most frequent dream was one of sliding from a place of great light back into my body. When I had this one, I would almost bolt into wide-awakeness, my heart beating rapidly. In adulthood, with the help of hypnosis and regression, I learned that the first two dreams were past-life recollections and the third was a vivid recall of returning to my body after astral traveling.

In early August of 1945 I had a brilliantly-colored dream of sitting somewhere high up, as if from the vantage point of a cloud. There was no sound whatsoever as I watched the blinding, fiery colors beneath me explode into a huge mushroom-like cloud. I told my grandmother about it. Several days later the front page of all the newspapers showed what I had seen in my dream. It was Hiroshima.

Dreams? I still don't always know what to make of them, but I ask for guidance and stay open to any messages coming to me from them.

Bodywork

In the pursuit of a healthy body, I oftentimes felt like the plate juggler on the old Ed Sullivan Show. He was the one who kept a whole row of plates spinning on top of tall sticks and was always running to keep them all up and spinning at the same time. So it seemed as I tried to do all the "good" things to care for this Temple of God, otherwise known as the human body.

I was grateful to have inherited good genes and a strong constitution. My body was constantly sending me messages for well-being.

Sometimes, I listened; sometimes, I didn't. Many, many years ago it took four annual bouts with pneumonia before I literally drowned a full pack of cigarettes in the kitchen sink. It was a spontaneous "*I quit*" ritual done in desperation after I had coughed up blood. It was a blessing in disguise as all my previous "quit smoking groups" and strategies had gone down in defeat.

Sessions of Shiatsu, lymphatic, and Swedish massage with Donelyn Larson assisted me in healing and balancing my body energies. I've experienced "laying on of hands" healings, Aromatherapy, Acupressure, and Reflexology. I am fortunate to have good friends that share their skills and expertise with me. Susan Ruebel has tackled my cellulite with her vigorous Cellulite Massage and her food combining and nutritional counseling. It works best when one is disciplined enough to follow the plan of supportive health habits. I do for a while, then fall off the wagon again. Kay Deaver, a committed friend, has not given up hope as she continuously makes her expertise in hot mineral bodysculpturing wraps available to me as my schedule allows.

Ten sessions with a gentle Rolfer, Kathy Robertson, opened up my body flexibility. As an unexpected bonus, a protruding rib I'd had since the birth of my children returned to its normal position during one of my hour-long sessions.

Being a "co-scientist" with aesthetician and makeup artist Joanne Isert has proved mutually rewarding. Her Skin Care Clinic often hums "after hours" as we experiment with new products and herbal and holistic approaches to expanded health, well-being, and beauty.

Rebirthing was another valuable tool I recently discovered. I could sense a block in some of my sessions when I wanted to go unconscious and go to sleep. I knew that the birth trauma affects our whole outlook on life and that I had more work to do in that area.

"Springing" on my mini-trampoline has been the most convenient way for me to get some exercise, though I'm still the Ed Sullivan juggler trying to keep all the plates spinning. Bodywork, meditation, exercising, colonics, fasts, vitamin-herb-nutritional counseling, hypnosis, and many other holistic tools along the way have each had their turn in contributing to my good health.

211

I've been collecting this tool box full of techniques most of my life. Unfortunately, they many times have their "day in the sun" and then find themselves sitting on a shelf awaiting my rediscovery. The trick of course, is to *use* them. Meanwhile, I keep an open ear and mind, always on the lookout for new discoveries.

Music

Whether listening or participating, music has always opened my heart to its healing vibrations. I experienced this deeply while hostessing a guest evening for Dean Tucker. He had put together an audio-visual experience called "Love's Awakening" that touched me deeply with its blend of spectacular photography and synchronized musical lyrics of inspiration. It would be difficult to be present at one of Dean's presentations and walk away with a heart unopened with awe, wonder, and *love* for this beautiful gift called life.

Singing uplifting songs in a group was another healing experience I participated in. Maitreya and Maloah Stillwater brought peace and love vibrations wherever they took their Heavensong celebrations. These musical festivals offered people of all cultures and religions an opportunity to gather together and experience a sense of unity and peace through music.

In a Spectrum workshop, Darri Heller shared about Hellerwork and led us through a process in which we could experience our entire physical body as the instrument through which we could hear and *feel* music. After leading our group into a quiet meditative state, Darri instructed us to lay on the floor while beautiful and titillating music filled the room. After a bit, I could *feel* the musical notes playing through the various parts of my body, sending electrical impulses clear to my fingertips. It gave me a deep appreciation for the magnificence and sensitivity of the physical instrument we call our body.

Whether "ooga-booga-ing" with the Alive Tribe, Sufi dancing with friends, "springing" on mini-trampolines to the music of Steven Halpern with a group of my ASSET "kids", or putting on a cassette tape by myself and letting my body create its own dance routine, music has helped me to release energies calling to be physically expressed. It has always left my body, mind, and spirit in a more harmoniously balanced state.

Movies

I've found that when I'm asking and seeking, God sometimes talks to me through unexpected sources, using whatever physical channels are most readily available to get a message to me. My job is to be sensitive to how my answers are coming to me and receive them. Mostly, it's a naturally intuitive gut-level "knowing" and/or a body sensation that runs through me when a message is *directly for me*—"goosebumps" and "confirmation chills." The movie *Flashdance* provided just such an experience.

The musical score was absolutely wonderful and the dance sequences made us want to get out of our seats and move our bodies to the pulsating beat. But somewhere near the middle of the movie a one-liner jumped out of the big screen and got me. Umph—a direct hit to the solar plexus and heart:

"When you let go of your dreams, you die!"

Instant tears filled my eyes and the lump in my throat felt like a rock stuck in my esophagus as I recognized the message for me in that statement.

As I looked back on some of my all-time favorite movies, *On a Clear Day, Resurrection, Somewhere in Time,* and *Gandhi* were a few of the ones I connected with most deeply. All, I later noticed, had mystical or spiritual overtones.

When I came out of the theater after seeing *Gandhi*, I went to my car and silently stared into space as I pondered its message. I thought long and hard about the part in the movie when an Indian had come to Gandhi's bedside. Gandhi had been on a fast until the rioting in his country ended. The man apologized for being part of the riot and explained that his son had been killed by a Pakistani and he had felt enraged and incensed by his loss. Gandhi had reached out to him gently and asked him if he would like to free himself from the hurt. The anguished man had nodded yes, anxiously awaiting the reply.

"Find a boy the age of your child and adopt him," Gandhi said. "Yes, Mahatma," the grieving father replied.

"And be sure the child you adopt is a Pakistani."

Television

If our thoughts and feelings are energy radiating and attracting experiences to us, what have we set ourselves up for when we look at the average evening's TV menu? Any seeds planted would grow even faster in our consciousness and reality when fertilized with intense feelings and emotions. We are the sum of our experiences expressing themselves. So what kind of experiences did I want to draw to me?

Writers, directors, and producers earn their living by creating *what sells*, but we can effectively filter out the negative energy projected on TV by becoming aware of the power of mind and thought and by acting upon the guidance of our "inner voice". Mine was telling me: "Do not fall asleep with the TV on, allowing material of questionable content to seep into your subconscious while you sleep. There are no neutral thoughts, feelings, or actions. Everything is an energy form and subject to the laws of cause and effect." The computer programmer's motto says it: "garbage in—garbage out."

The power of television can be used to unite people in common causes. The Olympics were a great example of people coming together in brotherhood and laying aside their personal differences for a brief period of time at all levels. Clearly, it was an occurrence of peace through a common, shared interest—sports.

My "inner voice" also led me to tune out some of the fear-inducing TV ministers. In my own experience, God is love and there is no duality about love. In the light of God and truth, right action is always done and the darkness of fear vanishes. What one directs his attention to expands. When someone is preaching fear to me, I very quickly choose love, and flip the dial.

The Candy Lightner story behind the organization Mothers Against Drunk Drivers (MADD) brought attention to the subject of drunk driving. It reminded me of a spiritual channeling I'd recalled while doing some automatic writing:

The soul can complete some of its unfinished earth lessons while in spirit form. However, drugs, alcohol, and other physical addictions need to be handled while still in a physical body. *Complete or repeat!*

The Adam Walsh story was another example of a seed of good coming out of tragic circumstances. Television has done much in this instance to bring awareness to the plight of missing children and their families.

And the recent telethons to raise monies for the hungry of the world—Band Aid, USA for Africa (We Are the World), Live Aid, and Farm Aid—showed what one man's idea can generate. Down deep the spirit of brotherhood is contagious and miracles happen when we pull together in a united cause. As Victor Hugo said:

> No army can withstand the strength of
> an idea whose time has come.

These programs proved to me that *everything* can be used to create negative or positive influences. We're each in charge of the dials of our lives, television and otherwise. Always, we are the *chooser* of the colors and emotions that paint our life experiences.

The Art of Organizing

A story about a king living in the year 1600 AD emphasized what we are all up against these days in the fast world of computers, jets, and instant video and audio communications. The king ordered all the printed information available in the whole world to be brought to him. All the printed information available in the year 1600 was roughly equivalent to the amount of information contained in a single Sunday issue of the *New York Times*. No wonder we human "computers" sometimes feel inefficient and overwhelmed by the infinite amount of data coming at us.

I tried at least three major organizational and/or time management systems before I found the best one for my needs. The first one I used was checkbook-sized. The next one was larger and looked pretty efficient, but it quickly proved inadequate for my needs. Finally, I discovered The Personal Resource System (PRS), a system that assisted me in organizing my thoughts and "mindmapping" my projects and dreams into physical reality and completion.

The instructional tape that came with the PRS was a mini-course in personal effectiveness. It had me gather all the scraps of paper I was carrying around in my wallet, purse, and assorted places and begin feeding them into appropriate sections. Life became simpler and frustrations receded as I began to use my time more efficiently. After using the PRS for many years, it would be hard to imagine functioning sanely and efficiently in today's busy world without one.

Astrology

My first formal introduction to astrology came from an astrologist named Alberta. My astrological reading was done in the comfort of Alberta's home; a cassette recorder made a tape of our session. While she interpreted my astrological chart, she held some 3" x 5" index cards. She was so accurate about what was going on in my life that I asked to see the cards to be sure she wasn't just "intuitively making it up" as we talked. Prior to my appointment, Alberta hadn't known a single thing about me except my first name and birth information, but from these bits of information, she was accurately relating to me intimate details of my life. I saw Alberta on a yearly basis two more times. At my last appointment she said I had made so much soul progress that I had somehow been rising above any propensities for negative happenings. She didn't think I needed to see her anymore unless I felt a specific need.

During the ASSET trainings, I had come in contact with another astrologist, Karen La Puma. It became clear to me that if one was working with an astrologist, it was imperative to choose one who emphasized the propensities for the positive and beautiful aspects of your chart in a lighthearted and loving manner. If thoughts create energy that attracts, I would certainly want my astrological interpretations to keep me focused on an uplifting path. Karen did this intuitively and well.

Most recently, my good friend from Los Angeles, Kay Snow Davis, felt intuitively led to record an astrological and channeled spiritual interpretation of the current forces influencing my life. I had just returned from travels in India. Her taped message let me know that major planets were transiting major positions at this time and the power of Pluto over my Mars was unusual, empowering breakthroughs in my subconscious. She felt that Bobby's death had played a major role in the development of my empathy and the shifting path of my destiny.

While she was channeling the reading, she said a lot she could only "feel," and it was indeed very powerful energy. She had to really work at staying fully conscious while the reading was coming through. She reminded me that we only get as much information from spirit as we can safely handle at the time.

Each of us has access to spirit and universal knowledge. We can ignore the "telephone line" that is *always* ringing from God or we can pick up the phone and *answer the call*. It is a choice every individual gets to make.

Numerology

A birthday present from Carolyn Ortega introduced me to the science of Numerology. I proceeded to listen to the cassette tape she had recorded labeled "I've Got Your Number," done for Shirley Joan Ferrero (the name listed on my birth certificate). As I listened to the reading, it became very clear that "threads of self-discovery" are available no matter where one looks. In life, one can run from many things, but *never* from oneself. Whatever lessons we've come to learn here in a physical body, they repeat until we've completed them. As with Shakespeare's quote: "Life is a stage and we are all players,..." the play named "Shirley" had its own themes to act out and it would attract into its life other actors specially chosen for their roles. According to Carolyn's spiritual interpretation ("...not psychic," she emphasized), my "birth path" number was a 33-6, and I had accepted a specific task to do before I was born. It was a path of service, seeking truth, and sharing it. It was important for me to learn to "walk my talk," simultaneously being a student of life as well as a teacher. The total number vibration of my name at birth was a 14-5. It was a karmic vibration and could be full of difficult "tests." If I passed the tests, super-comprehension could be gained through the experiences, and I would be given "tools" to bring inspiration out of them. This path would always be full of changes, challenging me to let go of old beliefs and programming.

My "outer personality" number was a six, a "motherly" vibration, and the numbers two and four were missing in my chart, indicating karmic lessons to be worked on during this go-around at life. The lack of twos indicated the need to learn patience and how to work with others in partnerships and relationships. The missing fours meant I needed to learn to lay sound foundations and organize, taking one step at a time whenever projects seemed overwhelming. I could sure validate this one; it was the old "how do you eat an elephant" routine—"a bite at a time", of course. However the various "number" interpretation systems worked, I noticed this particular reading Carolyn had done for me had passed my own *inner truth* test. It had uplifted my thoughts and aspirations to the highest levels I could imagine, and where one puts the energy of his thoughts and dreams, creation exists!

Graphology

A guest evening at Julie Traynor's home introduced me to Handwriting Analyst Diane Seaman. Diane's handsome brochure piqued my curiosity to hear more about graphology and discover what my handwriting might reveal. In the brochure, Diane's credentials listed degrees in psychology, counseling, and education with extensive graduate work done at USC, Stanford, and the University of California.

As the evening progressed we were each handed a sheet of plain 8-1/2" x 11" paper upon which we wrote our name, address, some sentences about ourselves, and our phone number. Diane read the last four digits of our telephone number so we could each identify our own reading as she was doing it.

As she read my telephone number, my ears definitely perked up. She said the person who had written on this sheet was creative, generous almost to a fault, and set high goals which may or may not become realities. The loop on my "r"'s marked me as having literary skills. The height at which I crossed my "t"'s gave away my tendency to set high goals and the inconsistency of balance on the crossed part of the "t"'s indicated that some of them may or may not be reached. The high uplift stroke with which I ended most of my words marked me as a generous person.

Intrigued, I spoke to Diane about the procedure for having a more in-depth reading. Workshops were available to learn how to use handwriting analysis in my own life or workplace, but I settled for a Profile Analysis. My instructions were to sit at a well-lighted desk or table, using my favorite ballpoint pen, and write about myself, my interests, and aspirations and mail them to Diane. I did so.

Back in the mail came my analysis. According to the results, my handwriting had disclosed me very accurately for Diane to read. Ah yes, even my sensitivity and inclination for taking criticism personally showed up in my reading, along with my dislike for monotony and sameness. It also pegged me as a spirit that was independent and unwilling to be controlled by others. A moderate capacity for self-direction was coupled with a strong determination to complete tasks and very responsive reactions to emotional experiences and situations. My handwriting revealed an ardent inner force causing enthusiastic interest and action. Family was important and so was the willingness to risk and put myself out to others and into my environment.

One could only imagine the value of an in-depth Compatibility Analysis of two persons involved in or planning on living or working together. A Vocational Analysis, Personnel Analysis, lectures, workshops, and classes were also available on this most interesting and scientific branch of psychology.

With this new info in mind, I noticed I was now consciously crossing my "t"'s higher and with a more balanced cross-stroke. Whatever works!

Tree Reading

There is such a thing as a tree reading—honest. It does exist and is more formally known as Arboromancy—the rare art and science of interpreting personality traits from drawings of trees. Arboromancy was innovated by a man named Abdullah Bawaney who I met at my MasterMind Alliance Group meetings. I offered to hostess a guest evening for him at my home.

A synchronistic connection clued me into wanting to know more about tree reading: my body chilled as I picked up Abdullah's Arboromancy brochure. Across the top was a picture of a gnarled, elongated, and bent pine tree. It was not anything unusual about the tree itself that caught my eye; it was, however, the *exact* same tree

I had asked my son Bobby to paint for me some ten years earlier. Bobby was skilled at charcoal drawings and I had a picture of a tree I thought would look great in my living room if it were done in oils. Reluctantly, Bobby began his first project in oils, and it had long since hung over our couch in the living room. I took the brochure home and compared it to Bobby's rendition of the same tree. It was *exact*, down to the placement of each of the seven birds in the picture!

On the guest evening my living room filled to capacity with friends eager to gain insights into themselves via a tree reading. We each sketched a whole tree in the space of an 8 1/2" x 11" sheet of paper. We were instructed not to use erasers or the broadside of our pencils as we each spontaneously drew what we considered to be a mature, full-grown tree. We were encouraged by Abdullah to put in as much detail as we wished.

To honor our privacy, our names were not read aloud as Abdullah began the round of readings. Knowing each of my guests pretty well, I was astounded at the accuracy with which the tree drawings were revealing each of us. I was particularly alert when he urged one guest to contact her personal physician at her earliest convenience. As it turned out, my friend did have a serious medical problem, discovered by her doctor after her tree reading, and was under the care of a physician for several months afterwards.

When my tree showed up for its reading, I could feel the red blush of embarrassment creep over me. I ranked my artistic skills at kindergarten level and I avoided sketching anything with a passion. Evidently it was not the degree of artistic ability that told the tale in a tree reading. Abdullah said the person who had drawn this very straight-limbed "sticky-looking" tree was a seeker searching for freedom and the higher spiritual values of life. After an evening with Abdullah and the phenomenal truths he shared as he examined each person's drawing. I was a believer in the value of tree readings.

Color Analysis

It was becoming fashionable to have your "colors done", so I signed up with a local Color Analyst who was doing personalized color fans. My color analysis, according to my new color fan, categorized me as ninety-five percent Soft; I was a Summer person. Quite quickly, I was also a *depressed* person. According to my Color Analyst, almost everything in my present wardrobe was wrong for me.

I purchased a couple of new outfits using my color fan. A flowered pink outfit and a soft blue outfit came back home with me. For a whole week, I wore soft summer-color combinations. My personality went *soft.* Here I was taking a class that empowered me to be in front of groups, and I felt less and less energy to do anything. When I looked in the mirror, I didn't even look much like "me" anymore. Maybe my makeup needed to be changed, so I went and sat myself down in front of a makeup artist at a local department store. I told her my tale and asked for her help.

"I've been in the makeup business for twenty years. Never, never," she said, shaking her head, "would I suggest that shade of blue for you. It brings out the yellow in your skin."

I showed her my color fan.

"I'd try another Color Consultant, if I were you. It's not your makeup that's off. It's the colors you're trying to wear," she told me.

I thought it over. The Color Analyst I'd chosen had a whole house full of the shades of color I was now trying to wear. Hmmmm, do I really have a nature-determined color scheme that rings true for me no matter what? Or, does the perception of "my" color scheme fluctuate and differ from Color Consultant to Color Consultant?

Through a series of quick events and workshops, the opportunity to have my colors done four more times came up to answer some of the questions hanging around in my head. All four of them were in agreement that I was Rich, an Autumn personality, and my new color palette was generously painted with shades of rust, greens, tans, and teal blues.

"Ahhh...," a sigh of relief as I held my color fan up and walked around my earthy-colored house. Intuitively, when I decorated it, I had been right on! It also started me thinking about the effect colors have in general and what results they might produce when consciously applied to obtain specific results in different kinds of businesses.

While preparing myself to take a group of ASSET training students out for a morning Sensitivity Process on the beach, I had another experience that further awakened me to the power of color in our lives. The bathroom I was dressing in was painted stark white with accents of brilliant primary yellow. The overhead lighting was florescent. Not my cup of tea, so to speak. Nothing was going right, and as I looked in the mirror, the circles under my eyes seemed exaggerated, clearly showing a lack of sleep. My disposition was cranky, to say the least. I needed to pull myself together better than that if I were to take fourteen sleepy-eyed ASSET participants out on the beach and spontaneously create a meaningful process. As I stared at the harsh reflection in the mirror, an idea hit me like a thunderbolt out of the blue. I was surrounded by colors that were inharmonious to what soothed and pleased me.

I gathered up my cosmetic totebag and clothes and moved into the downstairs bathroom. It had been decorated in driftwood, seashells, and shades of soft peachy rust and brown. The difference in my mood shifted dramatically! Soon I was humming and thoughts of a partnered "blind-walk-of-trust" process along the early morning seashore started creatively filling my head. Never again would I doubt the powerful support system the right colors for a person could create.

Hand Analysis

Thinking about my first introduction to palmistry brought about some funny pictures in my mind of a gypsy woman in an outlandish costume, complete with huge dangling earrings. I was about seven years old and attending a carnival event at the grammar school next door to my grandparents' ranch. The gypsy read my palm and told me to enjoy life fully and also to be *very careful*. There was a good chance that an illness or accident could threaten my life before I graduated from high school. I didn't want to listen to her impending doom message and didn't—for the most part. However, I sighed a *huge* sigh of relief the day after my high school graduation when I awakened and found myself *alive*.

My second encounter with palmistry came many, many years later. The science of hand analysis again crossed my palm in the form of a man named Richard Unger. Curiosity pulled at me to further investigate the subject. If the FBI could pick me out from everyone

222

in the whole world by the uniqueness of my fingerprints, there must be something else of value I could learn from hand analysis. A special guest evening was set up in my home after I heard a little more about Richard's credentials and style. He had read over 21,000 hands and had taught hand analysis at the State University of New York at Binghamton and at the Esoteric Philosophy Center in Houston. My Walnut Creek townhouse was filled to capacity with friends and their guests; even the staircase landings overflowed as Richard entertained us with a little of the "Palmese" language. We studied our own hands as he spoke.

After his talk, I, along with several of my guests, made appointments for a private reading with Richard that included a cassette tape and dated hand print for my permanent records. Others in the group signed up for the workshop that taught the basics of hand analysis to counselors and therapists.

Hand prints change as we experience life and thus form a record of the journey. The information received from Richard at my private session highlighted and dovetailed perfectly with information I'd received from other sources and/or data already known about myself.

"You're a chronic truthteller, Shirley," Richard explained as he noted my straight pinkie fingers. As he examined my thumb in profile, it looked like someone had been sitting on the crown of it, giving it a flat-tire effect.

"You give away your power and you are an overbearing perfectionist," he continued. "You need to give yourself permission to learn before you expect perfection of yourself. This right ring-finger bull's-eye pattern indicates highly developed artistic skills in a past life.

"You are equally comfortable in both the physical and metaphysical worlds and are a relatively 'late bloomer', a spiritual 'eager beaver' who has signed up this lifetime for some heavy remedial and emotional classes in the university called Earth."

The suggestion was made that I learn to play more in life. My creativity and intuitive inspirations would be released when I learned to let go of the perfectionist chatter in my mind. He joked that I was always "getting ready" in case God called me up for a date on Friday night and said that I'd probably have the audacity to tell God that I wasn't ready yet. Rigid self-control and discipline were useful but he expected they were blocking my creativity and suggested I relax more, have fun, and go for the limelight.

Having found "Nirvana" in a past life as a monk in a cave, could I please try and find it now by having fun? Richard suggested I try walking backwards when I left his apartment, for absolutely no reason at all, as a good place to start.

Toying with the idea as my appointment concluded, I chose to give the silly backward walking a try down a busy San Francisco street. It was very difficult for me to do it for "no reason". Passers-by looked at me weirdly and I noticed I was starting to play-act, as if I were searching for someone—a reason to justify walking backwards.

So many truths about Shirley, as I knew myself, came to light as I listened to my ninety-minute tape of the reading. A year later, I had another reading and hand print done. Sure enough, there had been some changes even I could see as we studied the present hand print and compared it with the one done a year earlier. Again, it validated what was going on presently in my everyday life. I began thinking that there was no place to hide from "me", because no matter what system I used for self-awareness, there "I" was!

TRAVEL

Hawaii

What a glorious feeling it was to wake up in a beautiful suite overlooking the Pacific Ocean. The view scanned the city of Honolulu, Diamond Head, and circled clear around to the lush green mountains. I'd been asked to come here to create a formal installation-of-officers ceremony, officiating as installation officer as well as past president of the Association of Plastic Surgery Assistants.

The moment I accepted the invitation, a vision popped into my head—flowers, candles, and crystals. I started a Mind Map in my Personal Resource System, capturing ideas there as they came through. Several months later, when I arrived in Hawaii, I had a well-designed outline of what I wanted to do. The words to pull the whole ceremony together hadn't yet come, though.

Time was getting short. In desperation, on the morning of the installation dinner, I stayed in my hotel suite. I went out to my lanai and breathed in the air, freshly scented and cleansed by a gentle morning shower. A rainbow reflected its brilliant hues of color from its point of origin over the mountains to my left. I quieted myself, sank into my balcony chair and started talking out loud to God.

"God, why did You bring me here? My creative thoughts are stuck. Please give me the words to bring this all together."

My friend Iris Jackson had loaned me a little book to take to Hawaii. I began reading aloud some of the "I Am" discourses. As I did, inspiration seemed to flow through me and the invocation and installation ceremony started writing themselves. The invocation spoke of gratitude for all the gifts life had bestowed upon us and a profession that allowed us to reach out and touch the hearts and lives of others with our skills, compassion, enthusiasm, joy, and love.

Part of the installation ceremony included using Austrian crystals hanging on gold necklace chains. I had chosen them earlier while shopping in California. Each one had a "name" that fit perfectly into the ceremony.

Since primitive times, I wrote, light has been used as the symbol of knowledge and wisdom. For this reason, we have used a lighted candle to convey and acknowledge the wisdom of our chosen leaders. The crystal is symbolic of the God-light that shines within and upon each of our newly elected officers.

As I was jotting words down on note cards, a sense of peacefulness came over me. Each newly-installed officer would be presented with a crystal necklace that symbolized her position.

The Camelot crystal was for outgoing President Jean Messerall. It was to remind her of the "shining moments" of her reign as Madame President. The addition of a bouquet of flowers and a "bouquet" of congratulatory balloons from the most recent past president, Jane Hambleton, would make this a special moment for Jean.

The Quan Yin crystal, for the newest Board of Directors member, Carolyn White, symbolized ruling with justice, mercy, and love.

For Treasurer Suzanne Pelley, the crystal pyramid stood for the strong financial foundation entrusted to her keeping.

Communications are the heart of any organization, and the heart crystal was chosen for Marie Thomas who held the office of secretary.

The multi-faceted emerald crystal symbolized the many hats a vice-president wears. It was for Del Bell.

For incoming President Floy Timms, the Empress crystal would bless her with the clarity to rule with wisdom, truth, and love.

The installation candles for the new officers had been lit, flowers presented, the banquet meal consumed, and the evening deemed a huge success. Several people came up to me to acknowledge the beauty of integrating the crystals into the installation ceremony. I was asked if I minded if the idea was used for other organizations.

"It would be an honor," I replied. "Crystals bring in healing, love, and light. This old earth can use all it can get."

It was reunion and celebration time and many of us gathered in the Bali room of the Hawaiian Hilton for after-dinner cocktails. A friend, Flip Nuñez, was singing and playing at the piano that evening—what a delightful and unexpected surprise. He invited me to do a couple of songs with him. The timing felt right and I accepted. Taking the mike in hand, I dedicated "My Funny Valentine" to outgoing APSA President Jean Messerall. "The Man I Love" was for a beautiful black lady, Joy Ann, and her man, a white man bound to the wheelchair he sat in. They were a dedicated and inspiring couple I had met the previous evening. Joy Ann's man beamed at her as he sat lovingly holding her hand.

I was amazed that the microphone in my hand wasn't giving me any paralyzing attacks of stagefright tonight.

Yippee! I thought, as the applause warmed my heart, maybe I've broken through another limiting mind-block from times past. I was grateful for the opportunity to be a part of "The Crystal Installation" ceremony. I basked in the splendor of Alohaland and good times with good friends.

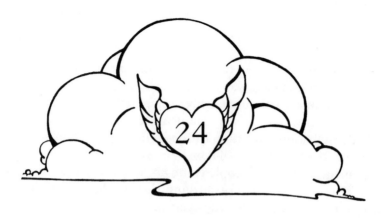

TEACHER
Tamara Diaghilev

During a conversation with Robin Blanc, I heard about a lady named Tamara who taught classes in psychic development and personal transformation. Before our conversation was finished, I *knew* I would be attending the classes along with Robin. In asking about Tamara's background, I found she held M.A. and M.S. degrees from the University of Bern in Switzerland and had been in the psychic field for over twenty-five years, doing clairvoyant readings, palmistry, past-life regressions, psychic house cleanings, and individual counseling.

If ever a class was divinely timed, this one was. I liked Tamara immediately when I met her. She had a very warm, caring way about her. It was exactly the kind of support I most needed when I found out my mother was terminally ill with cancer just before my second class in psychic development.

I was spending my days at a San Francisco hospital with my mother on the Oncology floor that housed cancer patients. By the time I'd arrived at Tamara's evening class, the learning to "run energy through your body" technique was exactly what I needed. Tamara taught us to cleanse and balance our various energy centers (chakras) as well as to channel healing energies. Her extensive European background was rich with beautiful and meaningful ritual ceremonies.

I loved the class in which we began learning to perceive the human aura. Occasionally I had done it before, without knowing that that was what I was doing. Usually, it had happened when I was in a white-walled lecture room and my attention was drifting. At that point, my eyes were not focused on anything in particular. Then I would "see" rings of different colored light around the speaker in the front of the room. When I tried to focus directly on the rings, they would disappear. I'd long thought I must be tired and my eyes were playing tricks on me.

Through Tamara, I rediscovered that everything has an aura (energy field), and that the living energy field never stands still but continuously moves and pulsates. We practiced "aura reading" on one another in class. Our energies blend with others at times and it was always necessary to protect yourself and also to ask permission of the other person before checking out their aura. No psychic "snooping" was appropriate. There was also another important process, that of separating your energy from another's when you had finished reading auras or doing psychic healings. I felt wise to be seeking guidance in these matters, as psychic realms were not a toy with which one should idly play and amuse oneself. There were spiritual laws one needed to be aware of and respect.

As we studied the seven chakras (energy centers), I came into more alignment with mine and what their purpose was. The first chakra is at the base of the spine and is the "grounding" chakra, also concerned with physical survival. Approximately one-and-a-half inches below the navel is the second chakra, the center of sexual energies. The solar plexus is the third chakra and is the "key" to our power. When balanced, it generates personal power and self-confidence. When out of balance, it is the great "beat yourself up" machine with its "shoulds" bombarding you and robbing you of your power.

The fourth chakra is the heart, the center of healing, affinity, love, and understanding. The throat is chakra number five, home of the communication center. My scruffy throat that evening was telling me I needed to work on this one. When this chakra is clear, we become clear channels for information to come through us. The sixth center is the clairvoyant chakra where things can be clearly seen with affinity rather than judgments. It is known as the "third eye." I remembered seeing "the eye" on the pyramid of a one-dollar bill and again pondered the profound spiritual wisdom of the founding fathers of this "land of the free" we lived in.

Chakra seven, the Crown chakra, is at the top of the head. It is the center of wisdom and cosmic energy. When this chakra is clear, we are in affinity with divine intelligence and all that is. The more I studied the fascinating subject, the more I realized that the "paths" of the ALL Games I had led lined up perfectly with the chakra information I was now receiving.

When we completed our beginning class on chakras, Tamara brought out what I would call a "divining rod." With it, we checked out each other's chakras. What fun! When a chakra was open, the arms of the divining rod would open up and swing out. When a chakra was closed, they would close-in tight, next to the body. It turned out that my self-evaluation was right on. That evening, my crown chakra was fairly open, my throat chakra was definitely closed down, and my heart chakra sent the rod expanding out as far as it could go. We laughed a lot as the divining rod would go "crazy," conveying its telltale revelations for each of us to think about.

I scheduled a private session with Tamara to work on releasing the blocks to "receiving" I'd set up in early childhood. When we'd finished, I tacked up my new list of affirmations on the bulletin board of my bathroom, with one in particular underlined:

The more I *am* open to receive, the more abundance and prosperity comes to me for myself and to share with others. I *am* joyfully connected to everything and everybody in an unlimited golden network of love!

When my mother was released from the hospital, she asked me to set up an appointment for her with Tamara. From this meeting she discovered and validated many things about her life's path and the lessons she had chosen to learn. Tamara's insights helped Mom to forgive and love herself and find another level of inner peace. Mom was smiling as I picked her up. "I'm not so bad or dumb after all!" she said.

Gratitude for the sensitive work Tamara does filled my heart. I sensed from some of the things that came up after the reading that Mom had probably already chosen, at some level of consciousness, to "check-out" with this round of big "C." I felt a little more at peace about the whole thing as I glanced at my mother's sleeping face that evening. The tense expressions of pain and anguish had softened and there was a faint smile on her face.

Mom, A Teacher
of Forgiveness of Self

Though my mother did not raise me past the age of four, her very absence nurtured a self-reliant independence in me. The life-long guilt Mom felt for giving my brother and me up literally ate her up over the years. After removal of a cancerous lung at age sixty-one, she survived another eight years before metastasis, showing up in the form of an inoperable brain tumor, claimed her life.

The brain tumor was diagnosed nine months before her death. Mom had fallen, and while she was being X-rayed for a possible brain concussion, the tumor was discovered. The exact diagnosis and prognosis were to be dependent on a long series of tests. For over two weeks following Mom's fall, I sat at her hospital bedside awaiting the final answers.

On the tenth day, hospital attendants wheeled Mom out of her room towards surgery for a brain biopsy. We tried to make light of her shaved head as we talked before the operation. In a short span of time, I watched four very different facets of Mom's personality surface and act themselves out on the stage of her face.

The first face Mom wore was one of an ancient-looking weather-beaten soul who was tired of playing this game called Life.

Next, her face became that of a small terrified child as tears and fears flooded over and through her.

Then came the "let's keep it all together" and bite your lip kind of braveness. "Just let me sign the surgical consent form and let's get on with it," she said. There seemed to be a lot of fight left in her.

As they rolled her away on the gurney, her face suddenly turned robot-like; she became a "go-alonger," waiting for someone else to render the verdict. She relegated the decision of whether she would live or die to her doctors.

The long-awaited results finally came in days later. Big "C" had returned and the tumor was inoperable. Radiation therapy was advised. My sister-in-law, Valerie Douglas, volunteered to come down from Redding and stay with Mom until her X-ray treatments were completed.

After two very long weeks at Mom's bedside, I found I was terribly depressed emotionally and "burnt-out" physically. I realized I was of no use to myself and certainly of no use to Mom in that state. What she loved most about having me around was my cheery attitude and loving energy. Neither virtue was anywhere to be found as Mom left the hospital. There and then, the realization hit me that it was not the quantity of time I spent with Mom that mattered as much as the *quality* of that time.

Rather than make the usual daily trips into the city to see her, I began planning special outings every couple of weeks for the times we would spend together. Mom *loved* it. After each outing, she had something to remember and talk to her friends about for days, and she had something to look forward to as we planned the next one.

Mom had never learned to drive, so though she had lived in San Francisco most of her life, she had never truly enjoyed all the riches of living in the "City by the Bay."

233

My friend, Bill Orlich, accompanied us on our adventures. He patiently played attentive chauffeur and loving support person, choosing the best and easiest routes and driving us as close to our destinations as possible so Mom could conserve her precious energy.

We visited Steinhart Aquarium, had tea and cookies in the Japanese Tea Garden, and sat and watched the colorful carp swim to and fro as Mom philosophized about her life and life in general. I was getting to know my mother from a new point of view. We enjoyed a Sunday brunch in Sausalito, watching the colorful panorama of sailboats gliding by from our seaside Spinnaker's Restaurant table. Mom loved the breathtaking view of the San Francisco bridges that she had never seen from this particular vantage point, as well as the San Francisco skyline. We had more philosophical discussions. They were all very precious and beautiful times.

Mom had been reading *Heal Your Body*, a book I'd given her. It was Louise L. Hay's book on metaphysical causes of physical illness. She looked up cancer and agreed with the "probable cause": "Deep hurt. Long-standing resentment. Deep secret or grief eating away at the self." Mom said it was absolutely true in her case. It had been very hard for her to give up custody of my brother and me. The Depression of the Thirties had brought many financial hardships and she felt it was in our best interest that our father have full custody of us.

She told me about the day she officially "gave us up." It had been a difficult and painful decision for her to make. She had walked the city streets crying and felt "guided" into a nearby shop. There in the window was a picture of a guardian angel hovering over a little girl and her younger brother. It was symbolic to her of all the love and concern she was feeling in her heart. Somehow, the "angel" would watch over her little son and daughter; she had to believe that was so. For some forty years now, the "guardian angel" picture had been with her. Everywhere Mom went, it went also. I was familiar with the painting though I was now hearing the story behind it for the first time.

Mom felt that I loved, forgave, and understood her now. Her one last regret in life was that Robert and she had never spent any time together. She had always imagined that he had felt deserted, rightfully so, and had no use for a mother who was mother in name only.

If that was the only thing that kept her from attaining inner peace at this point in her life, the solution seemed easy. After communicating what was going on to him, my brother Robert and his wife Mae invited us both over for a "Mother and Son" dinner.

Driving to Robert's Orinda home, Mom was as nervous as a teenager on her first real date!

"Do I look okay? Is my turban covering all the bald spots on my head? What should I say to him? Please put a little more of your powdered blush on my cheeks, Shirley, so I won't look so pale."

Dinner was an elegant affair-of-the-heart as Mom talked with the long-lost son she so much loved. Her china blue eyes sparkled and danced with new life. She blushed with happiness as she laughed and talked small talk with Robert. For a couple of precious hours, she looked fully alive again! As we left, my brother put his arm around her and kissed her goodbye.

"Robert said he loves me!" Mom beamed as we drove away.

"Of course he does," I laughed. "How many years have you been making it up in your mind that he didn't?" In that very simple and eloquent moment of reunion, I knew my mother had made peace with the part of her that had long nagged her with feelings of unworthiness and guilt.

Back at home, I tucked Mom's weary, but happy body into bed. As I kissed Mom's forehead and whispered goodnight, I glanced at the "guardian angel" picture and silently asked that the angel now turn her loving attention towards Mom. The little girl and boy symbolized in the picture were all grown up now and we were doing just fine!

Towards the end of the radiation treatments, Mom went home with my sister-in-law Valerie to Redding. She was very sick and didn't want to talk about getting well anymore. She just wanted reassurance that she would not be taken to a hospital full of rules, needles, and tubes. Being amongst those who loved her was what she wanted *most*.

I commuted to Redding to visit Mom. It scared me to see how much Mom had changed in two short weeks. She was very thin and pale and could barely move her lips. She was trying so hard to form a word. I flashed back on an illness of my own when I was totally conscious, totally aware of all conversation going on in the room, and unable to respond physically in any way. How frightening to be the "being" within with complete awareness but sealed in a body that was unable to physically communicate! I felt intuitively that that was what my mother was now going through. I began talking to her, telling her to relax, that I knew she could hear and understand me and it was okay for her not to use her strength trying to talk. A flash of what looked like relief flooded her face, and for an instant, we communicated deeply through our eyes.

As I left Mom that day, I knew her days were numbered and I would need to depend on my "inner voice" to tell me when it was time to return to Redding. It did.

Eleven days later, I awakened abruptly at 4:00 AM with a feeling of urgency to go to Redding. My daughter Kimberly said her "little voice" was urging her to cancel her weekend trip to Lake Tahoe and go to Redding with me. Her friend, Brian Rodde, volunteered to go along for whatever help and support we might need.

When we arrived, Mom was comatose and her frail body needed to be shifted regularly to prevent ulcerated bedsores from forming. I felt an immense gratitude to Valerie and Don for their courage and dedication to Mom's well-being. They had been on twenty-four hour a day call for some time now.

I helped bathe Mom and rubbed her shriveled body with soothing lotions. Soft peaceful music played in the background at all times. I lit the white candle at her bedside. There was little else to do now but pray that death be a gentle and peaceful experience of passing out of a physical body that no longer served her.

Kimberly kissed Mom goodby and tucked a small stuffed animal underneath "Grandma Mary's" arm. It was my turn. Life was so rich, precious, exciting, and joyful most days. There were also times like this when my heart ached deeply and it was time to say another "goodbye for now" to someone I loved. I kissed Mom's sleeping eyelids and whispered, "I love you."

As we drove the now familiar road away from the city of Redding and nearby Mt. Shasta, the sound of soft rain and synchronized windshield-wipers led the "symphony of goodbye" my heart was hearing.

Two days later, on St. Valentine's Day, my brother Don called from Redding to say, "Mom's gone." I cried. A voice within had been telling me that this was the most appropriate day Mom could have chosen to leave. It was my favorite day of the year—a day of the heart.

That evening, I joined some friends at a local nightspot in Walnut Creek. It was much too noisy. I made an excuse and got in Valentyne and started driving. Soon I found myself pulling up in the parking lot of Michael's Restaurant. The owner, who was also an old friend, Michael Gourkani, came over to my table to wish me a Happy Valentine's Day.

"What are you doing these days?" he asked. When Michael heard about Mom, he walked over to the gentleman playing at the piano bar. Over the microphone came a voice that said, "...and the next song is dedicated to a very special lady, Mary Edwards..."

"My Funny Valentine" filled the room and my heart with love.

Michael brought over a red rose and asked when I'd last eaten. I couldn't even remember. It was midnight as Michael escorted me and a friend, Sandy Shapiro, upstairs to the now empty dining room. The restaurant staff had already departed. Michael seated us and proceeded to personally prepare and serve us a candlelight supper fit for royalty.

It was appropriate that Sandy was my dinner partner for this special night. Both of us could look back to marriage vows taken on a St. Valentine's Day of the past—synchronicity again. Though the "dissolution of marriage" for both of us had happened some time ago, the day was still a very special one. Now it was filled with new dreams, hopes, and love. It was indeed a gift to have close friends such as Sandy and Michael tonight. We lifted our champagne glasses in a toast to Mom and to love.

"Mom, I send you a Valentine full of love and light, wherever you are this moment!"

Several days later a mortuary in San Bruno called. Mom's ashes were ready to be picked up. A strange feeling came over me as I entered the mortuary, signed a piece of paper, and walked out with "Mom." The small 8" x 8" x 8" box of ashes was symbolic to me.

"Mom," obviously, was not in the box but was a free spirit now. As the thought crossed my mind, bells from a nearby church began to chime on perfect cue. Synchronicity yet again!

After keeping Mom's ashes a few days, I took them to Robert's. He would keep them with him until Memorial Day when he would take them to his ranch in Modesto. There they would be freed amongst the almond trees where Nana's had been scattered on Memorial Day the year before.

It was just the way Mom would have planned it in her fondest dreams: driving around for a while in the back seat of a Mercedes, being talked to by her long-lost son, Robert.

A sense of release and deep peace embraced me.

26

TEACHERS
Children

Amongst the greatest teachers God has sent me are the five children that came into the physical world through my body. On our journey through time together as a family, our everyday lives and inner wisdom have been immensely enriched by our shared experiences and love.

Gregory

My first child came into the world with an "achiever" aura about him. He weighed in at 10 pounds, 1 ounce. We laughed as his father, Rick Bruno, and I walked down to the nursery at the St. Francis Hospital in San Francisco. Neither Rick nor I were very big people. My hospital roommate had a strapping big husband—a professional football player. Their newborn daughter weighed 5 pounds, 1 ounce. As the four of us stood at the nursery window to view our babies, the nurses were dumfounded; it looked to them as if we were claiming the wrong babies.

At six months, Greg was walking around everything in the house, barely holding on. He seemed in a hurry to grow up. He was seven years old when I married Bob Ruiz and our relationship shifted. He became even more of an achiever while trying to find what he had to do to be number one with me again. During the ASSET training, we had explored the issue in depth.

During high school, he dreamed of going to one of the U.S. Military Academies. He lived and breathed to obtain his goal and he did: Vice President Spiro Agnew awarded him with a nomination to the Naval Academy, but Greg opted for Congressman Jerome Waldie's backing for the Air Force Academy in Colorado Springs, Colorado, and became a "doolie." On Parents' Day that year, Bobby, Kim, Laura, and I drove to Colorado for our personalized tour of the beautiful academy that lay at the foot of the Rocky Mountains. It was a proud and memorable time for us all.

His freshman year at the Academy was no picnic and neither was the following summer "survival" training in which he got to taste what being a prisoner of war was like. It wasn't pleasant. During Greg's sophomore year, he and a few buddies attended a party given by friends at the University of Colorado. At the party, a marijuana cigarette was passed around. Greg joined in and the word got out. He and the others were called upon to resign and not cause a "drug scandal." They had taken an oath of honor not to use drugs of any kind and it had been broken. So was Greg's spirit when he called me. For five years of his life, all his energies had been aimed at being an Air Force fighter-jet pilot and now all his dreams came crashing down around him.

He came home and enrolled in the University of California at Berkeley. The short-haired "Mr. Clean" look soon gave way to a long-haired "hippie" mode of dress. For Greg it was an extensive period of finding himself again. Was there somewhere deep within him another "burning desire," another dream to nurture? Berkeley was a good place for him to earn his college degree and discover a love for helping people with a holistic approach to medicine. Palmer's School of Chiropractic Medicine in Davenport, Iowa, accepted his application and he was off pursuing a new career. He was learning how to heal with his hands, quite the opposite of his first fighter-jet pilot dream.

Often I looked at what transpired in Gregory's life and wondered about the "divine plan" that lies within each of us. Does it first whisper to us when we're off course and then finally have to resort to "hitting us over the head" with some crisis point to get our attention? It is the crisis situation that forces us to look once again at our lives without dodging the issues, to reassess, choose newly, and self-correct our course before getting on with life.

*   *   *

Steven

Steven, son number two, came into the world feeling insecure. He cried a lot. It was no wonder. It had been a most difficult pregnancy. Every other day I was reporting to my doctors for a shot to stop the nausea and vomiting. At four-and-a-half months, I was hospitalized with severe bleeding, in danger of aborting the child I was carrying. After ten days of hospitalization and off and on episodes of bleeding and severe abdominal pains, one of my doctors brought me papers to sign. They were permission forms to take me into surgery the next morning and take the baby as they felt my life was threatened.

Earlier that morning, I had felt "life" stirring within me, like tiny butterfly wings fluttering. There was no way I could or would sign that piece of paper. I pleaded with Rick not to go against my wishes. If it was God's will, the baby and I would both live. Luckily, the doctor doing rounds that day was a devout Catholic and heard my pleas. He agreed to wait an extra day and if the bleeding hadn't stopped by then, we'd have to re-evaluate. My doctors had to agree to a therapeutic abortion as a unanimous panel. Taking a life was not to be taken lightly under any circumstances, even life-threatening ones. They all felt, however, that something was most likely wrong with this baby since nature and my system had seemed keen on aborting this pregnancy from day one.

A miracle happened and my body resigned itself to spending the rest of my pregnancy in bed. Steven Richard made his 9 pound, 4 ounce appearance four-and-a-half months later, physically perfect in every way. We all said a prayer of thanks.

241

Steve reminded me of a cuddly teddy-bear with his large soft brown eyes. As a youngster he was much slower to learn than Greg. He was ambidextrous and easily confused. When he started writing he wrote with his right hand until he was tired and then switched to his left hand, reversing his printing like a mirror image. He struggled to keep up in school, also having started as one of the youngest in his class.

At age thirteen, he came into my bedroom one morning saying he didn't feel well. He had felt nauseated all night but hadn't wanted to awaken us. I thought he had the flu and suggested he might feel better if he took a warm shower. The moment he stepped into the shower he cried out in pain. Intuitively, I threw a robe on him and rushed him to the emergency room of the local hospital. His doctor didn't even wait for the completion of the lab tests before Steven was wheeled into surgery. He had a redhot appendix that was about ready to rupture.

Steven's recovery was weird. He had recurring fevers and never seemed "quite right" after surgery. When we sent him to school, he'd be sent home by the school nurse with a phone call alerting us that he was running a fever again. This went on for over a month and we were bewildered as to what was happening; so were his surgeon and pediatrician. By then his behavior was outrageously demanding and rebellious. No one knew what to do with him. One night he went into a rage that frightened us all. His doctor suggested we commit him to the County Hospital for observation. Afterwards when we went to visit, Steve did not respond to us at all; he was in a trancelike state. After many tests and several consultations, the three possible medical diagnoses given us differed drastically. It was possible he had contracted meningitis though spinal taps had not been taken early enough to prove out that diagnosis. Another doctor thought he had had a bad reaction to the anesthesia he'd been given in surgery, while the third doctor thought he was having some kind of nervous breakdown.

No one knew what to do with him next. He had supposedly threatened to run away or kill himself after he had been hospitalized for over a month. The hospital called to say they could no longer be responsible for him and I would have to transfer him to a private psychiatric hospital. Financially, it was out of the question. The only other suggestion was that we make him a ward of the court. Then the State would have to make room for him in the Napa State Hospital that was filled to capacity.

It was one of the most difficult things I ever had to do as a parent, going before a courtroom judge and signing my child over to the State of California. For Steven, it was the best thing we could have done to get him back on the road to recovery. When his stepfather Bob and I drove to Napa to see him the first time, we saw an immediate change. Steven had been taken off all the medications that he'd been taking to calm him down and keep him under control. He was actually happy to see us and showed interest in coming home as soon as possible. One month after going to Napa, Steven came home and went directly into high school, starting his freshman year three weeks behind the rest of his class.

Something had transpired within Steve: he was adamantly determined to succeed in school and do something with his life. He graduated with honors from high school and went on to put himself through college with honors at the University of California at Davis. His plan to be a veterinarian changed after he spent some time during a summer working with a local veterinary clinic. The following summer he spent some meaningful time with my dentist. Steve applied to dental school and was accepted at Georgetown University in Washington, D.C.

Steven took the training offered by est and after completing it, came to me with a "confession." Though he really had been sick when he was thirteen, it was also the first time he had ever had my undivided attention. Because I had a full-time job and five kids to mother, he had had to share me with his brothers and sisters. When he was sick, I would rush home to fix his lunch and take care of his needs in the evening before I did anything else. He liked it and had played up and dramatized his illness to the hilt to keep my attention. After "true confession" time Steve and I hugged as we dissolved any undelivered communications about the whole incident. Under my breath, I thanked a man named Werner Erhard, the founder of est, for a revitalized relationship with the wonderful son who had almost not made it into the world in the first place.

Robert

Robert Frank Bruno checked into the world two weeks after his grandfather, Frank Bruno, had checked out of it and three days before his brother Steven's first birthday. I had my hands full. Greg was just twenty-seven months old. It felt like I had triplets. Holding Bobby for the first time, I could feel he was a peaceful child.

At his birth I was a bit disappointed that "he" hadn't turned out to be a "she," but that quickly changed as I got acquainted with my newest son. He was too good to be true. He was hardly ever sick and always had a calming effect on me. He was not a trouble maker, and it took some doing, with older brothers like Greg and Steve, to not stir up a holocaust just by holding your own ground.

The first toy that interested him was an airplane and as soon as he could talk, he would say he was going to be a pilot when asked what he was going to be when he grew up. He soloed in an airplane on the first day he was legally old enough to do it.

Bobby was truly a peaceful old soul if ever I'd met one. A psychic friend who had done a reading on me and my children agreed. Only an old soul like Bobby could have handled the position of being youngest brother to high-energied Greg and Steve.

I wanted my children to be independent and self-assured and partially judged my own success as a mother by their *not* being Mama's boys or girls. I'd seen too many adults still tied to their mother's "apron strings." Holding a full-time job made it easy and necessary for me to ask them all to learn how to shop, cook, do laundry, and clean up their own messes. It paid off. When the boys went off to college, they could take care of themselves quite well. A letter from Bobby at Embry Riddle Aeronautical University in Florida said, "Thanks, Mom, for teaching me how to do laundry. Sure comes in handy when you're away from home."

Bobby continued flying and subsequently joined the Navy so he could continue getting his pilot licenses and afford to marry Kathleen, too. They went off to live in Japan for a year. On their return, they settled in San Diego until Bobby had completed his tour of duty with the Navy. By then, he had his instrument and instructor's licenses and returned to the Bay Area to fly commercial cargo flights for a company that chartered pickups for banks up and down the coast.

244

His future looked very bright, though the weather definitely wasn't, as his twin-engine Piper Navaho plane shifted course to take the company-prescribed alternate route. Through the pounding storm with winds up to 75 mph, Bobby's plane was tracked until 9:28 AM when the aircraft vanished from the radar screens in the vicinity of 14,162-foot Mt. Shasta.

One phone call later and the course of my life changed forever, too.

Kimberly

Of the five children I brought into the world, Kimberly Dee Ruiz was the only one I recall talking to before she was even conceived. Her dad, Bob, and I *knew* part of our coming together was to bring Kimberly into the world. It didn't strike us as strange to hold conversations with her. She was telling us to get our "act" together " 'cuz she was coming in soon"—ready or not!

Bob and I accepted as perfectly normal that a "soul" named Kimberly was communicating with us from the time we first started dating. Occasionally, I viewed it as "wishful thinking" on my part after giving birth to three sons in a row. It seemed then that my dream of having a daughter was one that would go unfulfilled. Then, in quiet times, I would *feel* the presence of someone around me. Bob felt the same way and we started communicating out loud with Kimberly. We even knew what she would look like—brown curly hair, hazel-green eyes, and a petite body frame.

The day we found out I was pregnant, we were ecstatic and never doubted that Kimberly had now come into our lives, physically as well as spiritually. All through the pregnancy, we talked with her. For a split moment as I headed for the delivery room, a thought that we might have a son instead of a daughter crossed our minds. Well, we'd soon know. Delivery of my fourth child was more difficult than I had expected and my physician, after being up all night with several of us noisy women in labor, chose to put me out.

My vision was foggy as I came out of the anesthetic in the quiet delivery room.

"Is my baby here?" I asked.

"She sure is, honey," the nurse answered.

"*She?* Are you sure?" I questioned.

The nurse brought over my newborn child and laid her in my arms so I could see for myself. I cried with joy! Little wisps of wet curly brown hair surrounded her very pink, still wet face. It looked like Vidal Sassoon had just given her a pixie cut. The nurse took her from me, saying she had to weigh her and clean her up some more. As she crossed the hall into the nursery, Bob caught a quick glance of his newest child. He saw the piece of umbilical cord and thought, for an instant, he had another son. As they wheeled me out of delivery, Bob could see I was crying.

"We did it, we did it, Kimberly is really here!" It took a moment for the miraculous new reality to really soak in. It was 9:00 AM in the morning and we had been without sleep for over twenty-four hours. We hugged, we laughed, we cried. Bob had two sons from his first marriage and I had three. Our prayers for a daughter had not gone unanswered; they had merely been saved for the most appropriate time.

From the time Kimberly was born, she was a well-behaved, adorable, and loving child. We could take her anywhere and she would contently occupy herself. Like Bobby, there was no effort in parenting required with Kimberly. She was a teacher of love and we were so grateful she had chosen us as her parents.

Laura

Such a teacher Laura was! From the first moment I brought this colicky baby home from the nearby hospital, I wondered if I hadn't bitten more off the block of motherhood than I could chew. Every wrinkle in my brow would be earned with my littlest "pooh." No matter what I said or did, didn't say or didn't do, she interpreted it as rejection.

How does a mother reach a "rejection" part of a child and assist her in replacing it with loving confidence? Everything I suggested to her seemed to invalidate her and indicate to her that she wasn't "okay" the way she was. Laura is a human dynamo of physical energy. Even as a baby, she could rock her crib clear across the room. As an adolescent, periods of just sitting, such as being indoors or in school, drove her nuts.

When her dad, Bob, and I divorced, it exaggerated her already troubled teenage world. She cut school, drank, and played around in the drug scene with her friends. At the time, I remembered stating that if things kept on as they were, it would take a miracle for Laura and I to both live to see her eighteenth birthday. In desperation, I pleaded with her to try some other lifestyles.

"Why don't you do the training that est offers with Bill Orlich and Kim next weekend?" I suggested one day.

Reluctantly, she agreed. Two weekends later, the training had made a difference at a meaningful level, and old habit patterns and peer pressure still had some holds on her. Nine months later, she chose to enroll in The 6-Day training for teenagers. It would take place at Kirkwood in the California Sierras.

Many other "hopeful" parents and I put our long-haired "toughie," skeptical, and solemn teenage sons and daughters aboard a bus in San Francisco one early Saturday morning in July. Seven days later, at the very same spot, we gathered to await the return of our children. You could *feel* the energy of the yellow bus before it even came into view. Nothing had quite prepared me, not even in my wildest hopes, for this moment. A radiant, shorter-haired, vibrantly alive Laura *ran* down the bus steps and over to where I was waiting, picked me up, and twirled me around. Joyful tears danced in our eyes. I had waited her *whole life* for the words she then spoke:

"Mom, *I love you so much*! I realized this week that all you ever wanted was to love and support me in being the best me I could be. *Thank you!*"

Seventeen years of a parental challenge and struggle named Laura dissolved into a loving reunion. My heart overflowed with happiness. From this point on, life became easier for her. Although old patterns of behavior still struggled to take charge of her energies, they now see-sawed with periods of great clarity and self-confidence. Then came January 22, 1981, and the news of her brother Bobby's death.

Out of her deep grief and shock, new spiritual dimensions opened up for Laura. She could now *feel*, sometimes "see," and even "join" Bobby in moving out-of-body experiences. Bobby, from his new dimension, was lovingly leading her into not wasting away her life. She kept hearing him say: "Go for it, Laura, you can do it!"

Out of inspiration from a dream I had of her in a uniform, happy and confident, she began to investigate. She took aptitude tests and talked with several recruiting officers. She was thrilled, when tests showed she had talents in several areas. She knew being chained to a stuck-at-a-desk job for the rest of her life would be an unbearable sentence. Her incredible energy levels needed to be focused and used through productive, healthy, and more physical outlets. One of the positions she qualified for that intrigued her was weather observer for the Air Force.

It was a privilege to be present when Laura, with tears in her eyes, was sworn in to the service. She was so proud of herself for having made a choice that offered her new options, places, training, and friends in life. Her 6-Day experience proved handy in Air Force boot camp. She *knew* she could exist on three hours of sleep a night and what going for it 100 percent felt like. It gave her a leading edge at Lackland Air Force Base and her confidence soared. She completed Weather Observation School at Chanute Air Force Base and received her first assignment—Zwiebrucken Air Force Base in West Germany.

I could *feel* the letters from Laura without seeing her handwriting as I picked them up from my mailbox. She was growing in leaps and bounds, taking every opportunity to see all that was available while she was stationed in Europe. Postcards came from Paris (on her twenty-first birthday), London, Brussels, Switzerland, and many places in between. The one letter I most remembered was the one about her first Christmas in West Germany. She had never been away from home and the family before during the holidays.

Having been in West Germany just a couple of months, the one and only person she knew was a friend from Boot Camp, Denise Attalla. Denise was stationed at nearby Ramstein Air Force Base. The need to create a new "family" to share the holidays with prompted Laura to offer spending her last forty dollars to treat Denise and her boyfriend to Christmas dinner. Denise questioned her as to how she was going to survive financially until the first-of-the-month payday if she spent her last bit of money now. Laura didn't know. The only thing she *knew* was that the three of them being together, sharing Christmas, was the only thing that mattered.

That evening, at a Christmas party on base, a smiling gentleman walked up to Laura and introduced himself. She smiled and wished him a Merry Christmas back. The next instant he placed a fifty-dollar bill in her hand.

"I don't understand. What's this for?" Laura asked, puzzled as to why a total stranger should suddenly walk up to her and hand her money.

"Every year on Christmas Eve, I take three fifty-dollar bills and ask to be guided to the people I am to give them to. When I came into the room and saw you, I knew you were one of them. Merry Christmas!"

Laura wiped away her tears of surprise and joy and said, "Thank you!" She now knew for a personal fact that what you send out into the universe comes back *quickly* and multiplied.

TEACHER

Werner Erhard

You and I possess
within ourselves,
at every moment of our lives,
under all circumstances,
the power to transform
the quality of our lives.

—Werner Erhard

What words can express enough gratitude to the man whose beautiful verse, imprinted upon a golden butterfly postcard, deeply inspired me to choose this spiritual journey path over the "grief puddle" path at the moment I was told of Bobby's death?

From the moment I enrolled in Werner Erhard's training, the very fabric of my life and all the threads that weave it shifted into an ongoing, rapid metamorphosis. Obviously, *something in my life was working*. Within a short period of time, sixty-nine relatives, friends, and co-workers; my doctor and dentist; and boyfriends past and present enrolled in the training to seek their own enlightenment experience.

New levels of communication opened up. Any victim-of-the-universe behavior soon disappeared as we all took full responsibility for creating the quality of our lives. Laura, Kimberly, Bobby, Kathleen, my mother Mary, my dad Lou, and stepmother Teresa, soon joined the family of Erhard training graduates. Sons Gregory and Steven had taken the training before us.

The most extraordinary things began happening as each person did the training and began clearing their relationships of past damage and undelivered communications. What bloomed was aliveness and love.

It was like being a person of unlimited love, joy, and creativity at birth and being covered slowly over the years with a huge pile of manure that symbolized all the belief systems and programming we had accepted and incorporated into our own truth. Little by little, our fears, judgments, and belief systems magnetized to themselves our individual dramas of life experience. For myself, I had taken my hands off the steering wheel of life and become a victim of whatever circumstance presented itself, not realizing that *I had created it*.

Once I opened to the fact that I create my own realities by what I think, feel, say, and do, miraculous changes began to take place overnight. I could take a sand pail to the pile of manure and tackle it, shovelful by shovelful, or do something powerful like the training or do nothing at all and stay stuck. For me, the training blasted open the top of the manure pile. I could now climb out and experience whole new levels of "seeingness and beingness" that I wasn't able to see from the perspective of being buried in a manure pile. Now, the pathway was open. Of course, being a human being with divine free will, I could also choose to climb back in and once again pull the manure back over myself and pretend that I didn't *know* any realities existed besides the perspective inside of the manure pile.

I chose to go for aliveness and took advantage of all the supportive seminars offered. I enrolled in the Guest Seminar Leader's Program (GSLP). It was quite a commitment. For six of the most intense months of my life, I held down my full-time job for Dr. Tolleth and Dr. Ransdell and participated fully in GSLP. Through my assigned homework, I impeccably cleaned up and organized my closets, garage, home, and car; balanced checkbooks; completed undelivered communications; and generally cleaned up my life.

I thought I would have less energy going full-blast sixteen to twenty hours a day, six or seven days a week. Nothing was further from the truth—I had much more. Weekend training sessions opened my eyes wide to what was true for me versus what I *thought* was true for me. I had always figured that when I was exhausted, I had no more energy sources to draw from, but I was wrong. We did a process in which we physically expended ourselves to what we thought was zero vitality; this was followed by an opportunity to create ten times more energy, and we did! Another belief system shot to hell— along with many others.

The next est experience I jumped into was The 6-Day training. There had been such a dramatic shift in my daughter Laura after she completed The 6-Day for teens that I could hardly wait a month for my turn.

My buddy for the six days up in the High Sierras was Alice Goble. We had done the first training together and now signed on as roommates in our Kirkwood ski cabin. We awakened each morning, to exercise and stretch at sunrise in the crisp 9,000-foot mountain air. About one hundred of us from all walks of life participated in this training.

My body groaned as it ran the one-mile course every morning. It was difficult to get my mind to stop chattering its nonsense long enough to allow my body to really "go for it" as I chug-a-lugged up the hills.

On the last day of running, we were encouraged to "go for it 100 percent" and see what that felt like. Assistants were planted all along the way, calling our names as we ran by and cheering us on to the next turn in the road. How could I give up on myself, I wondered as I puffed up the hill. Reaching the top, I could hear the theme from *Rocky* blare out. I felt supercharged, as tears streamed down my face. I opened up my running stride coming down the hill. To have tried to stop myself at this point would have been insane. I'd never in my life run like this. My body was so in tune, it was flying! Assistants gathered at the bottom of the hill and chanted our names as we came over the finish line to be greeted by a round of broad grins, tears of joy, and great big hugs. How many other times had I ever played the game of life at such a high level of commitment? This was *living*.

Though we were in a classroom most of the time, we did spend one whole day out in the mountains of Kirkwood, hiking, traversing, rappelling, and experiencing the zip-line. The Tyrolean traverse call-ed for me to pull myself across a ropecourse strung out between two mountains. The 6-Day physician had checked me out to make sure an old injury would not keep me from participating and it didn't. Halfway across the traverse I could feel my arms straining to pull my body weight across the ravine. We had divided into small teams for the day on the mountain, and I could hear my teammates sending me energy as they shouted: "You can do it, Shirley. Come on! Pull yourself one more time! Atta' girl, Shirl, you're almost there...come on! One more time!"

Their support and energies literally pulled me across. By myself, I might have quit and waited for someone to rescue me. Here at The 6-Day, I *knew* no one was coming to rescue me and I'd best put all my energies into completing what I was doing.

The next event was rappelling down the face of a mountain. My hands were sweating as I listened to the instructions while being harnessed up.

"Mom, when they tell you to fall back, do it. You can't walk down. They know what they're doing!" Laura had told me. She'd had a ball doing this one.

When my turn to rappel came, I took a deep breath and did what I was told. I fell back so totally I almost did a somersault. Quickly, I regained my balance and fell into a little jumping step, bouncing off the mountain like I'd seen in some movie. It was a blast! At the bottom, I could hear Alice calling my name: "Go for it, Shirl!"

When I reached the bottom, I sat beside Alice and cheered for my teammates who were still coming down. As I looked up the sheer mountain face I'd just rappelled down, tears welled up in my eyes, and I was filled with a sense of awe. I had really done it. Another "I can't" had been blasted out of my consciousness.

The third and last rope event our team had to do was called the zip-line. From high on the face of a mountain, the zip-line was a speedy trip to the meadow below. With a safety harness on, one reached up to the bar overhead for a good grip and then stepped off the platform.

As my turn came up, I awaited the protective helmet I was to wear. It was coming by rope from the meadow below and there was a jam somewhere. David, the ropes assistant, was having a difficult time getting the helmet up to where we were. I stood on the edge of what looked like oblivion. Looking down, my legs began to feel like soft butter. It was clear that these might be the last few moments of life on earth for me. By now, I felt light-headed and woozy. Then I remembered the secret of switching my attention somewhere besides myself. So I focused my attention on the struggle David was having instead. I started shouting a little—"Go for it, David"—chanting, feeding him energy to get the helmet up the mountain. The moment my attention shifted from my own thoughts of weakness to David's dilemma, my strength quickly returned. When the trainer next to me on the platform said "Go," my clammy hands grasped the overhead rail and I stepped off. My terror left as I surrendered to the exhilarating sense of *freedom* I felt as I flew through the air. I felt like I was breaking the sound barrier.

At the bottom of the zip-line, a fresh mountain stream invited us to top our day off with an invigorating swim. We all wanted to leave our "I can'ts" up here on the mountain. Each of us had done all three events. Young, old, male, female, weak, and strong had, with a "little help from our friends," done things we'd never dreamed ourselves capable of doing.

The final day of the training, I hugged my 6-Day friends and looked into their eyes. The difference I could see was incredible. Some of their eyes had actually changed color and everybody's were clearer and many times brighter. A controlled supportive diet with no red meat had proven of value as had the total nonavailability of any junk food. Diet, lots of water, exercise, the clearing and empowering processes of the training, and the healthy mountain environment had supported us all in discovering what "going for it 100 percent" felt like.

254

Being there in the supportive space of Kirkwood I felt as if I'd been playing on Mt. Olympus with the gods. People could really do and have miracles when they were totally supported in stretching to their limits to find whatever 100 percent participation was for them. There was so much love and support to be all you could be. It felt a bit scary to be returning to normal life—a place that didn't always love and support you; a place where judgments and competition separated people and created battlefields strewn with casualties in its wake.

Support groups formed as we realized that coping with life in the world below us might not be as safe and supportive as "Mt. Olympus" had been. Kit, Lee, Jane P., Don, Michael, John, Pat, Pamela, Edna, Gar, Jane B., Ada, Marti, Frogge, and I became a 6-Day family. In their presence, it would be difficult not to keep "going for it."

I remember hearing a song that talked about looking into space to find out who we were and felt a deep wave of love and gratitude go out to Werner Erhard.

A Tool and Teacher, and Watch Out!
It Can Lead You to Exciting Travels!
SYNCHRONICITY

*When two or more events take place at a given
moment of time without either one having caused
the other but with a distinctly meaningful
relationship existing between them beyond the
possibilities of coincidence, that situation has
the basic element of Synchronicity.*

—*Ira Progoff,* **Jung, Synchronicity,
and Human Destiny**

The word *synchronicity* was not in my Webster's dictionary
when I looked it up; however, it was operating in my life. Once I knew
what to look for, I could see it occurring all the time. Sometimes

SYNCHRONICITY

it alerted me to something or connected me with someone. At other times, it felt like the universe was directly answering my prayers or questions. Whatever "it" was, I was eternally grateful for the awareness of the principle. On the path of spiritual awakening, synchronicity was an invaluable tool. Guidance along the path came from everywhere if I was still long enough to listen and stayed open and receptive to how my answers were coming.

Synchronicity came from "ask and ye shall receive" types of questions. My answer might have come from anywhere—another person, anything, or just an awareness. My body notified me with a spine-tingling series of goosebumps to be alert to what was happening; it was what I called a confirmation chill.

When I asked to know when Bobby's body had arrived at the funeral home and moments later the lights blinked and phone trembled at the same vibratory rate, Kathleen and I *knew* Bobby had arrived.

At stepson Rob Ruiz's wedding, just after "I now pronounce you man and wife" was declared, Kim remarked, "I can *feel* Bobby's presence". The lights in the church quivered at the now-familiar vibratory rate. Kim, Laura, and I looked at one another with the same thought. It was Bobby's way of saying: "Congratulations!" Bobby loved his stepbrother and there was no way he would miss sharing Rob's happy day.

Laura had been trying to send me a single flower from West Germany for two weeks. A dozen flowers were no problem, but a single flower was much more difficult. She gave up and asked her spiritual guides to show her how if it was meant to be.

In a Spectrum workshop I was putting on in Redwood City, my energy was running low as I ate lunch. I asked God if I was really following my divine plan or if I'd gotten off on another detour. After lunch, Janice Hamby had put together an Acknowledgment Process for me. I was called to sit in a chair at the front of the room. Everyone in the seminar had a flower in their hand, and, one by one, they came to the front of the room and laid it at my feet. My job was to simply sit and let all the love in. Tears came to my eyes. The first person to come forward was my friend, Georgia Kahn. She had two flowers in her hand.

"This flower is from Laura. She wants you to know she loves you," were the words Georgia spoke. Had she been picking up telepathic messages from Laura when she acted on her inner urgings?

Being Bay Area Director of Spectrum Workshops was consuming all my time and I wondered when I'd find time to work on *Journey to High Places*. My ego voice was again nagging at me that my writing wasn't that important. After meditating, I asked God to show me the truth about the matter. Four hours later, a large colorful brochure from Peter Caddy arrived in the noon mail. My body chilled and tears came into my eyes. The front of the brochure was a picture of a mountain and across the front of it was written:

Peter Caddy invites you to...
experience the power of Mount Shasta.

At that moment, I did. I did!

TRAVEL

Mt. Shasta '83

What we have once enjoyed
we can never lose.
All that we love deeply
becomes a part of us.

—Helen Keller

Bobby's birthday was nearing again and I felt a pull-of-the-heart to return to Mt. Shasta.

"What better place to be on September 8th?" I thought, recalling the memorable sentimental journey nine of us had taken last year. I called Carolyn Ortega to talk about it.

"If you're going, I am too," she said. "I heard about some property for sale up on Round Mountain. It's supposed to have a marvelous view of Mt. Shasta. If we leave early in the day, we can check it out when we get there."

We were never quite sure whether we had checked out the property on Round Mountain or not. The directions we were given were sketchy as we bounced around some very dusty, bumpy wilderness roads looking for the property. It might have been a great place to try out for a "Jeep Olympics," but Valentyne didn't care much for the obstacle course we'd chosen for her.

The sun was setting, and it was becoming pitch-black quickly and getting a bit spooky. Carolyn and I got the urge to turn back at exactly the same time—like right *now*. Maybe our imaginations were running wild, but like the song said, we tried to whistle a happy tune to dispel our fears. We whistled, we sang, and hurriedly found our way back to civilization. The "big black bear" running towards us turned out to be a big black dog, followed by a beat-up pickup truck with three grubby-looking guys in it.

"Maybe we were trespassing. Let's stay out of there!"

We found a quaint motel in Mt. Shasta City and settled in. It seemed a lot colder than we remembered it being at this time last year. We brought in a bag of groceries and fixed a snack before turning in.

As soon as we awoke the next morning, we peeked out our motel window to see what the weather on the mountain looked like. Mountain? What mountain? Where did it go? The fog had hidden her from view. Still, it was Bobby's birthday, and we were going up, whatever the weather.

"Why don't we just drive as high as we can, light a candle, sing 'Happy Birthday,' and come right back to our motel," I said, shivering at the sound of the wind whistling shrill noises through the front door.

We loaded our tote bags with a camera, a glass-chimneyed white candle, munchies, and a tape recorder. With daughter Laura still in the service in Germany, we knew she would love to share this special time with us via cassette.

"I've brought along a brand new, precious little book chosen for this occasion," Carolyn beamed, stuffing it in her huge suitcase-like purse.

We were singing and laughing as we drove, circling up the mountain. As we rounded a wide curve, we saw a large beautiful eagle looking as if it had been waiting patiently for our arrival. It was sitting on a rock not more than eight feet off the ground and flew straight for the hood of Valentyne. Afraid I would hit the magnificent bird, I slammed on my brakes. The eagle appeared to touch the hood and then dip its wings in a salute to us as it soared off beyond the tall pine trees and out of sight.

It reminded me of the touch-and-go landings one does while learning to fly an airplane. Valentyne never had had a hood ornament like that before.

Carolyn looked at me, eyes wide with disbelief, as she reached into her purse and pulled out the book she had brought along to read at our impromptu memorial service for Bobby. The title of the book was *Prayers for the New Age* by White Eagle. Oooookay, synchronicity again. The hairs on our bodies stood up so straight they were literally waving hello to each other. Carolyn said the confirmation chill she was having was taking her breath away. We both agreed it was another of God's "clues" along the spiritual pathway of life, sent to confirm, guide, alert, and connect us with knowledge, people, and things invaluable for us at the time.

Occasionally, these everyday synchronistic events hit with great emotional impact. This one sure did.

"I think we've just been *formally welcomed* to the mountain," Carolyn said as she regained her speaking faculties.

As we pulled up to the lower Ski Bowl parking lot, the weather suddenly cleared. Big patches of brilliant blue sky showed all around us and the clouds resembled big puffy white angels holding hands and dancing around the mountain's summit. We hadn't come prepared for climbing, as the weather had looked totally nonsupportive earlier; we were both wearing dresses and sandals. It was so beautiful, we decided to climb anyway. Searching my car trunk, I found two pairs of thin nylon socks, a pair of jogging shoes and an old down jacket. We laughed as we looked at one another, dressed in our new climbing outfits. I had on a rust-colored multi-tiered towel dress, thin brown nylon socks that only reached half-way up my calves, beige running shoes, and a well-worn blue down jacket. My pockets were bulging with the candle, camera, car keys, kleenex, and other assorted goodies.

Carolyn had on a gray-and-gold plaid dress with matching gray hip-length jacket that sported huge pockets. She stuffed them full of matches, books, munchies, and crystals brought from home. My tape recorder hung from the belt around her waist. She put on thin forest-green nylon socks and some old waffle-stomper shoes of hers that were still in the car. The epitome of high fashion models we were *not*. We looked more like "bag ladies" and could hardly contain our laughter every time we glanced at one another.

We began climbing, searching for the perfect spot to build a mini-altar. After about half an hour, we chose a flat spot adorned with interesting rock formations and beautiful shrubby pine trees. Emptying out our pockets, we laid out the green quilt we had half-carried, half-dragged up the mountainside. I arranged some flat stones into an altar while Carolyn gathered some colorful lavender-and-yellow wildflowers she had found higher up the slope. She brought back a small mound of snow to "plant" the flowers in.

"God, Jesus, angels, masters, and guides of the mountain, come bless and join us today," I began. Carolyn opened the White Eagle book randomly and read a prayer for love and peace. We sang a couple of spiritual songs and chants followed by "Happy Birthday, Bobby." As we half-expected, the wind blew out our tall candle.

We turned to look behind us. Moments before there had been a smooth flat area; now, there was a large crater-like depression. Hmmm, were our imaginations playing tricks on us? We were certain it hadn't been there fifteen minutes earlier. A blue cloth waved in the breeze from the center of the crater. The blue was similar in hue to a pilot's uniform. Where had it come from? Surely we would have seen it while we were searching for rocks for the altar on our way up. The weather wasn't the only thing that could change quickly on the mountain.

We headed for the car, contemplating aloud the events of the day. The weather had suddenly lifted, inviting us to climb; we'd received an "eagle greeting", and a crater with a piece of torn blue cloth had appeared out of nowhere. How mystical the energies of Mt. Shasta can be! One could feel the spiritual vibrations anywhere on or near this majestic wonder of nature.

Back in town, Carolyn saw a sign in a restaurant that offered coffee for ten cents a cup and asked me to pull Valentyne over.

"It's getting near dinner time so we might as well eat here, too," my bag lady partner remarked. She ordered some liver while I

Altar on Mt. Shasta

looked over the limited menu and chose a cheeseburger. I hadn't had one in ages. It was a big mistake! When my cheeseburger arrived it looked like a burnt piece of leather. Carolyn's liver wasn't any better. "Oh, well, I've been toying with the idea of totally eliminating red meat from my diet. I think I just did," I laughed.

The next day we made a beeline for the Golden Bough Bookstore. Dorothy, the owner, was away this year. Calling our friend, Maureen Mitchell, we found out she was in Hawaii for a few days. Maureen had moved to Mt. Shasta after our trip here last year.

Later in the afternoon, we visited the new "I AM" Reading Room in downtown Mt. Shasta City. We had passed it earlier in the day, before it had opened. I'd been searching for a couple of their books ever since Iris Jackson had loaned me hers to take to Hawaii. A helpful gentleman named John Swenson answered a lot of our questions about the "I AM" group and about Mt. Shasta. Between the two boxes of books Carolyn purchased at the Golden Bough Bookstore and the ones we bought at the "I AM" Reading Room, the back seat of Valentyne looked like a library-on-wheels.

We walked down to the Fifth Season Sporting Gear Store to hunt up maps and info for climbing Mt. Shasta. The helpful fellows at the store told us we should have crampons and ice axes. They strongly advised we find ourselves a knowledgeable climbing guide. Walking back to the car, I looked up at the glistening snow-capped Mt. Shasta. I knew I'd be back next year to physically climb her "higher places."

TEACHER
Alexander Everett

My new job as Bay Area Director of Spectrum Workshops started off with a bang. Two big workshops were happening simultaneously in two different Millbrae hotel rooms. The "WOW" (Workshop of Workshops) was an opportunity to gather with a unique and empowering network of recognized teachers and founders of several consciousness organizations. I was in charge of overseeing the logistics. Across town, Alexander Everett was leading people "Inward Bound."

At the beginning of the WOW workshop, Alexander helped us kick it off by participating in a panel of eight teachers. The evening was a powerful and dynamic co-mingling of the multi-gifted teachers who had come to share with those taking the workshop. Most of these people were preparing to or were already putting on seminars of their own.

I *knew* I had connected with another major teacher on my spiritual path. Whenever Alexander spoke, a little cheering section

265

inside of me was agreeing with and applauding his every word. His resounding voice had a commanding presence that my inner knowingness responded to. I wanted to know more about the man who had been the founding source of Mind Dynamics. Other great consciousness leaders had come through his training program, including Werner Erhard of est, John Hanley of Lifespring, and Stewart Emery of Actualizations.

After the brief introduction to Alexander in the WOW workshop, I *knew* I wanted to do the next available Inward Bound training and so did Carolyn Ortega, Julie Traynor, and Robin Blanc. We found out the next one would be held on Alexander's ranch in Oregon.

With Julie's car fully packed, the four of us took off the following weekend for the ten-hour drive to Veneta, Oregon. By the time we arrived in Springfield, Oregon, where we had reserved a hotel room, it was 4 AM in the morning and raining heavily. We were sure if we drove around a little bit we would find the street our hotel was on but we had no luck and we were getting *very* tired. Pondering what we should do next, we half-jokingly called to the masters and guides that we were lost and needed help. Within one minute, a policeman's flashing red light appeared behind us and we were flagged over to the curb. We laughed—we had *asked* and now had to let go of *how* we *received*. Unbeknownst to us, we had been driving the wrong way down a one-way street. The policeman carefully checked over Julie's ID, listened to our "lost" story, and took mercy upon his four guests from California. As the policeman talked with us, an emergency call came in from across town, where our hotel was located. Our police "guardian angel" told us to follow him and he would signal us as we neared our hotel. With that, he turned on his red light and speedily escorted us across town.

Our Ramada Inn had a very homey dining room in which we found ourselves trying to awaken fully after only two hours of sleep. The restaurant was nearly deserted at that early hour and we were delighted with the good fortune of having a waitress who waited on us hand and foot and brought us herbal teas, honey, and an assortment of our favorite jams. We felt well taken care of this morning. We left our waitress a large tip and headed for Alexander's ranch.

The Alexander Everett Ranch was a perfect retreat with its trees, private lake, and large assortment of animals. At break time, all twenty of my classmates and I took advantage of our host's hospitality and went out to acquaint ourselves with the layout of the land and its many animals. I stopped first in the apple orchard and picked some apples fresh off the tree. It brought back wonderful memories of growing up on my grandparents' ranch. At an early age, I quickly learned how to pick the choicest, juiciest, ripest fruit whenever I desired it and I was spoiled. Memories of huge sweet blackberries, firm bing cherries at their ultimate moment of ripeness, and plums, peaches, apricots, and pears at their peak were forever etched in my mind and tastebuds. Here on Alexander's ranch the opportunity to scout out his orchard and fill my jacket pockets with crisp-tasting fresh apples was one I wasn't about to miss.

As I munched and walked, I came across some very pregnant miniature burros. They liked apples, too! A large fearless emu approached me. She or he was as tall as I was and confronted me for its share of the goodies. A llama near a far-off fence chose to keep her distance.

In a small fenced-off area, two small white deer-like animals of some kind were engaged in a horn-to-horn encounter. It was rutting season. In my curiosity, I almost got too close. One of the horns came through the wire fencing, brushing against my right arm. Startled, I stepped back and immediately felt something gently nudging at my left underarm. I quickly turned around and found a large doe trying to get my attention. She obviously had the run of the place and no fear of humans. Her name was Duchess. I petted and fed her and told her how beautiful she was. Then, quietly, I stepped back and gazed deeply into her eyes—what a breathtaking moment! I could feel the gentleness of her peaceful soul in this rare one-on-one encounter, and I felt honored that she had allowed me to be that close to her. How could anyone ever harm a creature-of-God such as Duchess after an encounter like this?

Back in our living-room classroom, we began meditating as Alexander's voice led us through the colors of the rainbow in his Centering Meditation. A deep state of peacefulness came over me, as I mentally observed the red, orange, yellow, green, blue, purple, and violet images in my mind. Fifteen minutes a day was all it would take to change our lives for the better. I bought the flute-enhanced Centering tape to use at home.

Inward Bound taught us techniques to tap into "universal consciousness", recognize intuition, develop creativity, and experience oneness. The philosophies Alexander shared were richly integrated with teachings from all over the world; they fascinated me. One experience he shared, although I was unaware of it at the time, would plant the seeds that would later enable me to hear the "call of India".

For some reason, I didn't take any notes in this class. I was allowing myself to fully experience being with this master teacher without getting too intellectual about it.

Alexander taught us how to tap into the higher parts of our consciousness, which *always knows* what to do in every situation, for answers. It proved valuable the first time I used it. After returning home from Inward Bound, I lost a brand new neatly folded one-hundred-dollar bill. A long time ago Dr. Tolleth had given it to me as a survival tool. It was not to be spent, but carried with me so that wherever I went, I would always have the crisp new one-hundred-dollar bill for food, room, or whatever I might need to bail myself out of an emergency. It had been with me, hidden away, for many years. But times had recently been getting financially tight so I gave myself permission to spend it to pay a pressing bill. When last I'd seen it, it was on my bed, still folded. Where had it disappeared to? I searched every nook and cranny, hiding place, and pocket I could think of.

In desperation, after looking at the mess I'd made in my search, I elected to try Alexander's process. That night before I went to bed I put a glass of water on my nightstand after drinking half of it and saying, "This is all I have to do to find the solution to my missing one-hundred-dollar bill". According to this process, the mind was in every cell of my body, and the water was a device I could use to psychologically trigger my higher consciousness to assist me. As I understood it, information could be retrieved in this manner from my memory bank, or that of others, or the universe. My answer could come promptly when I awakened or sometime during the day. I might also dream my answer. A thought or awareness could quickly hit me with my answer or a piece of the puzzle of whatever project I'd asked about.

Promptly on awakening at 6 AM the next morning, I drank the rest of the water, mentally thinking, "The answer to my question is now being revealed to me." Suddenly, I felt the urge to go through a big grocery bag full of garbage sitting by my bedroom door awaiting disposal. As I finished going through the bag without finding the money, I was disappointed that my first thought had not led me to it. In the distance, I could hear clanking noises breaking up the early morning stillness of our condominium complex. It was Tuesday, and the trash collectors were already busy at their tasks. Kim was usually the one to drag our big garbage can out to the front of the garage each week for pickup. But she had come in late last night, so I thought I might as well let her sleep a little longer and pull the trash can out of the garage myself.

I started to throw the bag of trash I'd brought down from my bedroom into the almost-full garbage can, but immediately I could sense my mind signaling me with a gentle urge. I saw another grocery bag full of throwaway mail peeking out of the plastic trash can in front of me. It was obviously trash from my bedroom, too. On an impulse, I tore into it. I couldn't believe my eyes! There, a "post-it note" had attached my money to the piles of junk mail I was throwing out. However the process worked, it did work. The timing was incredible—three minutes later, and my garbage would have been gone forever and along with it, my one hundred dollar bill. Ah yes, the gifts a master teacher can share with you can prove to be im-measurable on spiritual levels, and on occasions like this, financially rewarding on a nitty-gritty physical world level as well.

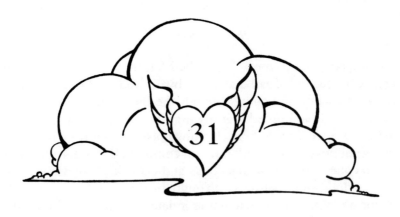

TEACHER
Bill Orlich

Bill was a teacher of unconditional love and support. With Bill, I *had* to learn to receive—I had attracted to myself a "giver". He assisted me greatly in breaking down some of the "thank you very much but I can do it myself" attitudes that had been with me since early childhood.

God, unbeknownst to me when Bill and I first met, had sent me a very unique friend, one who would assist me in many ways to heal my emotions and body after my second divorce. He was also my "midnight printer"; he helped me pull many a project out of the deadline fires.

We met in 1976 when he was a patient at Dr. Tolleth's office. The next time we met I was a volunteer working on the Daryl LaMonica Charity Golf Tournament. Our friendship blossomed when Bill saw me next in a leg cast, hobbling around on crutches. Newly divorced and hurting physically and emotionally, I was badly in need of a good friend. The nickname he gave me, "Cindy Seagull", stuck for a while; it was short for the combination of Cinderella and Jonathan Livingston Seagull. Bill saw me as an injured bird who just needed some tender loving care to regain strength and spirit before she soared to new heights.

Through the years Bill was a true "angel of mercy"—the refrigerator was magically filled when our food budget was tight. The gas tank of my car would register full, when it had been on empty before Bill drove it. Whether the garbage disposal was jammed or there was no more wood for the fireplace, Bill would show up and things would suddenly work. He was a friend who loved to window shop in Carmel every bit as much as I did and he ate Chinese food with chopsticks, too!

My study of past-life regressions revealed that Bill and I had known each other before: he had been a Samurai, I, a Geisha. Now, in this lifetime, roles reversed; the Samurai and Geisha have teamed up once again for we have much to learn from, and to teach, each other. So far our partnership has given birth to our printing company, Bill's Printing Center, and to Shastar Press. These enterprises have enriched both our lives and have provided us with the means to share our energies with the world.

Every person on earth should have one friend like Bill. Such a "divine friend" is always there, whether it is to dance the night away, give of his innate healing gifts through a tender massage session, assist you in bailing out a child in trouble, join you for a wee-hour jog around the park when you can't sleep, or plan an impromptu day of restoration and play in the tide pools at the beach.

Bill taught me to *ask* and then be open to *receive* assistance from another human being—with no "strings or hooks" attached. What a rare and priceless gift!!

TEACHER

Wingsong

*A great sculptor once asked for a certain
piece of marble. When asked why he had
chosen that particular one, he said,
"There is an angel in it and I want to
free it."*

—Wingsong Brochure

It never crossed my mind that I could channel mes-
ages from celestial beings. The first class I took at the Wingsong
Center, where I would learn this skill, felt different than other
kinds of classes. The Center had an ethereal quality about it as
I settled in to do a course on Manifesting.

"The laws of manifesting are as immutable as the law of gravity
and just as impersonal. They always produce results,

negative or positive, depending on the use we make of them," Lisa deLongchamps, creator of Wingsong, told us.

To *manifest* anything, it was important to be able to visualize as clearly as possible what we wanted and then to feel as though we already had it. The analogy Lisa used was one of a plugged-in coffee pot. It appears that the pot is cold yet you know it is plugged in and in the process of becoming hot. Our own individual acceptance level would dictate how much we allowed ourselves to receive. We worked on processes to clarify what we wanted and others to raise our acceptance level.

We were encouraged to make wish lists in a notebook or on a card, listing what we wanted to manifest in our lives and noting the results. It was powerful and effective. The first time I made my list, I made it an easy one—a new purse, a Champion Deluxe Army knife, some new silverware, and a weekend trip to Carmel. If I wanted something, I went out and did whatever I needed to do to have it. My manifestation list was completed before a week had passed by.

The next list was harder. I added mirrored doors for the closets of my home, outdoor carpeting for my two patios, and a VCR to my card and quickly manifested them all. It soon became a habit to look at and carry my manifesting card with me in The Personal Resource System.

We were also advised, "Rid yourself of excess so you may experience enough." In Wingsong teachings there was a clean-out time. By now, I well knew the value of lightening up and welcomed the homework of cleaning out closets and anything in my life that didn't feel impeccable; thus, creating a vacuum for what I wished to manifest.

"Does this include relationships?" someone from class asked.

"Yes! There is no space for a new love in your life if your bed is already occupied!" A lot of wide-eyed laughter filled the room.

The Twin-flame Workshop was a revealing opportunity to look at the relationships of my life. Again, it was necessary to impeccably complete the past before moving on. A daily process of forgiveness was called for. How well I now knew "complete or repeat". When manifesting the love of your life, it was important to give up the pictures of what he or she would look like and concentrate on what you wanted the relationship to "feel" like—nurturing, loving, peaceful, supportive, joyful, and so on. It could even turn out to be the old Frog-Prince story.

I went on to take the Visioning workshops. There, I learned to do a daily forgiveness process, using the violet flame to keep my forgiveness up-to-date. Forgiving others was usually quite easy for me to do. It was *forgiving myself* that was the most difficult.

Jesus talked of forgiveness in the Bible, and intuitively, I *knew* it was a must, if not *the* most important part of my spiritual growth process. I began calling forth the Violet Flame of Love and Perfection to "consume anything left unforgiven in my body, mind, emotions, and world affairs, past and present, cause and effect, and transmute it into perfect peace, divine love, ecstatic joy, and avalanches of prosperity and abundance". It fast became an ongoing part of my daily meditation ritual.

Lisa reminded us that it was crucial to have our forgiveness up-to-date in order to channel from an ascended master or celestial being. As I started to channel messages, always visualizing myself surrounded with light first, it felt like I'd come *home. All* messages I received were ones of love and inspiration. After a Wingsong class and a session of being a secretary for God's thoughts to come through, I always felt very light, very pure, and very *uplifted*.

TEACHER

Shirley MacLaine

Sitting in seclusion, working on this book, the phone rang. It was my friend Julie Traynor. She had just read an article in *The Ladies Home Journal* about Shirley MacLaine and her new book that she thought I should see. The book, *Out on a Limb*, was about Shirley discovering her spirituality. My body chilled and sprouted a healthy crop of goosebumps as I thanked Julie for her tip.

The phone rang again moments later. This time it was my daughter Kim who said she was going to the park to read a book on her lunch hour instead of coming home as she had planned.

"Mom, I'm reading the neatest book. Sounds so much like some of the things that have happened to you," Kim said with a happy singsong lilt to her voice.

Though somewhere in my mind I already knew which book, I asked anyway.

"*Out on a Limb* by Shirley MacLaine," she answered. "I just *love* her style!"

My body repeated its goosebumps and chilling act. Shrugging my shoulders, I put on my down jacket and headed for downtown Walnut Creek to hunt up my own copy of *Out on a Limb*. The synchronicity of the two phone calls in such a short period of time and the reactions I was feeling in my body were all I needed to clue me in that the book was of value to me.

The next few hours I virtually submerged myself in the book. Night turned into dawn, dawn became noon, and the afternoon wore on into evening as I read the book, cover to cover, taking time out for only the necessities of life. It was a wonderful, powerful, and moving reflection of the spiritual awakening and events in my own life.

Shirley MacLaine—a sister on the path! Another validation that spiritual awakening was happening everywhere. It felt so *right* for spiritual awakening experiences to be coming out of the closet now.

Celebrities, just by being in the public eye, can call a lot of attention to their experiences, many times for the betterment of all mankind. When Shirley Temple Black, Betty Ford, and Happy Rockefeller came forward and publicly discussed their bouts with breast cancer, it then became an okay subject for everyone to talk about. Because of their sharing, information and support became more commonplace, effective, and available for women dealing with this maiming, disfiguring, and sometimes fatal member of the cancer family.

Now another subject was out of the closet. I was grateful to Shirley for sharing her awareness and her skepticism about the spiritual awakening process. Much of it validated my own experience. It was crystal clear that Shirley MacLaine was teaching at the same time as she was being a student. She was a teacher-on-the-path with a humorous style. Her words stirred those ready to hear their own inner voice sounding the *call*.

276

The Alive Tribe

Our bodies are made of energy.
We are electromagnetic beings with an energy field.
We are that energy field creating a physical body
in a Universe of infinite energy.

—*The "Domain Shift Manual"*

As Bay Area Director of Spectrum Workshops, I met new spiritual teachers at an accelerated pace. I heard only good things about a group called The Alive Tribe. The founding couple of the Tribe were named Diamond and Angel Ecstasy. They would be coming to a workshop Spectrum was putting on. My curiosity was really aroused when I was informed two other members of the family, Summer Eternity and Crystal Paradise, were also coming. As I made up their name tags, part of me was smiling in disbelief that these names belonged to real human beings rather than some characters in a fairy tale. During the course of our first meeting, intense eye contact with Diamond revealed to me that the Alive Tribe meeting was no accident. There was much I could learn from being around them. Carolyn Ortega, Julie Traynor, and I promptly enrolled in their next workshop, called the Domain Shift.

If ever a name fit a family of individuals, The Alive Tribe name exemplified their essence. When I met the five Alive Tribe children of Diamond, Angel, Summer, and Crystal, I was fascinated watching this enlightened and loving family interact. All were in tune with the idea that "we create our own realities," including the small children. I watched the young boy named Ever get mad at one of the little girls. He immediately took responsibility for his anger and went over to the family mini-trampoline and jumped vigorously for about five minutes. As I watched him, it appeared he was blowing out his anger as he jumped. When he got off, he smiled at me and went on his playful way as if the anger had never existed. The anger he was feeling earlier was *his*, and he apparently took full responsibility for it and found a healthy, safe way to discharge it all by himself. Wow! If the whole world could learn this simple secret and each person took full responsibility for handling his own anger, frustrations, and pent-up emotions, a planet of peace and love would evolve overnight. Ah yes, the Domain Shift would be an interesting weekend. The lessons had already begun.

Diamond and Angel were co-facilitators of the training. Their combined talents and backgrounds had come together to create The Domain Shift and support staff called Multi-Dimensional Research and Expansion (MDRE). They were assisted by two other members of the Alive Tribe household, a soft, beautiful blond named Summer Eternity, and Crystal Paradise, a spirited blonde Registered Nurse. A happy soul named Choice came in each day to cook our health-conscious meals and they were deliciously, as well as lovingly, prepared.

The four days of the training took place at The Alive Tribe home, nestled in the woods of Mt. Tamalpais. It was like going to another planet. We learned several breathing techniques and experienced several forms of expression. It reaffirmed for me that each person's basic nature is one of *love* and *ecstasy*. When I was feeling fear, anger, guilt, or sadness, I learned to acknowledge that they were not bad; only emotions coming up to be expressed. As I had experienced, particulary since Bobby's death, whenever I appropriately expressed an emotion freely and fully, a wonderful sense of inner peace and tranquility would come over me. "The Domain Shift Manual" was a gift, a toolbox full of safe rituals and ways to return yourself to a state of *ecstasy*.

It was fun, too. My body loved the physicality of the processes we did. Carolyn and I both gave way to hysterical laughter when we obviously plugged into the same picture while doing an expressing process to free stuck sexual energies in our bodies.

There were times during the training when we expressed through dancing. After a session of "Alive Tribe Boogeying," the energy running through my body felt electrically alive and free. Rounds of group singing were woven throughout The Domain Shift. The songs were mostly creative and positive affirmations about the quality of life we all wanted to create for the world we live in.

There was time during the training for Angel to "retrieve a core belief" I was operating out of that no longer served me. Carolyn wrote it down as Angel worked with me:

> If I totally see what's possible for me I might die because everything might change *so much* and be *so different* that there'll be nothing familiar anymore and I might feel lost in my experience.

She was right—my life was changing values, scenes, and people so rapidly, I wondered what life was all about. Angel assisted me in forming the belief into a positive expansive perspective of the same theme.

Angel was incredibly perceptive as I watched her work with each individual. I realized there was a part of me in most everybody else's "core beliefs," too—old belief systems that had boxed in and smothered our aliveness and natural state of ecstasy for much too long:

"I *need* a man to love me to be happy..."

"I will die if I let go of putting other people before me because I only deserve to be alive if I take care of other people..."

"If I come into my full power, people will want to hurt me..."

"If I allow myself to be too feminine, men will control and manipulate me..."

"Women always try to mother and smother me..."

"If I own my power fully, the people around me won't be able to handle it..."

"If I tell the *real* truth to everyone, they'll all leave..."

As the process went on, my compassion for people and the belief systems that molded and shaped our lives grew immensely.

In a process expanding our multi-dimensional awareness, I started to cry. Bobby was talking to me, loud and clear. In disbelief, my mind questioned the validity of what I was experiencing. At that moment, the lights of the house flickered and the sound of an airplane could be heard directly over the house. Carolyn intuitively reached over and squeezed my hand.

The Domain Shift was so fulfilling that Carolyn and I signed up to repeat the class a couple of months later. After all, more is better. This time Sabrina Lee, Ellie Drew, and Robin Blanc joined us. It was no less enlightening the second time; it integrated what we were learning and experiencing to another level.

It was a privilege to hang out with Diamond, Angel, Crystal, and Summer. They had many valuable things to share and most importantly, they were spiritual teachers that *walked their talk*. After the second Domain Shift, I wrote in my PRS that if I had to leave Planet Earth right this minute and could take only three books with me, it would be the *Bible*, *A Course in Miracles*, and my "Domain Shift Manual."

TEACHER

Shakti Gawain

Where there is no vision,
the people perish.

—*Proverbs 29:18*

One of the last seminars I pulled together for Spectrum Workshops was "A Day with Shakti Gawain". I had long been a fan of her book, *Creative Visualizations* and was excited to be spending a day with Shakti in person.

The Saturday morning sky was a clear and sunny shade of blue and the place I'd chosen for holding the seminar, "The Barn" in Berkeley, was indeed the perfect quiet place for one to go within to look at the subtleties of one's inner thoughts and feelings. We sat around in a circle on the soft thick carpet of the upstairs loft and I began taking notes as Shakti spoke directly to the part of me that was already discovering universal laws and truth for itself:

"Everything reflects like a mirror and is a key to what needs to be improved."

"What do I *feel?*"

"*Back yourself up!*"

"Anger is your power that you put a lid on!"

"Happiness comes from the creative process; open yourself up as a creative channel. You *are* a *creator*, creating all the time anyway!"

"Your desire is the universe speaking to you. Be really willing to blow it (continually) in order to follow the inner voice and be a channel!"

"Trust your feelings—tune in at the moment to get your 'gut feeling'."

"A feeling of 'total turn-on' is where the universe wants you to be in the moment!"

"Decisions are out the window now. They're made from the head. Follow your inner voice; be constantly dialoguing with your inner self."

I loved it!

My pen could hardly keep up with the thoughts I was hearing. We looked at some of our "core beliefs", realizing that the most important thing was to begin recognizing them. Then, we were ninety percent home as we watched our own process without invalidating or judging it. This allowed our old "number" to run its pattern one more time, running itself out and being replaced with more expansive ones.

We each chose a current problem we were dealing with and took an in-depth look at the feelings and beliefs we held about the situation. Towards the end of the process, we faced our fear about the worst thing that could happen in this problem and released it. Next, we looked at the *best* thing that could possibly happen and really exaggerated seeing and feeling what we wanted, happening *right now*! The day was packed with universal gems of wisdom that rang true for me when I was in the flow, with my inner guidance totally in charge. I could also hear the truths that showed when my intellect was totally in charge, making decisions to make things happen. It certainly matched my experience since Bobby's death had sharply awakened the intuitive part of me.

At midday, we spent lunchtime in the beautiful garden at "The Barn". Spring flowers filled every flower bed and planter, bathing us in color and fragrance. My senses were heightened and I was fully open to any gifts available out of the processes we were doing with Shakti.

Things within me were being deeply stirred as I did a process that examined all my old patterns and memories of times when I "held it all together" out of the sheer force of incredible will and did not give my body the opportunity to fully feel and express its helplessness, sadness, and pain. I had not realized how much was still stuffed deep inside of me. This was one of the greatest gifts available to me that day and every cell in my body *knew* it. I wound up my logistical duties, bade the other participants goodbye, and hugged and thanked Shakti for the empowering and enlightening day.

As I watched Shakti and her assistant, Laurel, drive away, my body started shaking with chills. It had been a long time since I had been physically ill. As I entered my home half an hour later, all three telephone lines were ringing. My body was crying out "help" as I called up my friend, Bill Orlich, and asked if his couch was vacant. I needed some peace and *quiet* while I got hold of what was happening in my body.

"A Day with Shakti Gawain" had started things rumbling like an awakening volcano inside me. Old memories wanted to rise and be healed. For five days and nights, I stubbornly hid out from the world as fever and chills alternated with periods of great peace and mental clarity. The fever and chills seemed to go away when I was working on my book and return to knock the pins out from under me every time I thought about returning to my home.

In between writing, I found myself enthralled with reading the book *Initiation*, by Elisabeth Haich. It was an account of the events and experiences that contributed to Elisabeth's spiritual growth. It seemed I was going through "Initiation" with her. My hideaway allowed me to totally shut out the everyday world of people and telephones and just be with myself—my inner as well as my outer processes. For five days and nights I felt immersed in an unreal yet "real" dimension of reality. I did not want to leave it. Bill convinced me to visit Dr. Tolleth to make sure I was physically okay. On the way home, we picked up the prescription of antibiotics "Papa Doc" had prescribed.

Later that evening, as I finished reading *Initiation*, I realized part of me *knew* what to do and wanted to physically cleanse itself, much as I had felt on the day of "shock" after Bobby's funeral. I called my friend, Julie Traynor, to come over and assist me in doing some of the Alive Tribe release processes. Her telephone answering machine said she was not available. "Guess I'll just have to wait until later," I mumbled disappointedly. My body said *no way!* The chills returned at such intensity it felt like I was riding inside a can of paint when it was put on the paint-shaker machine.

I headed for the king-size waterbed in Bill's bedroom and dove onto it. All the times I'd held it together and not allowed myself to feel and safely express my pain, helplessness, and sadness wanted to be released from the cellular memory of my body. I totally surrendered to the process. It was a safe, appropriate place and time to empty out.

I hugged the king-size pillow and allowed my muffled screams of pain, sadness, and anger to escape. They were seemingly unrelated things that I had never communicated to important people in my life: a "deserted" child's pleas to her parents from a hospital bed; scolding words of anger at a child of my own who had repeatedly brought upsets into my life; heated words for an ex-husband who hadn't lived up to our financial arrangement while I had to take on a second job; the painful withholds when someone I loved very much appeared to have betrayed me.

Events and circumstances of the past kept flashing in my mind as I allowed the words I needed to say to escape into the safe space of a billowy pillow. The king-size waterbed was totally receptive to the flailing of my arms and kicking of my feet as I fully expressed all the emotions coming up and cleared them out of my body. Wow! I had no idea some of the incidents still had so much "charge" running around inside of me.

After what seemed a very long time, I felt "emptied out" and a deliriously peaceful sense of ecstasy came over me. Rolling over on my back and facing the ceiling, I thirstily drank in the elixir of absolute *peace*. My fever had evaporated into the night.

The next morning I awakened with my new sense of heightened awareness and inner peace still intact. I went out to the patio of Bill's apartment and stretched. I could see the freeway in the distance, skirting the bottom of the Walnut Creek hills. Paralleling it, a BART train jetted by. Before me lay the multi-colored green of the trees that edged the golf course below. A red-breasted robin tugged at a worm on the grass and bells from somewhere chimed out their melody. The morning breeze kissed my recuperating body with its refreshing briskness. I breathed in deeply. It was beautiful to *simply be alive*!

Back inside the apartment I picked up some paper and a pen to try and capture the feelings running through me.

> I am *free* now,
> living each day
> to the fullest,
> moment by moment.
>
> *Home* is wherever I am.
> No one can take
> it away from me.
> I carry *home* with me wherever I go.

What do I truly most want to do with my life, right *now*? I wondered. To research, write, and travel the world, was the answer I wrote down.

The next morning I returned to my townhouse. As before, all three telephone lines were ringing. When I entered, I *knew* I didn't live there anymore. I loved my home, but at this point in my life, I didn't own it, *it owned me*! Everything I was ever taught about how a successful life *should* look had been rearranged or disconnected inside me. The enormous burden of a large house and its financial entanglements was no longer where I wanted to focus my energies. A "For Sale" sign hung outside the door before another twenty-four hours had passed.

A journal I had been writing in opened to a page dated several months earlier. It recorded a vivid dream I'd long forgotten:

Getting on board an airplane. Daughter Kim and Robin
Blanc are also boarding. I say to the pilot, "I'm taking the
FLIGHT TO FREEDOM! It's *clearly* more important
than owning a house. So, HERE I AM, WORLD!"

It *was* time to free myself and give myself permission to seek and
explore some of the other things in life my inner voice was urging
me to experience. Thank you, Shakti, for being a powerful catalyst
to *freedom*!

TRAVEL

Puerto Vallarta

*...and so my responsibility to me
is to make my self enormous,
full of knowledge,
full of love,
full of understanding,
full of experience,
full of everything so that I can give it to you
and you can take it and build from there.*

—Leo Buscaglia
Living, Loving and Learning

My Golden Birthday was approaching and the family nest was almost empty. Kimberly would be leaving home this month. Just Nikki, our cat, and I would remain to hold down the family fort. Even those days were numbered: a "For Sale" sign hung outside our Walnut Creek townhouse. Soon I'd have to find a new home for Nikki and then one for myself. Strange, I couldn't remember ever living alone before. I had gone from being a child directly to being a wife and then a mother. Life was changing rapidly, reflecting the restlessness stirring deep within me.

Kim pulled together a big birthday party to celebrate "ole number fifty". Family and friends gathered to assist me in welcoming in the second half of my first century. As I opened presents, I unwrapped a suitcase from Kim. A note inside it told me to go home and pack this new bag immediately for five days of sun and fun. A vacation at a surprise destination was awaiting me. If this was an omen of what turning fifty was about, I loved it already. Funny, I didn't feel a half-century old—whatever I had imagined *that* would feel like. Life, to this point, had been a full spectrum of experiences and adventures. I could hardly wait to see what the next fifty held, especially given the accelerated path of spiritual seeking I was on.

The following Wednesday, we took off from San Francisco International Airport, headed for Los Angeles. When we deplaned, my daughter-in-law Kathleen was waiting to surprise me with her presence, a red rose, and a big banner that said "Happy Birthday, Mom—Love, Bobby and Kathleen". She was now studying full time at the Art Center Design College in Pasadena. I hadn't realized how much I'd missed her until I saw her radiant face. We had been through a lot together and our heart-to-heart bond remained strong.

Quickly, I was being hurried off to a different terminal of the Los Angeles International Airport to board another plane. The boarding sign gave away our destination—Puerto Vallarta.

In Mexico, Kim and I lazily drank away the days soaking up the rays of sun at the beach. That was about all we drank or soaked up. It was wonderful: the first vacation where I lost weight instead of gaining. We had been warned to drink only bottled water and pay impeccable attention to what we ate. We honored that piece of advice. It was my first real trip to Mexico other than one where I had made a quick visit over the border to Tiajuana. Here in the resort city of Puerto Vallarta it was fun bargaining for brilliantly-colored cotton clothing and small gifts to take home.

On the day we were scheduled to fly home we decided to take a taxi to a hotel on the southern end of town for lunch. The outdoor restaurant where we sat was decorated with carts of vibrant flowers. I glanced out towards the ocean. In the sky above the beach I could see a rainbow-hued parachute and coaxed Kim to walk towards it with me to check it out. Someone was parasailing! It looked like great fun and I offered to pay Kim's way if she wanted to try it as an early birthday present for her. At first she was hesitant. Suddenly, she shrugged her shoulders and smilingly said "what the heck" and proceeded to the harnessing area. At that moment, it became evident inside me that it was really *me* urging *me* to try it!

I watched Kim take off and sail above the turquoise waters. As I checked my wallet to see how much money I had left, I remembered that the young boys who ran the parasailing rides had said they didn't have any more change. I looked at the fifty-dollar bill in my hand, rubbing my forehead in thought.

As I stood there, blank as to what to do, my body trembled as I heard Bobby's voice saying: "Mom, this is *my* golden birthday present to you. Take *my* money and *come fly with me*!!"

I blinked my eyes in disbelief as I remembered the money that had belonged to Bobby when they had brought his body down from Mt. Shasta. It had been hidden away in a secret place in my wallet. I'd forgotten all about it after promising myself that I'd *know* when it was the right occasion to spend it. Flying high with Bobby—of course, *this was it*!

Pulling the money out of its hiding place, I walked over to the fellows that harness you into the parachute and asked if they could harness me up even though I was wearing a dress. They smiled and said "sure". I was carefully instructed on how to run along with the speedboat for takeoff and how to pull down on the strap of the parachute when the man in the speedboat pulling me blew his whistle. The second time he blew the whistle, I was to release the strap and float down to my landing spot on the beach.

I started running as instructed. The speedboat took off to sea like a shot, quickly taking up the slack in the tow rope. As the ocean and I were about to have a confrontation, my feet lifted off the ground and I was flying, climbing higher and higher. What a thrill! I could hear Bobby talking to me, and as I sailed high above the water, I had an inkling of why birds sing. The temperature up here

"Come Fly with Me"

was delightfully balmy and the views of the sea and swimming-pooled villas hiding away in this tropical setting were spectacular from this high place. I found myself singing, laughing, and crying all in the same moment. My experience, as I circled and sailed swiftly above all my eyes surveyed, was a distinct experience of being a *spirit* housed in a physical body, not vice-versa.

The second whistle sounded as I released my parachute strap and began floating down towards the beach. Two young Mexican boys were waiting to help break the impact of my landing. Wow! Such a birthday present!

GRACIAS, BOBBY, MUCHAS GRACIAS!

TEACHER/TOOL

Talking To God Directly

Ask, and it shall be given to you;
Seek, and you shall find;
Knock, and it shall be opened to you.
For everyone who asks receives,
and he who seeks finds, and
to him who knocks, it shall be opened.

—*Matthew 7:7-8*

Somehow while growing up, I picked up the absurd notion that one had to be the Virgin Mary, Joan of Arc, a rabbi, or a priest to talk to God directly. You had to be one of His special chosen ones. I often wondered how one knew if he was a chosen one or not. Did God tattoo you with a rose labeled Special Person somewhere on your body for you to discover one day?

It never consciously entered my mind that God was waiting patiently, through eons of time, to talk to His children, each when he or she was ready. He had given each of us the gift of free will and patiently waited for us to discover that He was our source and ask for His guidance. That process could vary a *lot* from individual to individual. For me, I came to Him through the "school of hard knocks". A crisis or tragedy had often times been the catalyst that brought me to my knees, to humbly and sincerely pray for assistance.

Weekly magazines like *The Enquirer,* with all its flashy gossip, ghoulish headlines, and sometimes questionable intentions, always had a strong thread of "miracle" stories running through the issues. One common denominator ran throughout the stories. A personal crisis had turned people to God for help because they felt helpless to do it "all by themselves". Whether they'd been cast adrift in a raft to survive the elements of sharks and sea, buried beneath an avalanche, attacked by a giant bear or man-eating tiger, they had called upon God, *asking* and *seeking.*

In my own search, I discovered that God was always there; His spark of divinity dwelled deep within each one of us. One must silence the chatter of his own mind to hear and be guided by the voice within. He longs to assist us in our journey. I realized that though I had often prayed, I had missed the other equally important part of the process: being still long enough to hear the answers.

When I first started meditating it seemed like an impossible task to quiet my mind. In fact, a small sense of terror would come upon me when I would sit and try to discipline my mind to be still. Transcendental Meditation (meditating with a mantra) helped me get the hang of it. Sometimes, I used a mantra; sometimes, I went through the colors of the rainbow with Alexander Everett's "Centering with Flute Music" cassette tape; at other times, I felt innovative and made up a meditation ritual for the day spontaneously as it came to me.

One of the things that most fascinated me was the challenge of discovering my "divine plan". Buried deep within us, we all have something in particular we came here to do. In my experience, it laid hidden amongst the things we do that make us happiest. God's divine plan for each one of us brings out our very best loving and creative energies. If we don't *love* what we do, it might be best to go out in nature and be quiet for a while. If we ask sincerely to be guided and we listen to the gentle signals, we will be led. Our divine plan will unfold, a step at a time, before our very eyes. It will be the kind of thing we love to do so much, we'd gladly pay to be able to do it.

Whatever the method of "be still and know that *I am God*", I have had conversations in my head or out loud with Him regularly. It used to be only about *big* things. Now I ask His advice on the shortest and best way to go somewhere, to bless my car each day before I start it, and to guide my thoughts, deeds, actions, and reactions, ad infinitum. Life gets simpler as you sensitize yourself and learn by experience how God sends His answers to *you*. We are each unique! Trust the inner voice, express gratitude for all you receive and have courage and patience. It's called "the Walk of Faith", or "Let Go and Let God".

A supportive system I have used consists of two plastic sweater boxes labeled God's "In" Box and God's "Out" Box. In the "In" Box I collect inspiring quotes and notes, cards, and letters from loving friends. On a low day, I sit with my "In" Box and bathe myself in its messages.

In my "Out" Box are reminders to send notes, books, cards, and any other thing I feel inwardly directed to reach out and send to others. After a quiet meditation time, I often feel like a steno that God sends goodies through. It may be a congratulatory note to new grandparents; a book or inspirational poem to a newly divorced or hurting friend; a few dollars to that child on the late news broadcast who needs financial support to have a life-saving heart transplant; adopting a hungry foster child in some faraway land; a jellybean card to the President of the United States when he has done something wonderful for a bereaved family (heaven knows, he gets enough of the other kind of mail!); a flower to a friend, or better still, a perfect stranger, for no particular reason at all. This "Out" Box is the place from which my own creative ideas can scatter seeds of compassion, support, and love out into the world.

The busier my God's "Out" Box, the richer and happier my life!

294

Freedom Day

In the future days, which we seek to make secure, we look forward to a world founded upon four essential freedoms. The first is freedom of speech and expression—everywhere in the world. The second is freedom of every person to worship God in his own way—everywhere in the world. The third is freedom from want... The fourth is freedom from fear.

—Franklin Delano Roosevelt

A newly hung "Sold" sign decorated the signpost in front of my house. Freedom at last! It had been a long ten-month process during which the condo had originally sold for cash, only to have the offer withdrawn at the last minute. My disappointment plummeted me to a low I hadn't known for a long time. I used it to reflect like a mirror what possible commitment in my life I wasn't living up to, and I didn't like what I saw. It had to do with a commitment to Bobby and God about writing a book that had been sitting untouched on my desk for some time. I was torn by the battle to support myself financially and the part of me that was learning to walk the path of faith and do what I knew my inner guidance was urging me to do—isolate myself and write.

There were times when fear wanted to take hold of my life and its terrorist energies seemed to have a stranglehold on me. How was I going to keep up on all my payments and write, too? My sister, Vickie Kovisto, knew of my inner conflicts and handed me a book. She felt spiritually guided to give me *Hinds' Feet on High Places* by Hannah Hurnard. It was a story, in allegory form, about Miss "Much-afraid" and the fears that came upon her to distract her from following the Shepherd to High Places. The book was a life preserver for me, thrown to keep me from drowning in a sea of new fears. I could see more clearly now that the fears I had created were a test of faith. Though my financial path for the next few months was still unclear, I chose to commit more time to writing my book and asked God to please let me know when I needed to go out and find a "regular nine-to-five" job. For four long months, I walked the narrow path of faith, a moment at a time, trusting that God was leading me every step of the way and that all my needs would be met.

Once I committed fully, unseen forces guided assistance my way at every turn of the road and most wondrous things began happening. Miracles of faith came to me, money to make it through yet another month. Out of a valentine card fell a check from my friend Sabrina Lee. It was a "love loan", without interest, to pay the mortgage on the house for the month of February.

My friend Bill Orlich kept the refrigerator well stocked and Valentyne's gas tank filled, as well as taking over some of my monthly financial obligations. Greg, my son, sent me a check from some of the money he had stashed away for his next semester of Chiropractic school.

A beautiful rainbow card that said "Follow your Dreams!" arrived along with a cashier's check from Kimberly. She said she believed in my dreams and wanted to help out.

A letter from Laura said it was a privilege for her to be able to support me "for a change." Would I please feel free to use the monthly

Air Force allotment checks she was sending me to save for her in any way that would assist me. "Finish your book Mom; a pair of 'angel wings' for your heart await you when you're done!" Laura saw the "angel wings" as a touchstone symbol from Bobby for the completion of the book.

Many times I was overwhelmed with the touching tributes of support from my family and friends. Julie Traynor presented me with another "love loan" to tide me through until escrow closed on my now-sold home.

From that little girl Shirley who could do everything by herself and never wanted to depend on others for anything, I'd come a long way. Humbly and with gratitude, I had learned to *receive*.

Anticipating the sale of the house at any moment, I'd long begun the selling or giving away of most of my material belongings. Finding "loving" homes for things I no longer wanted to lug around or store was fun. When I visited my friends, I could also "visit" things that had at one time been important in my life.

The big day of escrow closing finally came and I had a ball depositing the money and sending thank you notes with hearts all over them, along with checks that said "Thank you, God" under my signature. I paid off every single financial obligation I had in the world. What an incredible feeling of freedom!

Now it was time to pull together another dream, the one Laura and I had been holding in our hearts for over a year. It was for the two of us to have a reunion in Europe while she was still stationed in West Germany. It hadn't come together last year as we had originally hoped. Now it *was* the right time and everything was quickly falling into place. The "divine" timing was ever so evident as cancellations opened up for us, air fares magically reduced, and all signals were *go*!

Laura's schedule suddenly changed and I was left with a two-week block of time and no itinerary for it. A casual remark from a friend suggested I go to Egypt. She thought the high cheekbones of my face were definitely reminders of a past-life Egyptian heritage. Later that evening, I randomly opened my TWA book of tours. It opened to a tour named "Wonders of Antiquity," a two-week odyssey through Egypt and the Holy lands. My body chilled endlessly. So be it, Egypt and Israel, here I come!

My friends were almost as excited as my traveling companion Sabrina Lee and I were. Suzie Friedenthal called to set a date for a *bon voyage* lunch. Some of our male friends wanted to be included and lunch turned into a full-blown Fourth-of-July freedom party. Don Presson donated his top-of-the-hill home in Sausalito and Suzie, the party giver of party givers, began in earnest to create a party I would never forget!

The ballooned signs coming off of Highway 101 into Sausalito said "Park Here for Shuttlebus to Shirley's Party." It was quite a mind-blowing sight as we pulled off the freeway past the parking lot. At the front door to Don's place sat a life-size Uncle Sam with helium balloons in his hands. The entrance "ticket" to this party was a hat each of us had created that symbolized what freedom meant to us.

Such fun! I helped Sabrina Lee create hers—a long-haired china doll in a golden bikini. Beside her was a "treasure chest" of goodies. I thought long and hard about what freedom really signified for me. Right, now it looked like travel and opportunities to write when I pleased.

A trip to the local Buzy Bee hobby shop and some assistance from a wonderful lady named Dennie helped my freedom hat materialize. I spray-painted a straw hat blue and made an angel-haired "Mt. Shasta" to occupy the crown of the hat. A miniature angel with harp and crystal heart symbolized the spot where Bobby's plane was found. In front of it lay a book, a miniature of what *Journey to High Places* looked like in my fantasies. Over the mountain, flying on its pipe-cleaner base, was a golden airplane. Around the brim of the hat were miniature flags of the nations I planned to visit along with tiny trains, planes, boats, camels, skis, a see-through suitcase filled with goodies, and a miniature gold-leafed Bible. When I looked at it, the hat about said it all for me.

Dr. Tolleth showed up in a huge seagull hat carved out of white styrofoam. Elegant staircase's-to-heaven, travel tickets, and every other imaginable freedom to do what one most wanted to do in life paraded themselves around the room in the form of a hat. Everyone had come dressed in red, white, and blue attire and energies were flying high in Sausalito.

As each guest entered, they were handed a sheet of paper on which he was to complete the thought: "When I think of Shirley,

_____.'' What a gift of love Suzie gave when she handed me the box of love tokens from my dearest friends. The Shakespeare saying, "I am wealthy in my friends" was so true.

Since then, I've often used the idea to communicate to special people in my life what I think of when I think of them. It's a unique and thoughtful gift.

Guests took turns being video taped in their fantasy hats and speaking into the camera, accompanied with a lot of clowning around. When Suzie wants someone in her life to know how special they are to her, you *know*! Late in the evening she had everyone hold hands and form a huge circle that wove through two rooms. Lights were dimmed as she put a candle in my hand and lit it. From my lighted candle she lit hers and spoke a message of love and acknowledgment to me. Around the room the ceremony went, candles were lit and acknowledgments received. I noticed there was almost a limit as to how much ecstasy I was prepared to let in and absorb. I kept taking deep breaths, allowing myself to be saturated with the love and high energies flowing here tonight. What a send-off! This year, the Fourth of July fireworks were exploding in my filled-to-capacity heart. What a celebration and how blessed we all are to live in a country that takes a day each year to celebrate its most precious of gifts—*freedom*!

39

TRAVEL

Egypt

The World is my Country
All Mankind are my Brethren,
and to do good is My Religion.

—*Thomas Paine*

The July full moon shone over the Land of Pyramids when Sabrina Lee and I arrived. I had to pinch myself to believe I was really here. From the balcony of our hotel room, I could meditate and then open my eyes and gaze directly upon the Great Pyramid of Cheops. As the sun set and marked the end of our first full day in the Land of the Nile, it silhouetted the majesty of the Pyramids of Giza against a clear and brilliant apricot-and crimson Egyptian sky. It was a glorious backdrop for the Sound and Light Show being presented at the foot of the Great Sphinx.

We toured the city of Cairo; the ancient capital of Egypt, Memphis; and the early Step Pyramids. We really lucked-out with tour guides. We got a high-energied beautiful blonde Australian lady, Judi Bergengren. Her foreign country expertise started showing itself the moment she first met us and facilitated our entrance past the burly gun-toting Egyptian guards at the airport, without delay or incident. Her accent was delightful as was her sense of humor. Judi strongly advised us to drink bottled water only and *not* to eat *any* raw fruits or veggies. Sabrina and I listened. Others on our tour, to their deepest regret, did not.

A dinner cruise on The Nile Pharaoh took us to see Cairo from a floating point of view on the Nile. An exotic belly-dancer finished her evening performance by spinning around the room with a fully lit-up candelabra on her head.

Sitting by the window, staring out onto the ancient Nile River, a sense of sadness swept over me. I had a conversation with God under my breath, asking if this trip was "just" a vacation or did it have some deeper spiritual purpose to it? Within a moment, the maitre d' came over and laid a red rose in front of me and the band started playing an American song, "Tie a Yellow Ribbon Round the Old Oak Tree." The *synchronicity* of receiving my favorite flower, a red rose, and the song that was being played at the same time, made me shudder with massive chills. The weekend we were searching for Bobby's downed plane at Mt. Shasta we had all been wearing yellow ribbons, and the song was very familiar as it was played to welcome home the newly freed Iranian hostages. A red rose and one American song. A wild coincidence?

Hardly, Shirley, this is *Egypt*, my inner voice whispered.

The next day it was time for a closer look at the Great Pyramid of Cheops, largest of the three Great Pyramids. Sabrina and I chose to ride camels there, hoping we wouldn't get an angry one like the one spitting green stuff at the lady ahead of us. I bought one of the Arab headdresses to keep my head from burning in the midday sun. The Arabs knew what they were doing in wearing those white pieces of cloth; I felt degrees cooler the moment I put it on. We were told that we could climb to the inner chamber of the Great Pyramid if we were in good health, without back problems, and nonclaustrophobic.

Our guide appeared to be a very old man. I wondered how he could make the climb if it were such an athletic adventure, particularly in the high temperatures of a July day on the desert. I needn't have worried about the old man. It was Shirley who was huffing and perspiring as she climbed the uphill ramplike path, bent over, to the inner chambers of the Pyramid.

Every once in a while, the old man would stop his climb to look down the dimly lighted ascent path to see how we were doing. As I looked up at him, my eyes could not believe what they were seeing. Where his eyes should be, two long shafts of light were shining. I blinked twice thinking my eyes were playing tricks on me. Did all of our eyes look like that here inside the Great Pyramid, or was this "guide" somebody special?

There wasn't time to ponder on it much as we were approaching the inner chamber of Cheops' Great Pyramid, complete with sarcophagus and ventilation shafts. I listened to what our guide was saying as I arched my back, glad to be standing fully upright once again. The guide walked over to our group, singling me out and took me by the hands. I followed, wondering what he was doing. He led me to a certain spot in the chamber and adjusted where I stood until he was satisfied. Then he made two sweeping motions with both hands at the same time, as if he were drawing a large cross directly in front of me. He smiled and told me I was now "centered" in the Power Point of the Universe.

I bowed graciously as I thanked him, gazing deeply into his eyes, searching to see if there was anything unusual about them. A surge of powerful physical energy passed between us and the next thing I knew, we were hugging one another and doing a rocking back-and-forth dance around the center of the pyramid. A high voltage kind of energy was going through my body the whole time and I wondered who this "Holy Man" really was. No matter; I intuitively *knew* I had received a welcome and a blessing from him.

An overnight train ride beside the Nile River took us into riverside Luxor for a full day's look at the well-preserved temples and tombs of the Valley of Kings. By the time we reached King Tut's Tomb, I was glad Hollywood makeup man Marv Westmore's wife

302

The Great Pyramid and the Holy Man

had shared one of her secrets for staying cool on a hot movie set. She had had a lot of experience in hot locales while filming "MASH" episodes for TV. Joyce Westmore (aka Jennifer Davis) told me to mix some Sea Breeze Antiseptic with water and put some cloths rung out with the solution on the back of my neck or on my wrists. It worked and I also filled a small sprayer bottle with the solution and went around "blessing" members of our TWA group with a spritz of spray here and there. July was probably *not* the most comfortable time of the year to be traipsing around the deserts of Egypt.

A trip to the Khan-el-Khalili bazaar to shop for cartouches and custom-made garments of Egyptian cotton filled in the odd hours between touring temples, pyramids, and the Egyptian Museum, which houses the golden treasures of King Tut. It was extremely hot and stifling as Sabrina and I walked through the Museum. Maybe I was oversensitized, but the "vibes" of the Tut exhibit and feelings of *déja vu* made me weak in the knees. Wow—powerful history we were surrounding ourselves with—small wonder!

Our week passed quickly. It was time to head for Israel by air-conditioned motorcoach, via the Suez Canal. My body started getting weird sensations as we waited for the ferry to take our bus across the Canal. I couldn't explain it; I just wanted *out* of there. Days later we heard that mines had been discovered there shortly after we had passed through. It validated trusting my feelings and intuition.

Getting out of Egypt was no simple deal. One went through a long tiring process in Egypt, walked through a neutral zone, and then went through security on the Israeli side. We had to change buses, as neither our Egyptian bus or driver were allowed to accompany us into Israel.

We were getting quick lessons in security and political policies I'd only viewed in TV newscasts or in the movies before this trip. Watching petite blonde Judi deal with all the challenges traveling in a foreign land could conjure up, I was extremely grateful that she was leading the group. It was not an experience I would relish going through alone.

The experience with my "Holy Man" in the inner chamber of the Great Pyramid stood uppermost in my mind as I said "Goodbye" to Egypt. The mystery and stories about it fascinated me. When it was time for me to know, I knew I would understand more about what connection the Pyramids of old and I had with one another.

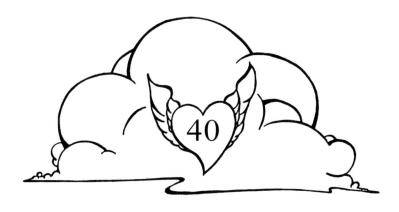

TRAVEL

Israel

God brings men into deep waters,
not to drown them, but to cleanse them.

—Aughey

The moment I crossed the Neutral Zone between Egypt
and Israel and saw a beautiful yellow flower blooming in a pot on the
hot desert floor, I knew I'd entered the Holy lands. For no apparent
reason tears flowed down my cheeks. I could *feel* the love vibration
here, and so much more. My deep feelings were instant, irrevocable,
and unexplainable. Given my mostly nonreligious upbringing and
the fact that I'd never before seemed even remotely interested in
coming to Israel, I *knew* I had been divinely guided to "come back"
to the Promised Land. Profound moments of *déja vu* and spiritual

stirrings were to be commonplace on my odyssey here and I knew it the moment my feet stepped onto the soil where many of the great religions of the world had found their origins.

It was great to be able to eat fruits and vegetables again and not worry about what we could drink. Iced tea and cold juices were a welcome shift from the very limited diet of Egypt. On the way into Israel, I had my first glimpse of the beautiful turquoise blue waters of the Mediterranean. They were a sharp and welcome contrast to the multi-colored golden sands of the Sinai Desert.

Our first stop was the bustling city of Tel Aviv. There we visited the Shalom Tower and the Old Jaffa's artist colony. That evening, Sabrina Lee and I walked from our hotel to the beach for our first Mediterranean sunset. Families were gathered on the beach, having supper picnics. I could sense the preciousness of freedom here and the privilege it was to gather with loved ones in peace.

The next evening we went to a nightclub to catch dinner and the colorful folk-song stage show. It was easy to overeat; everything tasted so good and it seemed so long since I'd had a several-course dinner. *Big* mistake! The next thing I knew dancers from the show were pulling me and a few others on stage to join them. The orchestra started playing "Hava Nagilah" and we danced, faster and faster, until I was on the verge of losing my dinner. I hadn't physically exerted myself that much since climbing the Pyramids and had to do some deep breathing before regaining a quieter pulse rate.

A drive north along the coast, took us to the seaside Roman ruins of Caesarea and its amphitheater with amazing acoustics. We traveled on by motorcoach to the Sea of Galilee and Nazareth's Basilica of Annunciation. Here I was walking in the footsteps of the Bible and world history that had been mostly names on pages before this trip. Sometimes my head would start spinning with light spells of dizziness because there was so much sensory input coming into me.

Our TWA guide Judi was with us overseeing the entire two-week tour, with local tour guides coming in to assist her on special segments. As our trip progressed in Israel, Judi introduced us to our Israel tour guide, an American lady named Susan, who now made Israel her home. Judi had worked with lots of guides over the years, wherever her tours took her, but she told me that she had never had a guide like Susan before. Susan had to have been *divinely* assigned to what she was doing. You could feel the intense love she had for this land—it came across powerfully.

Our TWA "family" had been traveling together for ten days now. Often we had arisen at odd hours or early (3 AM!) to cross deserts in the coolness of the night and early day, staying up late to explore wherever we landed for the evening and generally living each moment to the hilt. As I looked in the motorcoach around me, most all of my "Antiquity" buddies were asleep.

We were fast approaching the city of Jerusalem when Susan took the bus microphone in hand, *commanding* everyone to wake up! It would have been a perfect time to have a cassette recorder. The words Susan spoke escape me but the intensity of the emotions she stirred up were evident in the teary eyes of everyone on the bus. This lady knew how to awaken the deepest spiritual seeds that might be lying dormant within each of us. She was adamant that *no one* sleep through the sacred experience of entering the Holy City of Jerusalem.

My teary eyes didn't dry out for long in Israel. Everywhere I went I had to take in and release several deep breaths to keep my self emotionally and physically centered. We walked through the Old City of Jerusalem to the Mosque of Omar (Dome of the Rock). The blue tile on its exterior was exquisite and I recognized its huge golden dome from pictures I'd seen of Jerusalem. I felt comfortable being on my knees there praying to God in my own way.

As I approached the Wailing Wall, I covered my head in respect for the Jewish people praying there. Walking up to the wall, I placed my forehead and both hands on it. A lot of sadness and prayer had been expressed here—the wall vibrated with centuries of it.

Nothing had prepared me for the intense emotion I felt as I walked the Via Dolorosa (Avenue of Sorrow) marking Jesus's route to Calvary and His crucifixion. I could feel Mother Mary's pain for what was happening to her beloved son Jesus, and I could feel my own pain rising from its hidden depths for the loss of my son, Bobby. I was walking the stations of the cross and I was *living* them as we arrived at the Church of the Holy Sepulchre.

Walking in the Garden of Gethsemane at the foot of the Mount of Olives, I sat and meditated. It was time to go within and be still. So much was happening so fast. After a long period of silence, I opened my eyes to view the magnificent old olive trees before me. Some of them have been there since the days of Jesus and I better understood the natural affinity I have always felt for the gnarled beauty of old olive trees.

An afternoon excursion took us to the Grotto of the Nativity in Bethlehem, Manger Square, and Rachel's tomb. Again my body was responding with recognition chills—none quite so strong as when I entered the spot where the Star of Bethlehem had shone at the time of Jesus's birth. It was now enshrined with a marble altar and candles. I stood there transfixed by the energy running through my body. A tap on the shoulder alerted me to a man standing next to me who asked if he could take a picture of me sitting on the marbled area of this most holy place. I handed him my camera with a word of gratitude and sat down. A feeling of absolute "blissed-outness" overcame me as I sat there, trancelike, having my picture taken.

Two months later when the pictures were developed, a wide shaft of mystical ruby light could be seen coming from above me, through my hands, and disappearing into the depths of the "Star of Bethlehem." Who could find words to explain it? Not me—the experience felt too ethereal to capture in words of physical dissection.

Back in my Jerusalem hotel room, awaiting my return, were a dozen red roses, gift wrapped, and surrounded by delicate white baby's breath. A card lying beside them simply said "Shalom." There was no signature or florist's mark on the card. The hotel staff was at a loss to explain who had sent them to me or put them in my room. Under my breath I gave thanks for the unexpected gift and the blessing I'd received at the Star of Bethlehem.

On one of our free days in Israel, many of us took a bus trip to Masada. On the way, we stopped and swam in the Dead Sea and several of our group got into taking a mud bath. It was hysterical. After every inch of us was covered with the dark Dead Sea mud, you couldn't tell our black friend Ed from the rest of us. Oh, if the whole world could be here, covering itself with black mud, maybe the lesson, "we are all the same in the eyes of God," would sink in.

Swimming in the Dead Sea was an unbelievable phenomenon. I couldn't sink if I tried. And I did try. One really could sit upon the waters and read a newspaper just like the pictures in my travel brochure.

The "Star of Bethlehem" Blessing

When we reached Masada, a ski-lodge-type cable car lifted us up, very near the top of the Masada plateaus. I had only briefly glimpsed the spectacle of Masada on a TV movie about its history, back in the States. It was a high place to stand on the edge of and view the Dead Sea and surrounding desert from.

A lady in our group became hysterical as she got off the cable car to begin the narrow staircase climb to the even higher plateau above us. Susan, our guide, intuitively sent her down on the next cable car, saying she had never seen anyone react quite like that. My little mind was busy wondering if the lady had been here in a past life or something as the things she was muttering while crying—about dying if she went near one particular cliff edge— would make much more sense if heard from that point of view.

On another free day, I figured out an Israeli bus schedule and took a bus out to Hadassah Medical Center to view the Chagall stained-glass windows that filled the Synagogue there with their magnificence. I hailed a cab to take me to Yad VaShem, the national memorial to the six million Jews who perished in Nazi-occupied Europe. As I viewed the large metal sculpture depicting the cruelties that had occurred, I wept with overwhelming compassion and made a commitment to use whatever gifts and talents I had to help world healing so that this kind of inhumanity to man by his brethren could never happen again. Even with my eyes closed in silent prayer, I could feel and see the Eternal Flame of Yad VaShem.

It was time to leave Israel and I wanted to stay on for a day or two longer. It would have been difficult to change our plans at this late date and definitely would have cost a lot more. Sabrina Lee laughed when our early morning flight to Athens, Greece bumped us. With apologies, we were driven by a Mercedes taxi to a beach side Tel Aviv hotel and put up for the night, all expenses paid by the airline. Ah, watch what you ask for in life, *you just might get it*. Shalom, Israel, Shalom!

TRAVEL

Greece

*I am a part of all
that I have met.*

—*Tennyson*, **Ulysses**

"It's Greek to me" took on a new meaning when Sabrina Lee and I bid *adieu* to Israel and flew to Athens, Greece. As we looked at the signs around us, we realized it would be difficult to try and sound out or fake a communication or two in Greek. I couldn't identify which letter some of the symbols represented. Communicating with taxi drivers began to have weird destination consequences, so whenever possible, we had someone write it out for us in Greek.

Athens was covered in a heavy layer of smog the day we arrived and checked into the hotel which was to be our home away from home

311

for the next ten days. It was the chosen spot for a rendezvous with my daughter, Laura. That everything was going our way became evident when the small room we thought we'd be sharing turned out to be a top-floor suite for the same price.

Our suite had a large living room, a bedroom with twin beds, a refrigerator, and a sizeable bathroom, complete with bidet. An extra bonus was the thirty-foot patio from which we could see the Acropolis and most of the City of Athens. It was a great place to discreetly hang up our mini-clotheslines and catch up on two weeks worth of laundry. A huge bathtub, the sun, and a playful breeze made the chore easy. The sun ironed our cotton clothes nicely. I liked Greece already. Its people were hospitable, taxis were reasonable, and so was the food. We settled in quickly. It would be a treat to unpack and spend ten whole days at the same "home base".

Sabrina and I had a few days to explore before Laura joined us. We took a one-day cruise to the islands of Aegina, Hydra, and Poros to get the hang of nautical feet before the big cruise we had booked began.

Restaurants were everywhere. We ate Greek salads until they came out of our ears. We checked out the Plaka and other recommended shopping areas and caught the Sound and Light Show at the Acropolis. Generally, we were enjoying life at a leisurely pace for a change.

Laura thought she was to take a taxi into downtown Athens and meet us at our hotel, but we surprised her at the airport. What a joyous reunion! I hadn't seen my "baby" for over a year. Her normally very blonde hair had darkened a bit with so little sun for the two years she had been in West Germany. She was slim, trim, and glowing. We kept shaking our heads, holding hands, and enjoying the precious time we had so long been planning by letter. Now sightseeing in Greece could begin in full gear.

We explored the Acropolis and Parthenon by day and by night. It really was a "most perfect poem in stone". It inspired awe from any perspective. At night we could see it from our hotel room veranda as it lit up with different lighting effects for the Sound and Light Show.

After seeing much of Athens, we boarded a bus and headed North for a day in Delphi. The spectacular classical beauty of

Delphi basked itself in the midday rays of the sun on the slopes of Mt. Parnassus. We found our way to the Kastalian Spring where we drank of its clean, clear waters and fully splashed our bodies as well. It is rumored that tasting her waters cleanses your soul. We all filled our mini-water bottles to take some home just to cover all the bases.

We headed seventy kilometers south of Athens the next day to spend the afternoon watching the sunset from Sounion, The Temple of Poseidon. The hour-and-a-half bus trip in each direction was worth it. From the renowned Temple you could see several islands scattered randomly in the blue waters of the Aegean Sea. As the fireball of golden sunlight sank into the water, the Temple pillars were silhouetted against sea and sky; it was just like a postcard. We stayed and drank in its beauty until darkness and the next bus came.

The next day it was time to be on the move again. We packed our things and headed for the harbor of Piraeus to board our cruise ship, the World Renaissance. Neither Sabrina, Laura, nor I had ever been on a cruise before and we were excited to be taking our maiden cruise here in the Greek Islands.

It was quite an adjustment for three of us to go from our large luxurious hotel suite to a triple accommodation aboard a ship. It became evident the first day that compromise would be necessary if the trip was to be equally enjoyable for all three of us. The solution we found was to quit making plans as a group. We were each strong-minded and had our own ideas of how, where, when, and with whom we wanted to spend our precious Greek island times. Each of us had waited too long, come too far, and invested too much money not to have this "dream trip" be everything we'd imagined it could be.

Going our separate ways was a good solution; no one had to give up her individual style of enjoying things. Sabrina would go out with a group and tour by bus and Laura met up with some kids her age and viewed the Islands by mini-bikes and jeep.

I managed to find ideal companions for the day, share a Mercedes taxi and driver, and go by intuition after that. The neatest part about it was we always, island by island, ended up with the "perfect" driver, seeing twice as much as we would have on any bus tour, and geared precisely to what we wanted to see and when we wanted to see it. Ironically, our tour cost about half the price of the chartered bus tours.

Life aboard ship was just as depicted on the TV show "The Love Boat". There was an overabundance of scrumptious foods always available. Self-discipline, Shirley, self-discipline or your clothes won't fit for long. The most important thing to remember on this cruise was your *landing tag number.* Each passenger was assigned a tag with his number on it and they were placed in numerical order on the Landing Tag Board. You removed your tag whenever you left ship and replaced it immediately upon your return. This ensured the crew that everyone was aboard before sailing time. Not following this procedure impeccably could mean being left behind or holding up the ship's scheduled departure. The former would not make the left-behind passenger very happy; the latter could be embarrassing as your name was paged over the ship's intercom and the departure of a whole ship-full of passengers and crew awaited your being found. One could see how playing the Landing Tag game correctly served everyone. Landing Tag 157 and I quickly became bosom buddies.

Our first stop was the island of Santorini. Laura and I were on the 7 AM tender, a small boat taxiing passengers from ship to shore and vice versa. Once ashore, we had the choice of a cable car lift to the top of the cliffs or riding a donkey up the long steep trail.

We chose the donkey ride. As we climbed higher and higher on the mile-high ascent to the tiny village of Thera, a wall about four feet high kept us from falling onto the rocky ledges bordering the Aegean Sea below. A lady behind me started crying; a sense of panic overcame her when her donkey brushed against the wall. Mine had done the same thing and I noticed my palms were getting sweaty. Panic always spreads quickly and I knew I wanted no part of it so I started singing to my donkey to calm us both.

I laughed as I realized the song I was singing, "Hava Nagilah", was a song from Israel, not Greece. My memory bank was having a hard time recalling a Greek song. Giving up, the words to "If I Were A Rich Man" from *Fiddler on the Roof* came to me and I continued to serenade my donkey. At the top of the trek up the volcanic cliffs, a photographer snapped our pictures and an awesome Aegean panorama awaited us.

On the island of Crete, I had my first Mercedes taxi-tour adventure. New friends from Connecticut, Susan and Gary Kellman, and

"Donkey Serenade"

Joan Munsee, and another taxi load of fellow travelers, joined us on this one. We laughed all afternoon. Our driver, Georgios, kept us entertained as he told us jokes, reviewed the history of Heraklion's frescoed Palace of Knossos, and took us on a vineyard road where he pulled over and picked us each a bunch of ripe grapes from the heavily laden vines. Georgios thoroughly enjoyed life on this beautiful island.

He took us to the "Zorba the Greek" grave site and to a beautiful Greek Orthodox Church. There, he bought each of us a candle to light. Lighting candles in special places had become a ritual for me. On every opportunity throughout Egypt, Israel, and now Greece, candles had been lit for each member of my family and for a number of close friends spiritually connected to the journey I was taking. As I looked down at the gold chain around my neck, I could feel their presence and love. Kathryn Davi-Billeci's crucifix and a cross from Suzie Friedenthal were hanging on gold chains which also displayed an "OM" medallion and a fourteen-karat-gold replica of the Chinese symbol for love. In Egypt I had added a golden ankh. My find in Israel was a diamond-cut heart of gold. Within it was the Star of David. Often I would be asked about my religion and it became crystal clear to me that I was part of *all peoples* and *all religions.* My body had chilled when high above the world on the cliff sides of Santorini I sat and wrote how I felt:

> And I saw the world
> through the peoples
> and religions
> of many lands.

> What I saw was each
> Man's ETERNAL QUEST for
> FREEDOM, PEACE, ACCEPTANCE,
> SELF-REALIZATION and LOVE.

The ship's "Daily Programme" was invaluable for keeping track of what was going on shipside and what time to disembark or return to the ship. On this particular morning, my turn was last for using the bathroom. Sabrina and Laura had already departed when I finished showering. As I left ship, there was no one in sight. Everyone aboard had already left on excursions for the day. I felt left behind. Knowing that everything always works for the best even when I can't see it, I started having a conversation with God.

"What magical adventure do You have in store for me today?" I questioned as I started wandering along the pier on the island of Rhodes.

No sooner had I asked, than I turned a corner and ran into a couple I recognized from our ship, Gene Vaughn and Ann Vitiello. I had seen them dancing the evening before at the ship's tavern and had gone over to compliment them on their great dancing style. Now, they were inviting me to share their adventure for the day, complete with Mercedes taxi and driver.

"Yes, I'd be delighted!" I answered, giving silent thanks to God as well.

Our driver, Achilles, was about as handsome a man as one could ask to see and equally as personable and nice. He took us through the Palace of Knights and stopped along the coast so I could climb up on Katrina, the much-photographed camel, to have my picture taken. We were speeding along to the seaside community of Lindos when I spotted and remarked on the gorgeous tan of a brown bikini-clad blonde on a mini-bike. It was Laura! I yelled "Hi!" and waved as we passed her. Our arrangement to go our separate ways was working well today.

A short period of time had been allowed for us on the island of Patmos to visit the Monastery and the Grotto of St. John. Only the very committed were up early enough this particular morning to catch the 7:00 AM tender to shore. Susan and Gary Kellman, Joan Munsee, and myself hailed a cab to take us up the steep hill to the monastery. Inside it were some of the most beautiful jeweled crosses and crowns I'd ever seen.

We walked down the hill quickly, as time was precious and we wanted to visit the Grotto of St. John. It was here that St. John wrote the Book of Revelations. As we entered, a service was going on and it appeared we were being invited to partake of Communion. I gratefully accepted, and afterwards, we hurried to catch the last tender back to our ship.

Our next tour was to Kudasi, Turkey, and a trip to Ephesus. By the time we arrived, I almost missed a good thing. I had been traipsing through ruins of all descriptions from Egypt to Israel to Greece for the past several weeks and I was about "ruined"-out! A remark someone made about Ephesus being special changed my mind and the "four musketeers"—Gary, Susan, Joan, and myself—were off on another adventure. Again we were blessed, we got on the right bus—the only one that had air-conditioning.

Ephesus had once been the leading city of culture and religion in ancient Asia. Now, she was the most complete city ever excavated, made almost exclusively of marble. As Joan and I walked through the city, complete with the Library of Hadrian, a 25,000-person amphitheater, and a bordello, I could image vividly in my mind what this city must have looked like in its ancient glory. If I hadn't lived here in a past life, it must have been someplace that rivaled the regal beauty I saw before me now. "Confirmation chills" validated my thoughts and were a welcome visitor to my hot and sunburned body.

Back on ship, we sailed for Istanbul, 326 sea miles away. It was a change of scene to be at sea for twenty-four hours—we had time to sunbathe, visit with new-found friends, and play "Trivial Pursuits".While having a good time on deck, the word reached us that Actor Richard Burton had died in his Celigny, Switzerland, home. Leaving my group, I climbed to the top deck of the ship. I said a prayer for Richard's soul and silently stood there, contemplating the transition we call death, staring at the sea for a long, long time. The next thing I remembered hearing was a voice on the ship's speaker announcing we were now passing through the Bosporus, the natural channel which separates Europe from Asia.

After a Grand Buffet dinner that exhibited the chef's greatest culinary creations, I went back up on deck. We were coming into the Port of Istanbul, moments before sunset. Such a sight—the mosques and minarets of Istanbul were framed by the sparkling sea and a sky aflame with sunset hues.

Laura and I, as well as shipmate friends Jennifer Libbee and Bruce Cook from Los Angeles, again "lucked out" with the bus we'd chosen. Of the five buses carrying passengers from our ship, we were the only one that had the privilege of officially crossing over on the Istanbul Bosporus Bridge, the link between the two continents of Asia and Europe. The bridge looked very much like its twin sister,

318

the Golden Gate Bridge in San Francisco. Once on the Asia Minor side of the city, our driver took us to the highest spot, Camlica Hill, to view a most spectacular panorama, the Bosporus, quietly reflecting the twinkling night lights of Istanbul.

At a Turkish nightclub we were wined and entertained. The table Laura, Jenny, Bruce, and I were sitting at included a pretty blonde lady I had met taking communion at the Grotto of St. John. She introduced herself as Susan Wolf. Her husband, Werner Wolf, the well-known ABC sports commentator, pretended being shocked at the slithering behavior of a belly dancer while the club photographer snapped our pictures.

Touring the city full of magnificent mosques was a treat for the eyes, as we visited the Blue Mosque and St. Sophia's. By the time we reached Topkapi Palace and viewed its priceless riches, I was in a state of overwhelm. It was difficult to conceive of that much beauty and wealth. Thrones, crowns, daggers, pencil boxes, cups, and every other conceivable item were made of gold or silver and almost totally embroidered and embedded with diamonds, rubies, emeralds, and pearls of every size and description. Seeing the "Diamond of Kasikci" (eighty-six carats) stirred recollections of a suspenseful jewel robbery movie named *Topkapi.*

Then, if all that hadn't blown our minds, our trip to the Grand Bazaar would! Gary, Susan, Joan, and I agreed to stay near the main street of the several hundred shops in the Bazaar. Aboard ship we had been advised not to go there or at to least be careful as one could easily get lost in the labyrinth of tunnels, arcades, and courtyards which could take several days to shop. Joan and I separated from Gary and Susan and started making the rounds of leather and jewelry shops. Our Greek drachmae got tucked away while Turkish lira replaced it for the day. It was mind-boggling to comparison shop and then try to find a particular store you wanted to go back to. I hadn't purchased much before this, but here the temptation was too great. I'd just have to buy another suitcase and ship it home when we returned to Athens.

The last day of the cruise was spent in the friendly, international jet-set atmosphere of Mykonos. Walking along the sun-drenched beaches was quite different from home. Here in Mykonos, topless sunbathing was very much an "in" thing to do. Cubical whitewashed

319

houses and picturesque windmills dotted the landscape along with Paraportiana, said to be one of the most-photographed chapels in the world. The narrow, attractive passageways led to endless boutiques and chapels. Now and then I would see a familiar face from the ship, but mostly this was a cherished opportunity for me to wander alone by foot, taking in the Mediterranean beauty that surrounded me.

It was time to get back to the small pier and await a tender to take me back to our ship. As I was waiting, Bruce and Jenny appeared, wanting to take Laura and I to dinner here in Mykonos on the last night of our cruise. Laura hadn't been seen in hours so we decided to have dinner right near the pier so we could watch for her. Dinner was delicious and so was the sunset. It was time to catch the last tenders back to ship. Bruce said he would stay on shore a little longer and wait for Laura.

Back on ship I was getting a little nervous. By now, everyone aboard was time and landing tag conscious and not about to hold up the comings and goings of a whole ship and crew. I walked back down to the landing tag board. Many of the hooks were still empty. Wherever Laura was, she must have a few friends with her.

Finally, a tender returned with its load of "late" passengers. They had been eating dinner in a small hidden-away cafe when all the lights in town went out. It had taken them quite some time to find their way, in the dark, out of the labyrinth of narrow streets, back to where a bus could transport them to the pier. I breathed a sigh of great relief as we headed for the ship's Main Lounge. We had just enough time to exchange addresses and goodbyes with the many new friends we'd made.

Back in Athens again, Sabrina was not feeling well after a solid month of being on the road. She felt a strong urge to return home. That left me with the choice of either going on to Italy alone, returning home myself, or following Laura back to West Germany when she returned to Air Force duty.

I sat quietly reading my Unity's *Daily Word* and proceeded to consider my options, one by one. I knew I did not want to travel through Italy by myself, nor was I excited about cutting my trip short and going home early. The next step was to cancel my flight and hotel in Rome. That was no easy task. Using a phone in Greece and connecting with a hotel in Rome was a monumental task. I finally gave up and took a taxi to the nearby Holiday Inn and did it in person through the hotel telex.

Tiredness was setting in as Laura and I talked about what to do next. We walked over to an airline to see if there was space for me on the same flight Laura was booked on to return to West Germany in five days. There was!

We were making progress and it felt like changing all my original plans was the perfect thing to do. We sat on our luggage, resting and wondering what we were going to do with the five days Laura had left of her military leave. We had had enough of Athens and all flights and accommodations on Corfu and some of the other islands we might want to visit were already overbooked. A bolt of inspiration hit Laura as she walked over to a gentleman standing behind the Traveler's Aid desk and said "Help!" He took an immediate liking to Laura after hearing her story and told her to sit down while he looked at what he could do for her.

Ten minutes later, Laura returned smiling, with a name and address written on a piece of paper.

"I don't have the slightest idea where we're going, but we don't have many other options and my friend over there said 'trust me' as he wrote down this address. We're always divinely guided anyway, Mom, so let's get a cab and 'jam'!"

We *had* been divinely guided. The little hotel was appropriately named Paradise Inn and again our room was much upgraded from the rate we were being charged and included a large marble-floored balcony. We quickly checked in and put on walking shoes to explore where we were. To our delight, we were in the magnificent resort spot of Vouliagmeni. We wandered down to the beach area and discovered a Windsurfing and Waterskiing School and quickly made friends with the owner, Elias. He liked us and invited Laura and I to use the school's private beach for our sunbathing.

Mickey, one of Elias' windsurfing instructors, introduced Laura to the sport. Watching her taking lessons convinced me it was something I could live without trying.

Our precious five days were golden ones of sunbathing and swimming; speedboat rides with Elias as he took Rex, his German shepherd, out to sea for his daily one-mile swim. It was a riot to watch. Elias would slow the boat down and Rex would take the cue and dive into the clear turquoise waters for his swim. He loved it!

Laura would sometimes take Rex's daily swim time as an opportunity to go along with us, being towed on water skiis. Her proficiency showed as she zig-zagged on one ski behind us.

By now we were getting very tan and very spoiled with the Greek hospitality Elias extended to us. He invited us to his private beach party to celebrate the August full moon. The whole beach area was lit with large votive candles sitting on the sand.

As the full harvest moon rose steadily in the sky, the spirited atmosphere of the lavish beach buffet grew. The speedboats took Laura and a few other game souls out on the bay to water ski by moonlight. At midnight, no matter the age or shape, everyone went for a midnight swim in the calm and warm moonlit waters, many *au naturelle*!

Back at our hotel, we'd sometimes catch glimpses of what was going on at the Olympics. It would be at odd hours, sometimes after midnight. What a weird sensation, watching and hearing the commentary in Greek. I had to really pay attention to catch a clue as to who was winning all the medals and for what. The atmosphere got highly excited when Greg Louganis won the gold medal in the diving events. Every man watching the games wanted to be sure I knew he was Greek and that the games wouldn't exist today if it weren't for the Greeks originating them. They were proud of their heritage and rightly so.

With one day in Greece left, Laura and I found our way to the oceanside of the bay where we could go parasailing. My experience parasailing in Puerto Vallarta with Kim had intrigued Laura and she wanted to try it, too. When we got there, the sea was too rough for the boats to take us up and out. We signed up anyway and waited.

Before long, the parachutes were laid out and Laura was being hooked up in the harness. As I looked around I realized that takeoff would be from the cement pier we were standing on.

"Where do we land?" I asked, remembering well the impact with which I landed on the sandy beach in Mexico. The fellow pointed at the water and I swallowed hard. If I hit the water with the same force as I had the beach... I quit thinking about it and watched Laura take off and circle over the sea. She landed in the water, unhooked the harness, and swam to where I was standing on the pier.

"That was dynamite!! YAHOO!!" was all she could say. "Your turn, Mom!"

I totally surrendered to the experience that was ahead, laughing as the harness was secured about me. I ran just a few steps before the chute lifted me high enough to see all the beach areas around me and clear over into Vouliagmeni Bay. It was no less exciting this time than it had been on my first flight. I felt no fear as I let go and arched my back like a gymnast in flight, fully surrendering to the forces of sun and wind. I floated down into the water, very gently entering it. It was even better than a beach landing! Freeing myself from the harness, I swam to shore. A grin of ecstasy spread over my face.

Finally, it was time to pick up our bags and head for the Athens Airport and our next destination: Frankfurt, Germany. Greece and her islands had been my home for almost a month now, and I'd grown to love and appreciate her warm, hospitable people and gorgeous scenery.

"Yassas, Greece, yassas, until we meet again!"

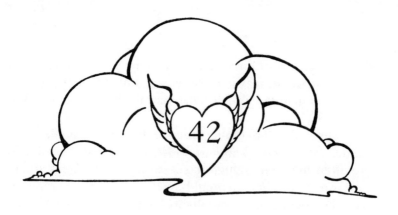

TRAVEL

Bavaria, Germany

*After silence, that which
comes nearest to expressing
the inexpressible is music.*

—Aldous Huxley

Our Lufthansa flight landed in Frankfurt, Germany, on time. What twist of fate had led me to cancel Italy and brought me here to Germany instead? The way my life had been so divinely guided, I was sure my question would reveal its own answer.

Laura and I were met at the airport by her Air Force friend, Jeffrey Hale. As we sped southwest in his car towards Zwiebrucken Air Force Base, it felt strange to be going so fast and still have cars passing us like we were standing still. Jeff explained there were no speed limits here. I kept seeing signs for "Ausfahrt" and remarked what a large town it must be.

"Mom, Ausfahrt in German means exit," Laura laughingly informed me.

"Time to shift gears one more time," I told myself. Egyptian pounds had given way to shekels in Israel, drachma in Greece, lira in Turkey, and marks in Germany. Sometimes my body would show its jet lag most when it was time to deal in a new currency or language. As I exchanged my American dollars for foreign ones, it struck me as funny that the oddly-colored pieces of paper had worth. A humorous new awareness about money having value only because you and I agree it does, came over me. The funny crinkled and torn piece of purple paper, appearing rather worthless to me, could in the right places, buy me a bus ticket or dinner. And if I were smart watching my exchange rates, the same American dollar could buy me more some days than others. This was a great time to be in Germany; the value of a U. S. dollar was at an all-time high—3.00 DM.

When we arrived at the Air Force Base, Laura got me a visitor's pass and there was a vacancy on base for me to stay at the Hill Top Hotel. It would do quite nicely as I checked around me—clean bathroom, large armoire for my clothes, and a television set where the characters spoke in English for a change. Jeff was my kind of guy—he had left a red rose in a bud vase, an orange Frangipani candle, and a bottle of Piesporter wine to welcome me to Germany. I rarely drink, but of all the liquor available, this was one of my favorites. We drank a toast to life bringing us more great reunions like this one.

The next morning, I *knew* why I'd come to Germany. Back in the States, when Sabrina Lee and I had been planning our original itinerary, my heart had been set on seeing the Passion Play at Oberammergau. The German play, depicting the last days and crucifixion of Jesus Christ, is performed only every tenth year. 1984 marked its 350th anniversary and it felt right for me to see it, especially after a spiritual journey through Israel. But no matter how hard I tried and which strings I tried to pull, my success rate for a ticket was zero. I had been disappointed but surrendered to the idea that "it wasn't meant to be, or it would have come together".

As we drove past the travel agency on base, I glanced up and looked at its marquee. Great emotion raced through me as I read it: "ONE CANCELLATION-PASSION PLAY-OBERAMMERGAU."

I told the travel agent that he had been saving that ticket just for me. He agreed. He told me he had been inundated with requests for tickets all summer but the play had been sold out for quite some time. He had put the cancellation notice up three days ago and had not had one single inquiry. Of course not, I smiled inwardly, *knowing* very well that this ticket had been *divinely* reserved for me.

Late the next evening I boarded a bus headed for Oberammergau and the "Fairy Tale Castle of Neuschwanstein", smiling at the precise split-timing that had brought me on this adventure. I was grateful and didn't even mind sitting up in a bus all night. My body was signaling me that it had not yet adjusted to the cool dampness of the German weather—such an abrupt change from the other countries I'd visited. I knew my lunch break from the play would be spent shopping for a coat. The Passion Play is sung in German, so I bought the English translation text to follow along.

I sat waiting for the opening scene, reading about how the Passion Play had come to be. In 1633, the inhabitants of Oberammergau were dying in large numbers of the plague. Members of the village parish prayed to have the epidemic checked and made a vow to give the Passion Play every ten years if it stopped. The Chronicle of Oberammergau reports that, thereafter, no one died of the plague. One year later, in 1634, the promise was fulfilled and has been faithfully kept for three-and-a-half centuries.

When the sixty-five piece orchestra and forty-eight member mixed chorus began filling the large Passion Theatre with its splendid sounds, I knew I was in for a moving experience. The lady next to me saw the huge goosebumps on my arms and handed me a spare blanket she had been sitting on. Gratefully, I wrapped it around me, not wanting to be distracted from the play by an uncomfortably cold body. The part of the theater we were sitting in was covered, the stage area was not. Rightly so, as the trees and mountains surrounding us added a beautiful dimension to the pageantry on stage.

Many of the places I had visited in Israel came together sequentially in the two-part, five-and-a-half-hour play, stirring me constantly with its realistic majesty. It was a beautiful sequel to my own personal experiences of walking in Jesus's footsteps. The re-enactment of the Resurrection and Glorification of Christ scenes held me spellbound with their impact and I gave thanks to this little "Village under the Cross" for honoring a commitment made to God 350 years ago!

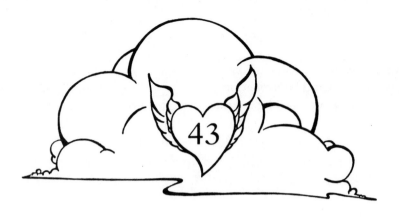

TRAVEL
Switzerland

*Though we travel the world over
to find the beautiful,
we must carry it with us or
we find it not.*

—*Ralph Waldo Emerson*

Traveling was becoming addictive. I was feeling more and more capable of handling anything that came up while living in foreign lands. For almost two months I'd been living life fully, moment by moment, willing to go wherever my intuition guided me. More often than not, life was full of quick changes in plans and unexpected blessings.

As soon as I returned from touring the beautiful countryside and castles of Bavaria, Germany, I repacked a small bag and headed by bus for a week in Switzerland. Quite gutsy now, I waved goodbye to Laura and Jeffrey as my late-night motorcoach headed southward on the Autobahn towards Lucerne, Switzerland.

It was getting colder as I watched the moon peek its crescent head up over the Alps. I was grateful for the wool loden-green hooded cape I had purchased in Oberammergau. It made a great blanket as I tried to find a comfortable position and catch some sleep, leaving the driving to an expert. If you could handle the discomfort of snoozing upright in a seat, it was a super way to cover a lot of kilometers, sleeping the night away.

We arrived in Lucerne in time for breakfast at our hotel. Wow! What else could I say as I took in the splendor of my surroundings. The boat on which I was riding toured the emerald and turquoise-green waters of Lake Lucerne and stopped at little villages along the shoreline. The flower beds bloomed extravagantly with brilliant color, and the surrounding mountains proudly displayed their grandeur. I sat in the back of the boat, letting the spraying waters refresh and bless me as we approached the docking area and headed back to the city.

The Chapel Bridge, bedecked with planters of flowers on both sides, was backdropped by Mt. Pilatus as we walked across it towards our hotel. A group of us had dinner at a local tourist nightspot where we heard yodeling and partook of the giant glass of beer being passed around. It was very touristy and *fun*.

A quick tour through Liechtenstein, Europe's tiniest principality, kept my camera busy after I finished waiting in line to have my passport stamped with the Royal Crown of Liechtenstein.

As we drove to the picturesque town of Appenzell, the lush green countryside never ceased to amaze me. It looked as if it had been freshly manicured this very morning, and the hills were alive with the sound of cowbells.

A day spent 7,000 feet above Lake Lucerne atop Mt. Pilatus treated me to an aerial cable ride that swung high enough to command a panorama of Switzerland all the way to the Black Forest. It also led to a breathtaking descent on the forty-eight percent grade of the steepest cog-wheel railway in the world. Whee!!

I was entranced immediately by the rich rosy-hued and gold-colored interior of the church at Einsiedeln and The Lady Chapel housing the Black Madonna. I'd seen many beautiful churches these past weeks, yet this one had a color vibration so high and warmly inviting that I felt like I had entered into the heart chamber of God Himself.

When some newly-made friends and I arrived in Interlaken, we were hungry and headed for a place Laura had recommended from her ski trips to the Alps. We found the Piz-Paz Restaurant and quickly devoured a large #16. She was right—it was the best seafood pizza I'd tasted in years. This famous health-resort city looked like a gateway to skier's heaven as I looked up at the Jungfrau and Eiger mountains in the distance.

The next two days were spent playing tourist in Berne, viewing the astronomical clock in the Clock Tower, the Bear pits, and the cathedrals of this capital city of Switzerland. The flavor of this city was a combination of bustle and charm, as the busyness of day settled into a peaceful atmosphere that led me walking the quaintly-lit streets late into the evening.

The stay in Zurich was brief, making possible a stopover at Rhine Falls on our return to Germany. By the time my new friend, Air Force Major Kathy Chalmers, and I had made our way to the falls, rain clouds and a hefty breeze were threatening to cancel any outdoor activities near the falls. In the center of the roaring waters of the fall, we could see a tiny pinnacle of an island, with a stairway leading to its top where a Swiss flag flew.

Making a split-second decision, we decided to go for it, take the small tourist boat to the middle of the turbulent waters, and climb to the top of the island. Meanwhile, the weather worsened. As our boat reached the island, the man who was in charge tried to keep the boat steady long enough for his passengers to disembark. He secured the front end of the boat and he thought the back was already secured when he told me to jump off and up to the ramp. I heard others in the boat yell at me not to jump but it was too late. I was already past the point-of-no-return! As I reached up to steady myself on the safety rails of the pier, the back of the boat slipped away, leaving me with nothing beneath me but the roaring waters of the falls. I pulled myself up with the help of people waiting on the island for the return boat to take them back to the mainland.

I normally carried my valuables in a totebag securely strapped on my shoulder at all times while traveling. This one time I had left the totebag with some people traveling with Kathy and me. Only my money, passport and camera were in my coat pocket. To my dismay, as I jumped from the boat, my camera, full of priceless photos of Mt. Pilatus and Interlaken, slipped into the turbulent waters of the fall.

At this point, I realized I had two choices. I could either be upset and let my beautiful trip be ruined, or I could be grateful I hadn't slipped into the waters, too. I chose the latter thought pattern. Given a choice, better my camera lost, than me or my passport.

On the bus heading for the Black Forest, I thought about what had happened and suddenly burst out laughing. A little voice within me was busy chattering, "Be careful what you ask for, Shirley. Your thoughts are getting more and more powerful all the time. You really set yourself up for this one."

Yes, I had! Throughout this whole two-month odyssey I had said, at least a hundred times, that I wished I had had a wide angle or telephoto lens. My little automatic 35mm camera was not made to use any specialty lens, and I would most likely not allow myself to buy another expensive camera while I still owned this one.

I could see how I had set it up where I now had to buy another camera if I wanted to take one with me to Mt. Shasta next month. This time, a little wiser, I'd get one with wide angle and telephoto lenses. An inner "smiley-face" was having a heyday with this one.

"Hmmm," I wondered, "what kind of camera should I buy next?"

TRAVEL

Germany

*All I have seen
teaches me to trust the Creator
for all I have not seen.*

—Emerson

I was back at Zwiebrucken Air Force Base and it was my birthday. Soon, it would be time to head back to the States. I was getting ready to take the bus into downtown Zwiebrucken to do some last-minute shopping when I heard the base loudspeaker announcing the base gates were now closed because a number of Peace Demonstrators were marching outside them. My first thought was how dare anyone cramp my birthday here in Germany. But after I had thought about it a bit the cosmic joke hit me: wasn't my birthday

332

the most perfect day to parade anywhere for love and peace? Wasn't that what my whole life was about these days? Much as the Air Force may not have appreciated it, I did. I thanked God for such a glorious tribute.

That evening, Laura and Jeffrey brought me some roses and took me to a quaint little countryside restaurant named Schweizer Haus for dinner. We'd originally planned to take the ten-minute drive across the border and have dinner in France. But it was Monday night and nearby French restaurants were closed. An air of sadness hung over us. It was time to say goodbye, again. They were driving me to the train station where I would catch a midnight train to Munich. I would spend my last four days there before my flight home to the States. It'd been wonderful being with Laura; thankfully, it wouldn't be too long before I would be with her again. Her two-year tour of overseas duty was about over and she was hoping to be home in time to climb Mt. Shasta with me on Bobby's birthday.

As we hugged our goodbyes, I encouraged them to go back to the base. They both had to be up bright and early and it'd been a long day. Once alone, it felt a little creepy. The train station was fairly dark and deserted. I sat down on a bench, feeling emotionally drained. My eyes were getting heavy—no, that would never work! If I fell asleep, I might miss my train. I had been warned that German trains are very prompt, quickly make their stops and are off again. I half-carried, half-dragged my luggage behind me along the platform.

"God, why do I have so much stuff?" I was thankful I'd shipped some things home from Athens and from Germany.

The train arrived on time to the minute and I boarded. I felt uneasy as I'd never ridden an express train like this and was uncertain as to the routine as I boarded and took a seat in the compartment next to the ticket collector. Finally, at 3:30 AM, I had adjusted to being on the train enough to doze off. I awoke with a start to a scene that was just like early-morning commuter traffic into San Francisco. Hordes of people, obviously dressed for work in the big city, climbed aboard the train and invaded my "private" compartment. What an abrupt awakening!

At 6 AM my train pulled into the Bahnhof (Railroad Station). What a funny feeling to have all this luggage and yet not have the

333

faintest idea where my hotel was. What to do, what to do? I decided to grab a luggage cart and proceeded to load my belongings on it. I could walk around a bit and try to get my bearings. Soon, I spotted the luggage lockers and dug up enough coins to store my two largest suitcases. I hoped I had enough change to get into the pay restrooms. I had discovered throughout most of Europe I'd visited that if you didn't have change for the bathroom, toilet paper machines, or maids, you were out of luck. After riding on a train for six-and-a-half hours, lucky for me, I had the right change.

My internal pleas for help had obviously been heard in the universe: a kind German gentlemen who spoke English offered to help me with my bags and walk me to my hotel. Once settled in, I lightened the load in my purse and began a walking tour of the city. Unstructured time was indeed a blessing. I shopped until my feet ached and my shopping bags were bursting. After three days, I knew my way around the city fairly well. I realized that with a little time and patience that would be true of anyone in any city.

On my bus ride to the airport at Munich, I thought about all the different cultures I had visited and how each had dispelled any inappropriate, hand-me-down archaic pictures I'd had about them and replaced them with ones of warm personal experience. For me, a smiling face and a happy ambience coupled with patience and gratitude could transcend any cultural or language barriers. Wonderful human beings came dressed in many-colored skins and costumes. This trip had opened wide my eyes and heart. Only time would reveal how deeply my soul had been touched.

It was time to fly home. Hooray for American telephones and salad bars! Besides my family and friends, I'd missed them the most. Home! I exulted, then it dawned on me—I no longer had a "home". I'd sold it. Oh, yes, life was indeed full of changes.

TRAVEL

Mt. Shasta '84

One day we will be able to believe
that God was not only involved in our grief,
but also had a use for it in our lives.

—*Beyond Sorrow*

After two intense "don't miss much" months of traveling through Egypt, Israel, Greece and her Islands, Turkey, Switzerland, and Germany, my feet were back on American soil. A joyful midnight reunion at San Francisco International Airport had brought out my dad Lou, my friend Kathryn Davi-Billeci, and Bill Orlich, red rose in hand. I didn't realize how much I'd missed everybody. I felt so much love when I saw their smiling faces that I wept.

Jet lag and the need for assimilation were making their bid for some quiet time. However, if I were going to be on the mountain for

Bobby's birthday this year, I only had a couple of days to pull together all the gear I would need. Bill Orlich invited me to hang out at his place on my return for as long as I needed. He was working up to twenty hours a day to realize the dream he had had for as long as I had known him—to own his own print shop.

I bought a new sleeping bag, foam bed roll, backpack, canteen, numerous hiking "goodies", and a new compact-sized 35mm Minolta "Talking Camera", complete with telephoto and wide-angle lens. That brought a knowing smile to my face.

The tentative plans were for daughters, Laura and Kim; daughter-in-law Kathleen; and friends Kathryn Davi-Billeci, Carolyn Ortega, Robin Blanc, Janice Hamby, and Julie Traynor to join me on this year's pilgrimage to Mt. Shasta. One by one, reason by reason, each one was detoured. I couldn't believe it. All I could do was accept that there was definitely a "divine plan" of some kind in the making. By now it was a well-accepted fact: "There are no accidents in life. Everything has its place, time, and purpose."

Doubt began to creep in: was I was supposed to go? Certainly my weary body, not appropriately conditioned for high-altitude mountain climbing, would cast a vote for staying home. I meditated and asked to be shown an unmistakable sign if I were to cancel the trip. None was shown so I continued to make the necessary arrangements. I would stay with my friend, Maureen Mitchell, who had moved to Mt. Shasta after our first climb in 1982. Boots suitable for climbing, ice crampons, and an ice axe were reserved and waiting for me at the Fifth Season Sporting Goods Store in Mt. Shasta City.

I had connected with my climbing guide, Shaun Wood, through a series of "no accident" events. Shaun first met daughter-in-law Kathleen and me at a farewell party for my son, Greg, shortly after Bobby's funeral. Soon afterwards, he became roommates with Kathleen and her girl friends for a short time. Recently, he had traced Kathleen through her parents and called her in Pasadena. In their conversation, he mentioned he'd been doing a lot of mountain climbing and was planning to climb Mt. Shasta again in September. Kathleen got excited when she heard he had climbed Mt. Shasta the previous year on September 8th. He had no way of knowing that I was also on the mountain that day or that it was Bobby's birthday. She told him to contact me as I was talking about going again, too.

336

Shaun and I briefly connected before I left for Egypt, leaving the arrangements loose. I had previously recruited myself another possible guide, my 6-Day buddy, Lee Parker.

Alert to any signs that I should cancel the climb, I was having trouble directly connecting with Lee. I knew his main goal would be to reach the summit if we went. Wondering if my jumbled-up missed communications with Lee was a sign to stay home, I called Shaun. If there was anything wishy-washy about his going, I would take that as divine guidance not to go to Shasta. To my surprise, he was not only ready and willing, he was *eager* to be my guide. In talking with Shaun I realized he'd already reached the summit of Mt. Shasta the previous year. This year his only goal seemed to be to support me in climbing as high as it felt right for me to go. That indeed felt comforting as I loaded my gear into Valentyne and headed North on Interstate 5.

I arrived in the late afternoon and drove directly to the base of the mountain and sat staring at it and the cloud formation around its peak.

God, she looks awesomely huge, I thought, studying the white icy markings of glacier snow cascading her slopes. Who the heck do I think I am, Superwoman? By now my ego mind-chatter was going hot and heavy and it was difficult not to buy into it. It was "put-up or shut-up" time. Tomorrow I would either cancel or begin the climb. Shaun and I rendezvoused at Maureen's. I was still hoping that one of my other possible mountain-climbing buddies would miraculously join us, but that turned out to be a definite *no*. Again, I'd missed connecting with Lee Parker and finally released it as "meant to be". We'd leave a message for him at the Ranger Station when we signed in for the climb.

My body ached when I awoke the next morning. I did some stretches and wondered if my ego was driving me to climb or if I was being divinely beckoned. No matter. I was at least going to start the climb and trust that my inner guidance would tell me when I should stop. I read the philosophical saying clipped to my Unity *Daily Word*:

It is *not* the critic who counts, not the man who points out how the strong man stumbled or where the doer of deeds could have done better. The credit belongs to the

man who is actually in the arena; whose face is marred
by dust and sweat and blood; who strives valiantly; who
errs and comes short again and again; who knows the
great enthusiasms, the great devotions, and spends
himself in a worthy cause; who, at best, knows in the
end the triumph of high achievement; and who, at the
worst, if he fails, at least fails while daring greatly, so that
his place shall never be with those cold and timid souls
who know neither victory nor defeat.

—Theodore Roosevelt

I meditated and prayed. Was this the egotistic part of me doing
what I said I'd do out of stubborn willfulness? God, use this opportunity of having me in this high spiritual vibration for my highest
good. Show me where my life's work to serve people should be
focused and how in the world I am supposed to support myself
financially. Funds from selling the house would soon need
replenishing, that was for sure.

Oh, yes, God, I added to the prayer, show me what I need to
know *gently*, please. I had read too many stories about people hurting themselves and ending up in a body cast and traction to be still
long enough to find God. That was *not* what I was asking for. Gently,
God, please make it gently.

Maureen accompanied Shaun and me to the Fifth Season. To
my dismay, the boots I'd reserved were rigid ski-type boots, suitable
for attaching ice-crampons. I had expected them to be soft leather
climbing boots. Too late now; I'd just have to carry the boots in my
backpack and climb Shasta in my tennis shoes. Maureen took our
picture, blessed us, and waved goodbye as we began our climb.

It was easier said than done. I had never backpacked or seriously
mountain climbed before. I'd definitely not been prepared for the
effect of a thirty-five pound pack on my back or the energy it takes
to climb at high altitudes. Shaun, bless his heart, saw the efforting
I was going through and took the heavy boots off my pack and added
them to his. He said he was only here to guide me to go as high as
I wanted to go. He had nothing he needed to prove for himself. He
was the perfect guide for me. No pressure, just encouragement.

338

Thank you God, You always know what You're doing when You set things up, even when I can't see it immediately, I prayed.

Shaun was great! He had the patience of a saint as we climbed along at *my* pace...s-l-o-w-l-y. The loose rock and frequent steep grades, coupled with the ever-higher altitude as we climbed, were taxing my body to the max. As I looked at the mountain before me, one of Robin Blanc's and my favorite sayings came into mind:

"How do you eat an elephant?"

"A bite at a time." It was a very useful perspective, given what I was doing.

We had started much later in the day than we had planned and were progressing slowly. The top of the mountain still looked to be very far in the distance. We must have made some progress, though, as I looked back to the area where we had started, now far behind and below us.

We found a nice, fairly level spot and set up our tent and built a small fire inside a ring of rocks. It was getting decidedly chilly. We heated some water and Shaun introduced me to a noodle-type soup, "Top Ramen". It tasted better than anything I could imagine as it warmed and filled my tummy.

The sun was painting the landscape before us with strokes of soft peach and gold. I took in a deep breath of the crisp Shasta air. My calves could already feel the effects of climbing. I massaged them lovingly, grateful my body had gotten me this far. The mountain was having an effect on my "beingness". I felt totally at peace and fully present in the moment as I crawled into my sleeping bag for my first night on the mountain.

At daybreak, the gentle rays of the sun awakened me to the clear skies of a new day. Thank God, the weather was definitely supporting our climbing adventure. Shaun was stirring, too. We had had a wonderful philosophical conversation last night. I thanked him for being my climbing guide. He said that he had also been gifted with me as a spiritual guide. Lots of changes were up for him and he now had some new perspectives to view them from.

The timberline was far below as we continued to climb. We checked our pulse rates when we stopped to rest and mine was racing, but I didn't feel too bad because Shaun's was, too. And he was twenty-plus years younger than I and very physically fit. The high-altitude climbing was burning my energies fast and my body was feeling pushed to the limit. Shaun went on to scout out the ridge ahead while I poked along at less-than-cruising speed. He called out to me to climb up to where he was; he had found something I should see.

On the top of the next ridge was a stack of large stones, a man-made monument of some sort.

"I think it's a monument for the young girl you told me about that died up here a couple of years ago," Shaun theorized as he lifted the top stone. Underneath was a photograph of a young person. I had told him a story about a teenaged brother and sister who were climbing Mt. Shasta together. The girl got tired and wanted to quit. Her brother told her to sit and rest while he went on ahead. He had carefully instructed her to wait for him so they could go back down the mountain together. When the boy returned, his sister was nowhere to be found. Finally, he himself went down the mountain to call for help. A couple of days later, the girl's body was found. She had apparently died from a fall. According to the story being told in Mt. Shasta, at the exact rock where the young girl had last been seen an ankh mysteriously appeared on the rock, (*ankh* is the Egyptian symbol for eternal life).

I stood beside the monument and put my hands on it to bless it. Immediately my body filled with intense feelings of sadness and I took a step backwards. As I did so, I twisted my ankle. Of all the places on the mountain to hurt oneself, this was ridiculous. It was level here. We sat for a few moments to see how much damage I'd done to my ankle. After a bit, I tried walking on it. It swelled a little but it was not an unbearable pain; just a nagging one.

As high noon approached, Shaun assisted me in climbing to the top of a steep slope. There, by prearranged time signals with my friends and daughters who were not with us, we lit the glass-chimneyed candle I'd been packing and sang "Happy Birthday" to Bobby. The view was magnificent from the crest we were standing on. Yes, yes, we had come a long way. Everything below us had grown much smaller in the distance.

All afternoon, we set little goals "to the next red rock" or "that big boulder formation up there" and kept on keeping on. Now and then we'd recheck my ankle. It wasn't swollen any more or any less than it had been. Its nagging pain kept reminding me it was there.

Other climbers passed us now and then. One man who was climbing with two young boys yelled out, "It's tough doing this kind of stuff when you're forty."

"Try doing it when you're fifty," I yelled back. He waved and commented on how amazing it was I'd made it this far without good hiking shoes.

"See you at Lake Helen and good luck," his voice echoed as he disappeared over the large ridge above me.

By the sheer power of Shaun's constant, patient encouragement, my stubborn willfulness, and God's blessing, we finally made it up to the white-glaciered bed of Lake Helen where we were to make camp for the night. I was exhausted. Shaun gently but firmly coaxed me into putting on my ice-climbing boots and crampons. They were *so* heavy as I lifted my tired feet up and put on my thick down jacket.

I picked up my ice axe and grumpily gave in and followed Shaun as we made our way across the ice bed. His senses were telling him I was probably not going to make the difficult climb all the way to the summit. He pointed to the "heart" of Mt. Shasta, a barren heart-shaped spot in the glacier. My whole body reacted to the word "heart" and I could feel the goosebumps beneath my heavy clothing alerting me that *this was it!* This was what I'd been climbing to reach—the heart of Mt. Shasta!

Shaun left me alone as I knelt in the snow and did a ritual of love and release. I thanked God for blessing my life this very day, twenty-nine years ago, with such a loving soul as Bobby. I thanked Bobby for the love, inspiration, and gifts of spiritual awareness he had given me and released any grief that still might hold him earthbound to me in that form. He needed to be free to do whatever his soul called him to do next. I bowed and visualized a big "hug" of light going out to my son as I also thanked Mt. Shasta for holding me in this high vibration of love, peace, and clarity.

I turned with my camera to catch a picture of Shaun, patiently waiting below me. It was time to turn back to camp; soon it would be dark. We arrived at our tent just as the sun slipped out of view, leaving only a broad band of orange sky behind her. The nearby peaks on our right were dark craggy silhouettes standing in bold contrast to the last hues of a peachy-crimson sunset.

Heart of Mt. Shasta

The winds were cold as they came off the glacier snow and blew our tent relentlessly. Sometimes it felt like the tent would be picked up, parachute-like, with us in it, and blown to who knows where. A full moon rose boldly over the mountain range to the south: it was a spectacular sight! The sky was so blue and full of stars and the clarity at this altitude was as close to heaven as I could imagine being while in a physical body. I braved the wind and stepped out of our tent to take a picture of it. It was a funny commentary: my new Minolta "talking" camera wanted me to move closer to the moon. It kept asking me to "check distance"! I took the picture anyway.

The icy rocks beneath my sleeping bag and the howling wind snapping at our tent made it difficult to sleep, not to mention the forces of a full moon doing whatever it does to the human body. We were amongst a small community of fellow mountain climbers, asleep in nearby tents. Ninety-five percent of those up here were males. This high on the mountain there were no private spots to go to the bathroom—certainly there were times when being a male was advantageous! I lost my shyness and quickly did what I had to do.

The next morning I felt I'd completed what I'd come to the mountain to do. It was time to start the long journey down. To go to the summit was, for me, at least another four-or-five hour, physically demanding trek up the glacier face of the peak. Climbing up I might have thought about, but coming down was a different story. One had to "ski" down the steep descent on his shoes and crampons or sit and slide by the "seat of his pants" using the ice axe as a rudder. Old-timers told tales of reaching speeds of up to sixty-five miles per hour coming down. More than one climber had been "gaffed" by his own ice axe if he lost control. I might have inborn stubborn qualities but I wasn't stupid.

With a candle in front of me, I meditated while Shaun packed up the tent. The wind started quieting down as the sun came up. Again, I thanked the mountain for her inspirational influence and bade her adieu.

Going downhill uses a different set of leg muscles from those used for climbing up. Looking down was scarier than looking up. I consciously searched for sure footing. I looked at the glacier paths on the side of some of the rocks and yelled to Shaun that I wanted to try glissading down for awhile. He heartily agreed it might be fun, challenging, and definitely faster. It was! The seat of my pants was quickly soaking wet from falling, but I was getting the hang of it. It was like skiing without skis.

Too soon the glacier snow was behind us and I began using my ice axe as a cane to steady myself so I could move faster across the loose rocks. A sort of rhythm was developing—sometimes we were almost jogging. I had to keep a firmly disciplined grip on my mind as it wanted to imagine all the terrible accidents I could have along the way. I did fall a couple of times but not in the places where it was dangerous to human limbs. My wrists and fingers were swelling from catching my falls.

As we descended, the heat of the day grew intensely. The lower we got the hotter it became. The constant jolting that coming down the mountain dealt to my body and bladder was becoming extremely painful. My heavy pack cut off my circulation such that my fingers were numbing and extremely swollen. As we finally approached the spot where we had parked the car, I went off by myself into a heavily wooded area. There, I sat on a shaded log and allowed myself to release the now unbearable pain I'd collected in my body. I sobbed for several minutes until I felt emptied out—literally as well as figuratively.

Back at Maureen's, I drank lots of cranberry juice to help ease the pain kicking up in my bladder and took a Vanquish. I went into the bedroom to be alone with the pain and my thoughts. After about a half hour, Maureen came in to check on me and sat down to talk. After telling her about all the adventures and insights we'd had, I casually mentioned the monument Shaun had found. We felt it was for the little girl who died on the mountain after Bobby did. I also told her about how crazy it was that I hurt my ankle there instead of any one of the more dangerous places.

Maureen was silent for a long moment and then spoke. "Why do you suppose that little girl is trying to get your attention with a 'nagging' ankle?"

It was my turn to be silent for a moment, and then it hit me like a ton of bricks. I had asked God to *gently* show me the direction I was to focus my energies. He had.

When I put my hands on the monument to bless it, I had psychically picked up the sadness and grief of the person who had built it. It was obvious that he or she was feeling "called" back to the

344

mountain, just as I had been for the past three years, to have climbed that high to build it. My work, perhaps through my book, would be to help others make it through their grief. Whew! A "light bulb" had gone on in my head!

I hugged and thanked Shaun and Maureen for being part of this journey to the mountain. Physically feeling a little better, I began the long five-hour drive home to Walnut Creek. I hadn't seen Kimberly since before I left for Egypt and she was driving up from Los Angeles to spend some time with me.

Arriving home at 1:30 in the morning, I dove onto the warm waterbed, clothes and all, and fell into a deep exhausted sleep.

When I awakened it was 10:30 in the morning and Kim was knocking on the door. It was hugging time! I gave her several presents I'd brought back from Europe and told her all about the reunion with Laura. Suddenly we realized that this was Bill's first day in his new business. He had always been so supportive of the girls and me. The least we could do was get him a congratulatory card and plant.

We picked up a large flowering plant and headed for the nearby Hallmark Gift Shop. I immediately looked over at a whole wall of cards on my left. One of the cards "beckoned" me. Whatever the card said inside, I'd adapt the message to fit Bill's Opening Day. The card was one of those foot tall ones and had a picture of two little kittens peeking over the edge of a brandy snifter on it. It carried its own "private joke" message. Bill had once said I was the "kitty" Pied Piper of his apartment complex; our patio was often full of kitty visitors.

As I opened the card to read what was inside, I *knew* I had received the answer to the other question I had asked God to answer on my Mt. Shasta trip. How I was supposed to support myself financially? Bill had asked me before I left for Mt. Shasta if I would be interested in being his partner in the Printing Center. I had said I didn't think so and really didn't have the time even to think about it then. Now as I read the message inside the card I'd so intuitively chosen I had my answer. The card simply said:

WE'RE IN THIS TOGETHER!

Kim and I delivered the plant and card to a smiling-faced Bill. This was his long-awaited day and happiness shone from his alive

345

clear blue eyes. On the spot, I filled out and signed the partnership DBA papers. That was it! "Ask and ye shall receive!" Less than twenty-four hours down off the mountain and I was now in the printing business.

I threw myself wholeheartedly into the office management part of the business, setting up invoices, filing systems, and an appropriate decor that felt good to be around. It was a great partnership. Bill had been in the printing business (for someone else) for thirty years. His creativity could now bloom fully its own way in our print shop. I had the organizational, public relations, and office management skills to round out the other half of the business venture.

We reupholstered all the second-hand furniture and covered long boards with rust-colored fabric. Inspirational messages were framed for the walls and the place began to feel like "home". It was clear that the business would take a lot, if not all, of my energy for the better part of a year or so. When would I ever finish writing my book after putting in sixteen- and sometimes eighteen-hour days, six and seven days a week?

I sat at my office desk, pondering my life's priorities. Having one of my under-the-breath conversations with God, I asked if He had really guided me here or if I had just made the whole thing up. Ten minutes later, the phone rang. It was Robin Blanc asking "Is this the Divine Printer?" She went on to tell me that Reverend Terry Cole-Whittaker's classes were being given in San Francisco and "would I be their Divine Printer?" If that didn't make a *believer* out of me— there must be thousands of printing shops in the San Francisco Bay Area and we got the job. We weren't even listed in the phone book yet. Divine Forces were at work again. With God, who needs the yellow pages?

346

TRAVEL

India

Start the day with love,
fill the day with love,
end the day with love;
this is the way to God.

—Sai Baba

Ever since I had sat in Alexander Everett's Inward Bound class and heard him talk about India "calling" him and his visit with Sai Baba, the Holy Man, a "seed" had been planted in my mind. What does "you'll just *know* when India calls you" feel like? I could only imagine the telephone ringing... "Hello!"

"Hello, Shirley Ruiz, this is India calling. Please come *now*."

Alexander had said, "It is rumored you only get to see Sai Baba when you are 'called'." He proceeded to share stories about the

Avatar, the *vibhuti* (sacred ash) he manifests out of thin air, and his experience of having a personal audience with Sai Baba. I laughed, wondering if India or Sai Baba would ever "call" *me*, and tucked the thought away in the back of my mind.

Now, some two years later, I *knew* what India "calling" felt like. It happened while I was sitting in a Terry Cole-Whittaker "Mastery of Faith" class in San Francisco. I was sitting near Robin Blanc and Julie Traynor, totally peaceful, listening to the class announcements preceding our evening break time. "There are a few spaces left in the 'On the Road God Training with Three Masters in India' available. Loy Young, Sondra Ray, and Terry Cole-Whittaker will be leading the group", I heard Jim Fundingsland saying.

That's all I heard before my body began to shake and tremble, totally covered with hair standing straight up. Julie and Robin *knew*. How could it be I *was* going to India? I hadn't even thought of physically going there, but something deep within was unmistakably notifying me this very instant that I *was going*. There was no rational understanding of it as no "mind-mulling" was even faintly involved in my choosing to go—at least to my knowledge. My whole being *knew* I was going and that was that.

This certain knowledge didn't stop the panicy chatter of my frantic mind. Driving home from class, I asked my commuting buddy Julie Traynor to hear out all the considerations of my mind running out its objections to my taking the India trip.

"I don't meditate enough. Who do I think I am, traveling to India with the likes of Terry, Sondra, and Loy? I'll probably eat half a box of oatmeal cookies when I get home and really start thinking about this trip. It will blow what's left of my nest egg. With a brand-new business, I can't just up and take off to India for three weeks. I'm not self-disciplined enough. It would be next to impossible to pull it all together in such a short period of time—money, office help, visas, shots, and clothes suitable for life in an ashram. Where in the heck would one find a sari around here? I've only been rebirthed once. I don't even like the taste of curry." On and on I went, emptying out every thought that came into my mind for the entire half-hour trip home.

Julie quietly listened to all my gibberish thoughts. When there seemed to be nothing left for me to say, she asked, "So when are you enrolling?"

"Tomorrow morning if there is still any space available."

There was! I was beside myself with excitement. Wow, how powerful, just like that...and I *am* going to India.

I recalled my palm reading session with Richard Unger: he had said I was always getting ready in case God called me up for a date on Friday night and that I'd probably have the audacity to tell God when He called that "I wasn't ready yet!" I closed my eyes as Richard's words echoed in my head. A beautiful picture appeared in my mind's eye of white puffy clouds parting to reveal a golden stairway. A reverberating voice was saying "come!" At that moment, I *knew* that *nothing* on this physical earth was reason enough to keep me from answering the "call to India". I was ready—ready or not!

Excitedly, I told my printing business partner Bill Orlich about my revelation and going to India. "Go! Do what you have to do!" was the blessing he gave.

After meditation the next morning, I called Kathryn Davi-Billeci, Deena Jackson, Carolyn Ortega, Suzie Friedenthal, Georgia Kahn, and Romi Lea to see if India was "calling" them, too. Suzie's new job had her tied down and Carolyn thought her gift in this was not to go, not to make it happen. Deena felt torn between a heart that was telling her to go and a recently operated-on body that might be at risk to travel abroad so soon. Romi was still thinking about it. Georgia had already enrolled and Kathryn was on the phone to San Diego to make her travel arrangements.

Coincidentally, Kathryn found a book on her bookshelf about Sai Baba, which she brought over for me to read. Who was this Avatar Sai Baba? I sat up all night reading to find out. The book confirmed that no one comes to Sai Baba without him calling them, even if a hundred people "persuade or drag or push".

"That without His will, no one can start the journey to Puttaparthi. He cannot reach the place where Baba is." That was true for some; for others, "everything becomes easy. Leave, money, and companions become available quickly and all obstacles are removed." I *knew* I was one of the latter and soon everything began falling into place: passport, visa, shots, information, money, and an exhilaration that was unbelievable.

The big fat envelope arrived from the God Training Office containing lists of recommended "to dos" before leaving: travel items to pack, brief pointers for living in India, information on appropriate dress in an ashram, and complete step-by-step pictures on how to wrap a sari. More information about Sai Baba was included, as well as a glossary of Sanskrit terms and our itinerary.

Excitement surged through me as I sat down with my world globe to see just where in the world I was actually going. It appeared that the spot in India where we were headed was almost exactly half-way around the world. The group departing from San Diego was to connect along the way with groups leaving from Los Angeles, San Francisco, and Honolulu. There, we were to meet up with the first two of our teachers, Sondra Ray and Loy Young. Terry Cole-Whittaker had gone to India ahead of us with a crew to film some shows for her Sunday Morning TV Ministry. We were scheduled to rendezvous with her at the Taj Hotel in Bangalore, India.

My personal "to do" list grew endlessly. I knew I had to get into and stay in high gear to be ready to leave on Singapore Airlines Flight 1 as scheduled.

The Monday before we were to leave, Kathryn called to tell me she wasn't going to India after all. She had been ill for a couple of days and felt strongly guided to cancel the trip. My disappointment couldn't be captured in words, it was so intense. Together we had carefully laid out our itinerary for after the God Training time at Sai Baba's ashram. We were continuing on to Agra to rendezvous with Kathryn's foster daughter, Asha, whom she had long supported through a Christian relief group. She had never had the joy and privilege of meeting Asha in person.

The cherry on top of the cake, for me, was a visit to the Taj Mahal on Valentine's Day. Had I still been married to Bob Ruiz, it would have been our twenty-fifth wedding anniversary. Somehow, the Taj Mahal seemed the perfect place to spend the Day of Hearts, close to God, in a magnificent marble monument to love.

After the Taj Mahal, we had planned our free airline stopover in Japan. So many long-dreamed-of places to be seen in one trip. Kathryn's cancellation seemed to blow it all out of the water. There wasn't enough time to find a new travel partner and *make* the side trip come together. Besides, I knew that things always happen for the best, and even though I couldn't see it now, there was a higher reason for this sudden change of plans—both for Kathryn and myself.

In my meditation that morning I asked for guidance about why all this was happening to our "perfect" trip. My answer was a sense of "do nothing". I did nothing about rearranging my itinerary and kept tackling the endless items on my list that needed to get done.

The noon mail brought an envelope from Miracles Unlimited, a gift shop in Wailuku, Maui. It contained a letter from my good friend, Romi Lea. It was not appropriate for her to go to India with me at this time, she wrote. Was it possible though that I stop over on my way home from India and bring the essence of the India trip and myself to Maui?

"Your fifth-floor bedroom, overlooking gorgeous Maui sunsets, awaits you, dear friend." The internal "click" I often heard when something was really right for me was loudly signaling—yes, yes, yes! A week of rest, recreation, and reunion in Maui with Romi couldn't exactly fall into the category of being a booby prize. Could it be that my inner being *knew* that following the God Training and being in the presence of Sai Baba, a time of integration and rest would be much more appropriate for me than an intense week of sightseeing? Must be, must be. I called and arranged for my free stopover on the way home to be rerouted to Hawaii.

The long-awaited moment to depart arrived. A joyous late-evening send-off at San Francisco International Airport awaited me as Robin Blanc, Jim Fundingsland, and several other "Mastery of Faith" classmates, as well as Bill Orlich, my daughter Kim, daughter-in-law Kathleen, a friend of hers, and my parents, Lou and Teresa Ferrero, gathered for goodbye hugs.

In Honolulu we got off the plane for an hour layover while the remainder of our growing group, including Sondra Ray and Loy Young, joined us. Georgia Kahn had spent the past week on convention in Honolulu. It was good to see her radiant face as she boarded the airplane. We were about to share another adventure together.

The 'On the Road God Training' officially began as Sondra Ray handed each of us a beautiful lavender, white, and gold workbook. It was entitled *Drinking the Divine*, and had been put together to make study of *A Course in Miracles* easier. On the inside cover, a handwritten and signed welcome from the author, Sondra herself, said "Welcome to The God Training and my life." The eleven-and-a-half-hour flight to our next stop, Hong Kong, went quickly as I read and highlighted my entire 190-page workbook.

The last page of the book gave more information about the God Training. I read the list of prerequisites for doing the standard two-week training. It had been given for the first time in 1984 at Mt. Shasta! I had *known* from the moment I flew there to search for Bobby's downed plane that there was something very spiritual and magnetic about being in the proximity of this majestic mountain. "Mt.Shasta keeps popping up in my life wherever I go," I said, shaking my head in wonder. A confirmation chill ran through my body.

A brief stopover in Hong Kong was long enough for most of us to do some quick shopping in the airport gift shops and stretch our legs a bit—a welcome change from sitting in one place for nearly twelve hours.

Several hours later, we arrived in Singapore. By then, I had given up the game of keeping track of what day and time it was back home and in India. After crossing the international dateline, I chose to go with the flow of whatever was happening at the moment and slip into a more peaceful, centered state, taking life a moment at a time, forgetting clock and calendar as much as possible.

It was a good lesson for the whole group to learn, even the teachers and logistics team. The trip was to hold many unplanned adventures and challenges, and going with the flow, without expectations, would float us over some experiences that could be upsetting if we allowed them to be so.

A very recent change in visa requirements meant leaving Robert Young, Loy's husband and the man in charge of logistics (and our luggage!), behind when our plane took off from Singapore for Madras, India. (He rejoined us later.) That meant a switch in how we would handle all the luggage. Ah, ha! This was a letting go of how we all had planned the trip and an omen to let it just spontaneously unfold.

Georgia and I had put in a last-minute request to be roommates when Kathryn cancelled her plans to be my traveling companion. The switch connected well. Georgia and I checked into our joint Singapore Hotel room. There, a surprise reunion with an old friend took place that slid into the category of "one-in-a-million" odds of happening.

352

Three years earlier, I was assisting Christi Ana Davidsunn in leading an All Game Intensive. We were again using the Walnut Creek apartment of Bill Orlich and Bill was one of the participants. Another gentleman in the training was a man everyone called "Captain Thom". Thom brought a brass Captain's clock for Bill to try and fix for him. He left it with Bill and seemed to disappear from the face of the earth.

Much time passed. When I sold my Walnut Creek condominium, and was going through my things, I discovered the clock and remembered my intention of finding Thom for Bill and returning the clock to him. I tried, and again every lead to find Thom came to a dead end. It was the only thing on all my moving "to dos" list that went uncrossed off. Finally, wanting to feel complete, I sort of jokingly talked with God and told him that I was appointing myself caretaker of the clock for now. If I was to return it to Thom, God would have to give me some more clues on where to look for him.

Georgia and I were investigating the contents of our hotel room refrigerator when there was a knock at the door. Georgia opened the door and in came a bearded man who said he had a room across the hall from us. She had immediately recognized him as a fellow student in the God Training.

Our guest and I stared at one another searchingly. He asked me if we hadn't met somewhere before. We had; it was Thom! Halfway around the world, and we are neighbors across the hall in a Singapore hotel! It astounded all of us and yet, we were also accustomed to things happening in our lives, on a regular basis, that were beyond our human explanations.

Thom went on to tell us that he had been in a bad accident after the All Game Intensive. He had sold his boat after many months of intensive medical care and, for some reason or other, ended up walking into a Terry Cole-Whittaker event in San Diego. When he heard about the India trip, he *knew* he was to go. And here we were, thousands of miles from home, exchanging hugs in Singapore. Thom told me the clock was mine and he would send me its winding key.

Such blessings! Our schedule allowed for a day-and-a-half in Singapore, sightseeing and shopping. We visited temples and scenic areas. I was impressed by what a strictly enforced litter-law had done for this dynamic island republic. The city streets and vicinities were immaculate. So unusual for a big city, and so very much appreciated by my tourist's eyes.

Georgia and I joined others from our group and descended upon a local shopping center where bargaining for expandable pieces of luggage seemed to be the "hot" purchase of the day. Thank God I chose one with wheels. We were toting our own bags a lot these days and I wanted to pare down to a minimum of things. We were allowed to store our unneeded things at the Marco Polo Hotel until our stopover on the way home. Being a Virgo and having raised five children, there now seemed to be an inner battle going on between taking everything I could imagine one could need for emergencies, and the other part of me that loved being a free spirit and traveling *very* light. It ended up being a compromise. Bathing suits, most of the clothing I had brought along and my jewelry stayed in storage at the Marco Polo. The thin foam bed roll, towels, vitamins, "magic" healing potions, bags of trail-mix, and my *Daily Word* magazine from Unity were packed in my new burgundy roll-along expandable tote bag, as well as a flashlight and several candles.

Late that evening, we boarded another plane, headed for Madras, India. Arriving in Madras, we went through a long wait for our buses and by the time we arrived at our hotel, it was nearly three in the morning. Only two buses instead of the three ordered arrived to pick us up. No one really fussed much, tired as we were, even when the hotel we had been booked into didn't have space for us due to a layover of the group that had preceded us. Our group had the blessed ability to adapt to anything with a sense of humor and patience. India was training us well.

At our hotel, we were able to catch a few hours of rest before we were up again to catch an early-morning flight to Bangalore. There, we were turned loose to get our U.S. dollars changed into rupees and do some quick shopping for clothes more appropriate for life at the ashram. The fellows looked at cotton shirts and pants while we gals quickly spent our rupees on saris and punjabi outfits. The trick would be learning to wrap the saris so no inappropriate parts of our bodies were showing. The humid weather was making me wish strapless tops and short wraparound skirts had been mentioned in the dress-code list.

354

We met up with Terry Cole-Whittaker and the TV camera crew in time to board three buses for the nearly four-hour ride to Puttaparthi and the Ashram of Sai Baba. The road conditions varied from okay to being a bumpy dirt road. At one point, our buses were asked to wait while a road crew dynamited nearby. Still, good humor prevailed. The logistical plan of having us divide into small groups, each with an appointed "captain", had gotten us through airports, customs, and several side trips by bus without losing anybody.

We were beginning to look out for one another, becoming little families. Everyone seemed pretty enlightened and in tune with the premise that we each create our own realities. The very acceptance of that reality makes the bumps and boringness of long travel dissipate into challenging opportunities to transcend possible upsetting circumstances.

The big moment approached: we finally neared Puttaparthi and the ashram of Sai Baba. Appropriately, we shifted from the boisterous songs we had been singing to more spiritual ones and began "Om"-ing. Our buses passed the university and the merchant shops outside the walls of the ashram. A gated wall separated the ashram from the small village skirting its perimeters. As we got out of the hot buses, it felt good to be here and I was surer about the saying, "no one stumbles upon this ashram by accident." It had been a long journey and we had been passing "little tests" along the way, even before the actual traveling began.

Our housing was a large cement-walled and floored building we were to share as a group, men and women alike. That was unusual for India. There were no private western-type bathroom facilities where we were housed. One had to venture between and behind the cement buildings to use the available bathing and toilet "amenities". I had not had much time to think about, and had purposely not allowed myself to set up, any expectations in this department. "When in Rome, do as the Romans do." Ditto for India. All would be part of the great adventure of living in India.

The 'On the Road God Training' group consisted of about fifty students, both males and females, plus support staff for the three teachers and a camera crew. In India, protocol called for males and females to be separated for most activities. A special compensation had been made for our group and, for whatever reason, we were all in the same sleeping quarters. Each of us, males on one side, females on the other, staked out a small space on the floor and began unpacking our belongings and laying out whatever sleeping mats or bags we had brought from home. "Privacy" was a part of the Western world we'd left behind.

This was an incredibly resourceful, sharing, and creative group of people I was sharing Building 11 with. It took only a trip or two to the village before the cement building we were living in was transformed into a holy temple. Silk saris, when they weren't being worn, decorated and glorified the windows and walls. Indian mats and colorful pillows decorated many a person's sleeping space. Candles of all shapes, sizes, and colors, brought from home, lit up the dark evenings. Shadows and flickers of candlelight played around the mini-altars several people had set up. Pictures of Jesus Christ and crucifixes, as well as other religious pictures, were in full evidence about the room. Fresh flowers bought from the young flower vendors just outside the ashram gates adorned every window and many a lady's hair. It was clear that this group knew how to make the most of whatever life gifted them with.

The only electricity available was the overhead lights, and they went out at 9:00 PM each evening. After that, it was flashlight, candles, and silence.

By 3:00 AM each morning, someone was usually stirring. One by one, people spontaneously awakened, again in silence, to prepare themselves for going to the *mandir* (temple) at Prasanthi Nilayam (Abode of Perfect Peace, Sathya Sai Baba's residence). By flashlight I washed my face with water from the bucket of water Georgia and I had fetched from the only water faucet in our vicinity. When it was on (there were times when it would be turned off for hours), we each were responsible for collecting enough water for our own needs.

Georgia and I had two large plastic buckets and two smaller ones. "Captain Thom" had brought along water purifying devices which several people bought and shared. It beat the taste of iodine tablets in our water. I dissolved a packet of Emergen-C nutritional drink in a cup of water and drank it as my breakfast for the day. When I had first made this wondrous liquid a part of my daily life, it had been highly endorsed by Sylvester Stallone, John Travolta, and many other celebrities who were into physical fitness. It got my added vote, whatever it was worth. My body time clock was confused and it felt that the most supportive thing I could do for it was to drink my Emergen-C, lots of water, and go easy on strange food for a couple of days.

It was nearing 4:00 AM as I ran a brush through my hair and wrapped a scarf around my head, being careful to cover myself appropriately to enter into the *mandir.* With flashlight in hand, I quickly found my shoes amongst the fifty-odd pair lined up outside our door.

The revered silence of the early morning hour was heightened as I stepped out into the mystical light of a large full moon. Quickly and silently, women were gathering on one side of Prasanthi Nilayam while the men met on the opposite side. Everyone who entered the grounds did so barefooted. I parked my shoes, as did Georgia, beneath a tree just outside the entrance to the sacred grounds. We walked around and around, circling the Prasanthi Nilayam in silence and prayerful modes. I watched to see what the Indian women were doing and followed their example. In the profound silence I could hear the loud pounding rhythms of my heartbeats. It was a sacred privilege to be here and every cell of my body knew it.

Soon I was sitting in a line with all the women, waiting for the moment when we were allowed to go inside the temple. Coming to the *mandir* for morning prayer was left up to each of us and our inner calling. It was not a required part of the God Training. As I looked about me and surveyed the sea of covered heads, I could see that a good many of our group had felt as I did—called inwardly to participate in every moment of sacred ritual we could experience.

As we were motioned to begin entering the temple, you could hear people clearing their throats, as absolute silence was to be observed once inside. The reverence I felt as I sat, knee to knee, with others gathered to pray together, was awesome.

Again, inside the temple, men sat on the floor on one half of the room while females occupied the opposite side. The interior of the *mandir* was lit mostly by small lights on the altar, and portraits of Sai Baba and Shirdi Sai Baba (a previous incarnation of Sai Baba) could be seen in the soft lighting. The silver-figured focal point was a statue of Sai Baba of Shirdi, who looked like a wise old man I might encounter climbing a mystical mountain.

The darkened silence was broken by the sound of a deep male voice giving us instructions. The next sound was the sound of an "Om" filling the temple with its almighty vibrations. As I joined the others in "Om"-ing, I became aware of strong sensations traveling up my spine. I had "Om"-ed in a group many times before, but it had been mostly an audio experience of the sound. Now, the sound of the "Om" filling the temple was a "tuning fork" of sorts and I could feel its strong reverberations climbing up my spine, aligning my chakras. Chills ran through my body as if I were a flute and the breath of the twenty-one "Oms" was playing its own melody of praise and worship to God through my body. "Shanti, shanti, shanti," we sang out— peace, peace, peace. No matter the language, the word felt the same in my heart. There was a short period of silence and we were instructed to remain silent while specially chosen vocalists sang the Suprabhatam, an invocation to awaken the Lord in each individual heart. Something was definitely stirring within me.

As we exited the temple, Georgia and I followed the Indian women to where they were gathering and lining up, several abreast. We joined in the Nagar Sankirtan, a procession of barefooted women singing *bhajans* (devotional songs), awakening the whole ashram to the name of God. Somewhere in the ashram, the men were doing the same thing. You could hear the richness of their male voices echoing through the streets. Though I didn't know the words, I hummed along, wondrously on tune. The ritual of the pre-dawn walking with devotees of Sai Baba through the ashram grounds was a deeply moving, peaceful, and centering experience.

When the procession ended, it was evident that neither Georgia nor myself wanted to break away from the mystical ambience enfolding us. Simultaneously, and without words, we each headed for one of the trees that ringed the palace courtyard. I sat beneath mine, my gaze transfixed on the temple and the soft lights emanating from it.

After a period of time we got up and retrieved our shoes and started walking towards our ashram quarters. On the way, we came upon the huge, building-high sculpture of a lotus. I stopped to take in fully the sight before me. From where I was standing I could see only the outline of the lotus, silhouetted against the indigo blue sky. Positioned *dead center* above the lotus was the February full moon. A rainbow aura encircled it as it prepared for its descent in the

358

The "Lotus" Full Moon

western sky. Inside me some kind of mystical ritual was going on. Tears freely flowed down my face. The voice within informed me that "the male and female energies within you have united as one, *the divine marriage* at last!"

I walked away feeling truly blessed. Behind me was a spectacular daybreak canvas of dusty purples, lavenders, rosy hues, and beams of gold the Divine Painter was using to welcome the new day.

At 8:30 each morning and 4:30 each afternoon, we would head back to the Prasanthi Nilayam for darshan. The glossary I had described *darshan* as "seeing a holy person and receiving his blessing". We would first line up outside the temple grounds. The first person in each line drew number lots which established the order in which each group entered and took their place on the temple grounds. Needless to say, front-row ground seats were highly desirable. Soon after everyone was seated, men on the Eastern side, women on the Western side, the wait for Sai Baba began.

Quietly, he appeared in front of a group of women to our right. He was of slight build, clothed in a long orange robe. His hair was in an afro-looking hairstyle, and as he walked before his devotees, you could easily sense the effect his presence had upon the adoring crowd. Sometimes, he stopped to say a word or two to a devotee or accept a letter held up for him. Other times, he would hold up his hand to bless and quiet the crowd that was clamoring for his personal attention.

It is said that Sai Baba can read minds, so I noticed some of my attention was on the thoughts wildly racing through my head. Part of my thoughts were pleading for a personal audience with Baba while another part of them were trying to figure out how I should be behaving in his presence. Other thoughts were trying to find the rhyme and reason when someone was singled out for the honor of having a personal audience with him.

While my mind was filled with fleeting thoughts, my eyes were glued to watching Sai Baba's hands. When his hand started to make small circles at about waist level, he was manifesting *vibhuti* (sacred ash) out of nowhere. As closely as I watched, it was beyond my human understanding to explain what was happening. My fondest wish became one to view him at a closer range when this was happening.

Every morning I went to the 4:45 AM prayers at the *mandir*, and twice a day I attended darshan. Within the group, we were hoping at least one of us would be granted a personal audience, or better still, be invited as a group for a private meeting.

As I thought about all that was happening, I found no inner conflicts between what I was experiencing and the teachings of Jesus Christ. What was happening here rang true in my heart and aligned with my own personal sense of truth. At the highest levels of spiritual awareness, all illusions of separation vanished; only oneness with God remained. To awaken and lead each of us to that very point of awareness appears to me to be the whole purpose of Jesus's presence in our lives today.

After morning darshan each day, we would climb the hill up to the big Banyan tree known as the Tree of Wisdom and Meditation for classes with Terry Cole-Whittaker. There was time, sitting here on the ground surrounding Terry, for sharing what was going on with us. She was every bit as beautiful and vivacious physically as I had sensed her to be spiritually after watching her on a video screen. Her loving and high spiritual levels of energy came across clearly no matter what form I viewed her in. It was especially powerful to spend time with her in person at this point in our rapidly changing lives. The best part of being with Terry for me was that I could sense her willingness to tell the truth, her own personal truth, whatever the subject—no matter what. Her personal sharing came directly from her heart, thus connecting directly with mine.

Our classes were being filmed by the TV crew, and it was fun watching them hook Terry up for sound and use reflectors to get better lighting effects here under the shade of the large old Banyan tree.

Terry's morning classes were times for us to look deep within at where, to whom, and when we gave away our power and what that felt like in our bodies when we did that. Business partners, mates, and my children were some of the "soft spots" to whom I often gave my power away. Other than a few sparse notes, my class notebook remained blank. I was deeply entrenched in the experience of what I was feeling and not much into writing. India was doing all the writing, deeply etching her own message onto the pages of my heart and spirit.

Afternoon classes were held back at our sleeping quarters. It was one of the few places we, male and female, could gather in the same place and interact freely. Our western style of spontaneous hugging and walking with our arms entwined around one another was not being respectful of many of the customs of India.

We were called as a group to hear a lecture about it shortly after our arrival at the ashram. After that, we dressed, walked, and spoke in a more appropriate manner. Sometimes it was hard to contain all the joy we were experiencing. Here in India we had none of the conveniences and trappings of our Western culture we thought necessary to experience happiness. *None!* Yet the consensus of most of the group was that they had never felt more joyful and happy. Back at our ashram "home" we could let some of our inner exuberance freely express itself.

Alternately, afternoon classes were taught by Sondra or Loy, and sometimes they would combine their teaching talents. Terry joined us on a couple of afternoons. One particular instance that stands out in my mind was an afternoon when we moved around the room in silence, pairing up at random with whomever was next to us. The process called for us simply to *be*, holding hands and keeping eye contact with one another until we made contact with the "essence" of the other being.

My cup was already full by the time I paired up with Terry Cole-Whittaker. When our essences finished making contact, "my cup runneth over", overflowing voluptuously until tears of ecstasy danced down my cheeks. The sense of love and of each person's own precious and awakening divinity brought tremendous energy into the room. Talk about a high!

We had rebirthing sessions with Sondra Ray and her assistants on the floor of our massive ashram bedroom. She emphasized the need for us to keep chanting and breathing fully.

"In the presence of the Guru, anything you're stuck on gets stimulated!" She went on to tell us how chanting and rebirthing were powerful spiritual purifiers. I wasn't sure if I was resisting rebirthing or whether my body figured it was a great time to take a nap. Often I would be awakened by the voice of a rebirther standing next to me gently instructing me how to breathe.

Sondra shared the story of how she had been guided to take the God Training "on the road" to visit the ashram of Sai Baba. She also told about how she went into solitude in Bali to write one of her books. Though I had not known anything about Loy Young, our third teacher, before the trip to India, she soon earned my highest respect. Her classes covered many aspects of Eastern as well as Western philosophy and psychology. She told us being in India was like going to a new planet and we should be open and view things with devotion and respect.

"Just surrender and let things happen on this planet, look for the beauty in the simplicity of life and the people."

Loy gave us each a colored chart, "The Evolution of the Soul to Immortality" (Through Service to Humanity). Reading it and looking at my own life through it was like bringing a map on a slide screen into proper focus for viewing. I knew this map was a useful reference point for staying straight and narrow on the spiritual path to immortality. The tempting detours in life could be more clearly spotted when you had a road map in front of you, and you could choose to stay focused on the place you were going to.

Through the map, I could clearly see the "initiation" points of my own life. The two most painful ones, my divorce from Bob Ruiz and Bobby's death, had been the times when my consciousness had taken the biggest leaps of expansion. I had joked that surviving the big "Ds" (Divorce and Death) had pushed me out into life like I had never been pushed before. One of the sayings attributed to Sai Baba certainly fit my life: "The Lord has ordained sorrow, for without sorrow, man will not cling to God." At crisis times like these, one's values are apt to shift drastically.

Another part of Loy's teaching that really appealed to me was "whatever lesson in life you have learned, turn around and help twelve others, a half-of-a-step behind you, through the same lesson and teach them to turn around and help twelve others." If this was followed to its logical conclusion, I could see how the world could be healed and become a Planet of Love and Peace very quickly. It further spurred my energies into completing *Journey to High Places* as quickly as possible.

While shopping in the village outside the ashram walls, Georgia and I encountered a beggar woman asking for money. She looked rather pathetic in her worn and torn sari. Instead of money, we thought a colorful new sari would please her. Georgia picked out a beautiful sari and after we had paid for it, we smiled and handed it to the beggar woman. There was not one iota of gratitude coming from her and as some other Americans were approaching, she quickly tucked the new sari out of sight and went back to her begging. I realized from this that until her consciousness changed, she was stuck in being a beggar. Had she worn our pretty new garment, it would have blown her beggar "act". It was the only way she knew of to survive so anything given her would probably never be "enough". It reminded me of Maslow's pyramid of survival: until a person's basic "survival" needs are met, they are not open to the next level of higher consciousness and ultimately, self-realization. Except in this case, her consciousness was the obstacle to her transcending the "survival" level.

Another afternoon of browsing through the village shops brought an experience of great joy. Georgia and I were looking at the sandalwood *japamalas*, religious necklaces that contained 108 beads to be fingered while contemplating God. I was thinking about what beautiful fragrant gifts of love they would make for some of my friends back home.

I shut my eyes momentarily to think about who would most appreciate them. At that moment, I heard an inner voice say, "Buy the lady some beads." A bit startled, I opened my eyes to see who was near me. Georgia was to my left and a silver-haired Indian lady with her back to me was on my right. I talked to the owner of the small booth and asked if the lady next to me spoke English. He spoke to her in her language and told me she did not speak English. I handed him the beads I had planned to take home to the states and asked him to tell the Indian woman to pick out a *japamala*. I told him I felt guided and would consider it a privilege if she would allow me to buy one for her. He translated my message and the woman turned to face me. She had the most loving, beautiful countenance about her. A tear rolled down her face as she took the beads, smiled, and bowed in gratitude. My heart felt full and I reached out and hugged her in a touching encounter.

The next day as we left the temple grounds after darshan, my new friend and the man she was with appeared and approached me. He introduced himself and thanked me in English for what I had done for his mother-in-law and proceeded to introduce me to his wife and young son. His mother-in-law had been praying to Sai Baba for some beads for several days when I heeded the inner voice that directed me to buy them for her. He said she was most grateful and would like to show her appreciation by making some treats for me and my family.

I thanked her and mentioned that "my family" consisted of about seventy-two people in total and that would be too much to ask. My new friend felt like a mother to me and she acknowledged that I was given by Almighty Bagawan Sathya Sayee (Sai Baba) to be a loving daughter of hers. Language may have been a barrier, but none existed when we hugged and gazed into one another's eyes. I now had "Amma" and a whole new Indian family in my life.

Despite having "outhouses" for toilets, and having to fetch water by the bucket for toilet needs, bathing, or showering; having only a half-inch-thick four-foot-long foam-rubber pad to sleep on, and food I didn't particularly care for, I couldn't remember when I had felt more ongoing joy and peace for such a long period of time. Our six days of ashram life were passing too quickly. The evening before our last day at the ashram had arrived. We had all felt sure at least one of us would have been granted a private audience with Sai Baba. There was a moment of disappointment as I thought about the missed opportunity.

It was time to begin packing for the return trip home. I heard an excited voice enter our sleeping quarters. Word had just been received by Malia Wagner, the Hawaiian travel agent so instrumental in pulling this trip together for us, that we were to be granted a private audience with Sai Baba after darshan early the next morning.

What moments before had been a quiet, library-like atmosphere became as alive as a buzzing beehive. Suddenly people were heading to the showers to shampoo their hair and scurrying through their clothing trying to decide what to wear for the great occasion. It reminded me of a last-minute Senior Ball invitation when everyone was looking through their best silk apparel for "the" gown to wear to the ball. I was so ecstatic I could hardly sleep and wondered exactly what lay ahead as there was so much excitement stirring inside of me.

Two months ago, I had only barely heard the name of Sai Baba. Now, the thought of having the rare privilege of meeting with him privately in the *mandir* felt like fervent prayers of some kind had been answered. I was so glad the village girls had come and done some of our laundry. Now, what will I wear, what will I wear?

A bit of sadness crept over me the next morning as I walked the now-familiar path from our sleeping quarters to the *mandir* for morning prayer in the pre-dawn silence. Starting each day in devotional prayer and songs to God had quickly become a meaningful and empowering part of my life. Somehow I *must* find a way to keep this great sense of peace and contentment when we returned home to our Western way of living.

At the 8:30 AM darshan, males and females alike from the God Training wore scarves, headbands, or ties of the same hot pink fabric so we could easily be identified as a group when we were beckoned to the temple to see Sai Baba. We ladies all sat close together when the time came to await quietly the morning appearance of Sai Baba.

I could hardly sit still, so much electricity was running through me. Suddenly and silently, Sai Baba appeared in the courtyard and came directly over to us. Usually, darshan went on for a half-hour or so, but this time, after motioning to our group, Sai Baba headed straight across the cleanly swept golden sand of the temple grounds for the *mandir.*

Our group rose to their feet simultaneously, like one body in motion, to follow. I wondered if my feet were actually touching the ground. It felt more like I was gliding on a cushion of air as I walked proudly in my long emerald-green-and-gold Indian dress. This must be something like what Princess Diana felt when she took that long walk down the aisle to marry her Prince Charles.

The men in our group joined us inside the *mandir.* We sat on the marble floor as Sai Baba, in English, told us bits of wisdom. The soft words he spoke floated through the *mandir* and I drank in the essence of what he was saying.

"Turn off your monkey-minds. You are awakening to your divinity. Love. Be happy!" He stopped to talk personally to several of our group individually. He smiled as he told Terry Cole-Whittaker she was doing good work.

I was seated where I could get the best view, next to the men. Sai Baba was conversing with Dennis, the gentleman sitting directly in front of me, and after first getting his permission, began transmuting his present ring into a Sai Baba ring. My eyes were glued to what was happening right before them. The vision my eyes could physically see could not capture the manifestation process. It was almost as if I were frozen in a suspended frame of time while the ring was being created in a realm outside of time. Dazzling bits of energy seemed to be pulsating in front of me and words failed to verbalize what I was seeing and feeling. High energy for sure!

Shortly, Baba began to distribute packets of *vibhuti* to each of us. As I held mine, I put a bit of it on my tongue. It had a pleasant and breath-freshening taste to it. As our audience with Sai Baba ended and everyone started leaving the temple, Georgia and I lingered long enough to take pictures of one another up against the silver altar. When we finished Georgia went on ahead. It was time to go to class under the Meditation Tree. Somehow, I wanted this moment in the *mandir* to go on and on.

As I went out into the courtyard, I sat down and leaned against one of the pillars.

"Time for a little contemplation, Shirley," I heard my little voice saying. After a few moments of staring at the outside of the *mandir*, I glanced over a few feet to my left. There sat Georgia. We communicated by sign language and each snapped a picture of the other leaning by a pillar, soaking up the bliss.

Back under the Banyan tree everyone shared their insights and feelings about the audience with Sai Baba. Matt Garrigan had tears in his eyes as he described viewing us ladies as we walked across the courtyard. He said we were a walking rainbow of color and freshly scrubbed radiant faces, absolutely gliding across the golden sands.

"Amma", my newly-adopted Indian "Mama", and her family were waiting for me and invited me to follow them to their abode. "Amma" had been up since early dawn preparing treats for me and "my family". She had made one hundred of Ganesha's (the name of the elephant-headed God, son of Shiva) favorite food for us to have tonight, our last night at the ashram. Her daughter marked the spot between my eyes with a red Indian *kumkum* dot. I felt accepted and deeply honored.

Later that evening, Sondra Ray led us through another rebirthing session. After being in such close proximity with a master, she felt it doubly important we all do more deep breathing and releasing tonight before we began the long trek home. She congratulated and thanked us for being courageous enough to participate in this unique adventure, the first 'On the Road God Training' and for enriching her life. Terry and Sondra had a moment of mutual love and acknowledgment that brought tears to my eyes.

We held a little goodbye party by candlelight as we tasted of "Amma's" labors of love and exchanged addresses and hugs. In the early light of day the group would be breaking up, going in several directions. Some people were staying on at the ashram and Southern India for a few more days. Others were headed for Northern India and Tibet. Australia and Japan were calling to others and a large number of us were stopping over in Hawaii before returning to the mainland. It was a happy, yet tearful time. India had given us some peak experiences of *ananda* (bliss) that had touched our souls. Its timeless gifts of love, devotion, and simplicity were forever stored in my heart.

*　*　*

It had been about fifty-seven sleepless on-the-go hours, if my mental calculator was still functioning correctly through all the time zones and International Date Line change, since leaving Sai Baba's ashram. When I finally arrived at the airport in Maui, Hawaii, buses, airports, flight after flight, brief stopovers here and there, and a long line through U.S. Customs had all taken their toll on my body. Suddenly, it no longer knew or cared what day or time it was. It was putting me on notice that it was very weary and on the verge of complete exhaustion and collapse.

As I looked down at my feet, there wasn't even a hint of a thing called ankles. My feet were so swollen that my thumbprint left a lasting crater a dime could fit into. Food hadn't been digesting properly either for the past twenty hours and my vision was playing tricks on me. I felt like I didn't belong anywhere and kept leaving my body and spacing out. Breathing itself felt like too much effort as I dragged my overstuffed suitcases beside me. I was grateful that at least one of them was on wheels.

My friend Romi Lea's tan, smiling face soon appeared through the crowd. Her loving hug felt so good, like the giant transfusion of energy I needed to take even one more step. It was no accident that I dubbed her "Minister of Miracles"!

A fifth-floor ocean-view bedroom and a glorious crimson Maui sunset awaited me. What a welcome sight! I kicked off my shoes

368

knowing it would probably be next to impossible to get them back on. Romi's friends gathered in the living room that evening to view some Ramtha video tapes. I was placed on the couch in the middle of the most loving and caring friends, old ones and a whole group of new ones, too.

Romi brought me some freshly cut papaya to aid my digestion and pillows to elevate my "elephant" legs. I watched the Ramtha tapes and took a series of delicious cat-naps at the same time. Every time I opened my eyes, a new pair of hands was doing its own unique style of body work and massage, helping my body to release some of the extraordinary amounts of fluid trapped in my legs and feet. Alohaland, ah, yes, *paradise*, and at the same time, I was receiving my introduction to J.Z. Knight, the physical channel the wisdom of an old entity named Ramtha had chosen to come through. It was fascinating, and much of what I heard was echoing some of the truths I had been validating for myself and some I'd absorbed from India and from being with Sai Baba. I knew I'd connect with the Ramtha teachings again when I was more consciously alert.

The next morning we all headed out for a beautiful stretch of quiet seclusion called Sacred Beach. Everyone had prepared and brought their specialty dishes to share for the gala Valentine's Day picnic. I enjoyed being and interacting with beautiful, loving, and spiritually aware souls.

Burt and Nonnie Hotchkiss were there. He was on a world tour with his book, *Have Miracles, Will Travel*. Maloah and Maitreya Stillwater were readying their Heavensong World Tour. Through their loving ministry of music, they taught the eternal principles of love and *A Course in Miracles*.

It was a wondrous opportunity for a reunion with another dear friend I hadn't seen in some time—author and lecturer Eve Weir. She introduced me to her new husband, Lloyd Curtis. Marriage and Hawaii agreed with her. She radiated love and joy that overflowed as our eyes met, allowing me a moment of interacting deeply through the china blue windows of her soul.

My spirit was ecstatic and my body wanted to go off by itself and rest quietly in the sun. With these kinds of friends, no excuses were necessary. Everyone encouraged me to walk along the sandy beach, letting the ocean lap at my balloned legs and feet.

Thank you, God, for guiding me here. It's the most supportive and loving place I could think of to be this day of St. Valentine, I prayed.

The next day Romi made an appointment for me to have my first experience in a Samadhi tank. She felt that it might accelerate the healing and alignment of my body energies. It did. An hour of floating in the perfectly temperatured saline solution worked miracles. At first I wondered if I might feel a little claustrophobic being enclosed in a dark tank of tepid water. I was given the choice of leaving the door ajar or not, and having music piped in or not. Might as well go for the whole new experience, I thought as the door closed behind me.

Floating in the water was a pleasurable experience, no physical or mental effort was even faintly involved. I imagined all the healing forces of the universe were silently nurturing my body as my mind drifted off, hitchhiking a ride on the soothing sounds of music that were floating through the chamber. Pure ecstasy!

The next thing I knew, three rapping sounds on the door of the tank were bringing my consciousness back into alignment with my physical body and notifying me that my "floating" time was up. Some professional deep body work and massage were next on the agenda. My masseur knew his art well. A catlike part of me began a purring you could surely hear for blocks.

It was assimilation time and Maui was the perfect place to do it. Romi and her friend Ed took me out sailing the next day to do some "whale watching". Our eyes searched the seas until we spotted one spouting off as it migrated through the warm Hawaiian waters.

The day before I was to return to California, Eve, Lloyd, Ed, Romi, and I returned to Sacred Beach for a day of sea, sun and solitude to whatever degree we each sought it. It was perfect. My body was feeling much better and my thought processes rang with tones of perceptive clarity. After some time talking with the others, I chose to go off by myself for awhile.

An inner calling led me to a place where the warm gentle turquoise waters played flirtatiously with the clean-swept golden sands of Sacred Beach. Across the waters, I could see the islands of Molokai and Lanai. I positioned myself in a crossed-legged position

Namaste, Bobby, I love you!

and took in and released several long, slow, deep breaths. An occasional wave swirled itself around my body, baptizing me with its holy waters before leisurely returning to its origins. "Mother Maui," as she is so often affectionately called, sure knew how to nurture the children that came to rest in her caring arms. I closed my eyes to meditate on the perfect state of peacefulness I was feeling.

After a long while, I began "Om"-ing. When I opened my eyes, a most expanded state of awareness gifted itself upon me. I was a part of everything: earth, wind, sun, and water. There was no time or space as I had always known it, just a sense of timeless peace. As I looked upon the vision of paradise before me, radiant rays of sunlight twinkled and sparkled as they beamed through broken clouds, mingling and merging with the dancing, deep aquamarine waters. The balmy tropical breeze blessed my countenance with her gentle breath.

Contemplating my thoughts, the Ken Keyes book, *The Hundredth Monkey*, floated across my consciousness. I could see the truth of the theory at work in the world. As awakening souls everywhere, like myself, went within and called forth the powerful loving creative forces of the Lord God of their Being, the collective consciousness of the whole planet was being raised. After a certain point of critical mass was reached (soon, I feel), *voilà*—"The Hundredth Monkey" phenomenon in action! The world will then be lifted into the light, the long awaited Golden Age, the second coming of Christ. My body shivered an affirmative confirmation.

I smiled as the thought "How do you eat an elephant?" skirted the fringe of my mind. "A bite at a time", of course, of course. It applied itself well to the writing process of the book I now longed to return home to and finish.

Reflecting back upon January 22, 1981, I felt humbled by its impact on the course of my life. Looking at the tropical sky above me, the clouds seemed to form a misty image of Bobby winking and giving me the "high sign". His death, or transition, as I have now come to know it, has been a *powerful catalyst* to the speeded-up evolution of my soul. It has led me directly to the deepest, most sacred and holy part of myself, the God-self within. Truly, a Journey to High Places!

372

I AM
a Spiritual Being
residing in
a physical body
for whatever
span of time
allotted me
in this lifetime.

To Live, to Learn
to Love, to Share
God's Gifts
of an Abundant
and Peaceful
Way of Life.

Until the Day
when
my Soul
has completed yet
another classroom
of Learning,
I will live
and fully embrace
Life with
my whole Being!

Then,
I will graduate,
be freed
to return to
my Maker.

Rising to new dimensions
as a crystal-winged Spirit,
up through the ethers
journeying...
to the Golden Mansions
of Oneness
and my Lord's
High Places.

Author's Note

You may have picked up this book for any number of
reasons. The one I urge you to look at most closely is *your* inner voice
urging you to tune into your own divine guidance. Its mode of communication is through your intuition, *not* your intellect. We are so
programmed to process everything through our intellect that it often
shuts out our intuitive guidance. This guidance awaits only our call
for it to lead us to an enlightened perspective of this Earth existence
we call "life".

The inner calling awakening you to who you *really* are can be as
subtle as a gentle whisper or as earth-shaking as mine was: the death
of a loved one. This is not airy-fairy stuff. In my reality, it is more real
than anything you can experience in the physical world of illusions.
It is the treasure at the end of the rainbow we've long been searching
for in places where it is not. This treasure is the all-knowing essence-
spark, the God-self that fires the life-force of our being. The path

to it is not found outside of ourselves. The great treasure lies within and the path to it is an inner one.

Searching outside of ourselves leads to lifetimes of birth, pain, separation, and death. The inner path leads to knowing you are not your physical body but the spirit essence that dwells within and commands the physical vehicle. It *frees* you! We are unlimited and immortal images of and co-creators with God. The universe awaits our choosing to awaken and claim our inheritance.

METAMORPHOSIS
Caterpillars we've been,
Butterflies we're becoming;
It's the 'green-gooey'
in-between stage
that tests our faith
and strengthens us!

Do what you truly dream of doing—follow *your* divine plan. It may lie hidden deep beneath the piles of society's "shoulds" you've unknowingly accepted as your own. Hunt relentlessly for it in the things you most *love* to do. Your divine plan lies somewhere amongst the activities or projects that bring you feelings of inner peace, joy, satisfaction, love, self-worth, and "total turned-on-ness"! Don't invalidate, judge, or belittle your worth or talent at any stage of its development or expression. Every single one of us chose to be here and play our one-of-a-kind role. There's no one who can do it to you or for you. Be willing to do whatever it takes, including letting go of belief systems and relationships that are complete and that no longer serve those involved. Ask, seek, and sensitize yourself to the unique way in which your inner guidance *will come forth*. Then have the guts and faith to follow it!

Once you hear the guidance of your inner voice, however faintly, and choose to answer its call, your life will have new meaning and energy flowing through it. It is not always easy to tread the spiritual path. It takes commitment, courage, and unshakable faith! You are a spiritual pioneer mapping out the journey as you travel it.

Empower and call forth your Higher Self, the Christ within, the Lord God of your being. You are a *co-creator!* Every thought you

375

think, every word you speak, every action you take is creating your present physical world existence. That divine power has already been irrevocably decreed to you by your Creator. *There are no neutral thoughts!* Everything is an energy form and accountable to the immutable laws of the universe. By the Law of Cause and Effect, every action has a reaction. Be the chooser, the disciplinarian of your mind. Do not feel loyalty to a thought running through your mind you no longer choose to accept, "fertilize", and manifest. Stop it *mid-thought* with a self-command of "cancel", without feeling one iota of obligation to finish or further explore the unwanted thought form. No longer choose to perpetuate any life patterns that do not serve your highest good or that of mankind and replace them immediately with thought patterns that do. *Choose your reality!*

Once you *know*, there's no forgetting your new knowingness. You will not want to turn back. You will hunger for more and more spiritual awareness. Only its food will still the pangs within. It is the most satisfying, exciting, and loving thing you can do for yourself. So, "Keep on keepin' on!" "*Ask* and it shall be given to you." And don't forget to still the chatter of your mind long enough to sense or hear the answer coming to you through the blessed silence!

Planet Earth is speeding up its vibration. Hang around like-minded beings of love; they will remind you who you are. Your relationships will nurture and empower you while you bring forth and express your highest virtues and creative gifts. The formation of love-and-light networks is much needed and happening everywhere. They will support the present transition period as the Aquarian Age of peace, love, and oneness anchors its energies in. *You* are a crucial part! Awaken to who you are: co-creator with God. Call forth and empower the Christ self within, the Lord God of your being. This is a time of great change, and definitely the time to choose and affirm how you want the quality of life on this planet to be, right *now*!

May Rainbows full of God's magnificent and unlimited gifts of creativity, inner peace, joy, truth, light, radiant good health, prosperity, and love accompany you on your spiritual journey.

I Love You!

Resources

An infinite number of sources and resources have contributed to my evolutionary journey. This particular resource list gratefully acknowledges the Teachers and Tools mentioned in Journey to High Places.

*   *   *

AUTHORS, BOOKS and PUBLICATIONS

"A Course in Miracles"
Foundation for Inner Peace
P. O. Box 635, Tiburon, CA 94920

Richard Bach
"Illusions"
Dell Publishing, NY

Rusty Berkus
"Life is a Gift"; "Appearances"; "To Heal Again"
RED ROSE PRESS
P.O Box 24, Encino, CA 91426, (818) 981-7638

Leo Buscaglia
"Living, Loving and Learning"
Fawcett Columbine, NY

Melba Colgrove, Ph.D.; Harold Bloomfield, M.D.;
    Peter McWilliams
"How to Survive the Loss of a Love"
(58 Things to Do When There is Nothing to Be Done)
Bantam Books, NY

DAILY WORD
Inspirational Affirmations, Insights and Thoughts for the Day
Unity Village, MO 64065, (816) 251-3580

Richard Dwyer
"The Sky's the Limit"
Pocket Books, NY

Kahlil Gibran
"The Prophet"
Alfred A. Knopf, NY

GOLDEN BOUGH BOOKSTORE
Metaphysical and New Age Books and Gifts
Missi Gillespi, Proprietress
219 N. Mt. Shasta Boulevard, Mt. Shasta, CA 96067,
(916) 926-3228

Elisabeth Haich
"Initiation"
Seed Center, Garberville, NY

Louise L. Hay
"You Can Heal Your Life"
"Heal Your Body"
HAY HOUSE
Books, Video and Cassette Tapes, Workshops and Seminars
1242 Berkeley Street, Santa Monica, CA 90404, (213) 828-3666

Napoleon Hill
"You Can Work Your Own Miracles"
Fawcett Gold Medal, NY

Burt Hotchkiss
"Have Miracles, Will Travel"
Harlo, Detroit, MI

Hannah Hurnard
"Hinds' Feet on High Places"
Tyndale House, Wheaton, IL

"I AM" Reading Room
The Ascended Master Teachings of St Germain
P.O. Box 832, Mt. Shasta, CA 96067, (916) 926-4775

Carolyn Keene
"Nancy Drew Mystery Stories"
Grosset and Dunlap, NY

Ken Keyes
"The Hundredth Monkey"
Vision Books, 790 Commercial Ave.
Coos Bay, OR 97420

Elisabeth Kubler-Ross
"Death, the Final Stage of Growth"
Simon and Schuster Inc., NY

Shirley MacLaine
"Out on a Limb"
Bantam Books, NY

John Gillepie Magee, Jr.
"High Flight", poem

— Ira Progoff
"Jung, Synchronicity, and Human Destiny"
Dell Publishing Co. Inc., NY

Gail Sheehy
"Passages"
Bantam Books, NY

Eugene E. Thomas
"The Brotherhood of Mt. Shasta"
DeVorss and Co., Los Angeles, CA

White Dove, Ida Partridge
"Golden Moments With the Ascended Masters"
"Spiritual Bouquets from the Ascended Lady Masters"
10420 Mercury Drive, Grass Valley, CA 95945, (916) 272-7788

White Eagle
"Prayers for the New Age"
White Eagle Publishing Trust, Liss, Hampshire, England

Chelsea Quinn Yarbro
"Messages from Michael"
Playboy Paperbacks, NY

CASSETTE and VIDEO TAPES

AWAKENING HEART PRODUCTIONS
"Love's Awakening", Presentations and Videos
Dean and Mark Tucker
5914 Channel Drive
Santa Rosa, CA 95405
(707) 539-3535

Steven Halpern
HALPERN SOUNDS, Cassette Tapes
1775 Old County Road #9
Belmont, CA 94002, (800) 544-4444 or (415) 592-4900

HEAVENSONG
Maitreya and Maloah Stillwater
Worldwide Songfest Presentations and Cassette Tapes
P. O. Box 450, Kula, Maui, HI 96790, (803) 878-6415

"Oxygene"
Jean Michel Jarre
Polydor Recordings

"The Prophet"
A Musical Interpretation Featuring
Richard Harris
Atlantic Recording Corporation

COUNSELORS and THERAPISTS

Abdullah Bawaney
ABOROMANCY (Tree Readings)
1815B El Parque Court, San Mateo, CA 94403, (415) 572-2629

Elaine Christine
Metaphysical and Spiritual Counselor
Crystals Used in Individual Healing Sessions
P.O. Box 83782, San Diego, CA 92138

Kay Deaver
FASHION FIGURES
Hot Mineral Body-wrap Sculpting
3769 Peralta Boulevard, Suite G, Fremont, CA 94536
(415) 792-9605

Tamara Diaghilev
Metaphysical Teacher and Counselor
Classes, Workshops and Private Sessions
2168 15th Street, San Francisco, CA 94114, (415) 861-7616

Joanne Isert
JOANNE ISERT SKIN CARE CLINIC
A Holistic and Herbalistic Approach to Beauty Needs
Customized Make-up Consultant
Prescriptive Therapeutic Make-up Formulas
1372 N. Main Street, # 200, Walnut Creek, CA 94596,
(415) 945-6876

Karen LaPuma
Astrologer and Metaphysical Counselor
457 Oak Manor Drive, Fairfax, CA 94930, (415) 459-1442

Donelyn Larsen, C.M.T.
Therapeutic Massage
Shiatsu • Swedish • Lymphatic • Reflexology
3738 Mt. Diablo Boulevard, Lafayette, CA 94549, (415) 284-5077

Meta Mergy, Licensed Practitioner
HEALING THROUGH TOUCH
Reiki, Jin Shin, Shiatsu, Acupressure
1406 Maria Lane, Walnut Creek, CA 94596
(415) 946-9689

M.G. Westmore Academy of Cosmetic Arts
Marvin and Joyce Westmore
15445 Ventura Boulevard, Suite 8
Sherman Oaks, CA 91403
(818) 906-1815

Kathy Robertson, RPT
Licensed Physical Therapist, Electroneuromyographer and Rolfer
Hypergravity and Stress Consultant to NASA, The School of Aerospace
Medicine and the F-16 Fighterpilot Program
Olympic Athlete Consultant
Consultant to Brian Orser,
   Men's 1987 World Figure Skating Gold Medalist
1844 San Miguel Drive, Walnut Creek, CA 94596, (415) 934-6078

Susan Ruebel
TRANSITIONS
Cellulite Therapy and Nutritional Counseling
1844 San Miguel Dr., # 301A, Walnut Creek, CA 94596
(415) 944-1559

Diane Seaman, M.A.,Ph.D Candidate
Certified Handwriting Analyst
INSTITUTE of GRAPHOLOGICAL RESEARCH
Workshops,Analyses, Graphotherapy and Private Consultations
610 Lochmoor Court, Danville, CA 94526, (415) 866-1995

Kay Snow Davis
Healing Consultant
Box 17863, Boulder, CO 80308-7863
2531 Sawtelle Boulevard, # 97, Los Angeles, CA 90064
(213) 259-4825

Richard Unger, Director
Teacher, Lecturer, Personal Growth Consultant
INSTITUTE OF HAND ANALYSIS
P. O. Box 1313, San Rafael, CA 94915, (415) 461-1128

CREATIVE VENTURES

Sharyn Abbott
GREAT IMPRESSIONS
34 Chance Lane, Walnut Creek, CA 94596, (415) 930-8424

ROBIN N. BLANC PROMOTIONS
P. O. Box 2491, Del Mar, CA 92014, (619) 226-5266

Kathleen Bruno
Artist
c/o SHASTAR PRESS
P.O. Box 30186, Walnut Creek, CA 94598

Sandy Emerson
HI-TEK CONSULTING
SYSTEMS ENGINEERING SOFTWARE
M.P. O. 18L Riverside Drive, Washougal, WA 98671
(206) 837-3844

Russ Fischella
Photographer and Make-up Artisan
37 Orben Place, San Francisco, CA 94115, (415) 563-5397

INSTITUTE OF COLOR AND DESIGN
Naomi Tickle
1929 Union Street, Suite B, San Francisco, CA 94123
(415) 346-8305

John Lykes
Artist
814 5th Street, #4, Santa Monica, CA 90403

MATRIX PRODUCTIONS
Kim and Merrill Peterson
Editing, Design, Publication and Production Services
430 Estado Way, Novato, CA 94947, (415) 892-3298

MICHAEL'S
Michael Gourkani, Restaurateur
1536 Newell Avenue, Walnut Creek, CA 94596, (415) 934-5337

MIRACLES UNLIMITED
"Maui's Spiritual Network and Retail Center"
Books, Gifts, Cassette Tapes and Crystals
81 Central Avenue, Wailuku, Maui, HI 96793, (808) 242-7799

Bill Orlich
BILL'S PRINTING CENTER
1207 Arroyo Way, Walnut Creek, CA 94596, (415) 932-4640

THE PERSONAL RESOURCE SYSTEM (PRS)
Lee Berglund
11588 Sorrento Valley Rd., # 17, San Diego, CA 92121
1-800-621-0852

PERSONAL STYLE COUNSELORS
Joan Songer, Founder
Personal Color and Style Consultants
and Affiliated Support Services
458 Santa Clara Avenue, Oakland, CA 94610, (415) 832-1714

Michael St. James
Photo Retouch and Restoration
38 Orben Place, San Francisco, CA 94115, (415) 563-5397

SEMINARS, TRAININGS and WORKSHOPS

ADVENTURES IN ENLIGHTENMENT
Terry Cole-Whittaker
Workshops, Retreats, Video and Cassette Tapes and Books
P. O. Box 528, Rochester, WA 98579, (206) 273-8861

The Alive Tribe
Multi-Dimensional Research and Expansion
DOMAIN SHIFT
Diamond and Angel Ecstasy
Workshops, Integration Journal, Cassette Tapes and Books
Box 4068, Aspen, CO 81612-4068
(800) 331-MDRE (outside Colorado), (303) 923-5806

The A*L*L* Discovery Process
JOURNEY INTO ONENESS
Christi Ana Davidsunn
P. O. Box ONE, Niwot, CO 80544, (303) 444-0011

ASSET
Awareness, Sensitivity, Spiritual Enlightenment and Transformation
Larry Jensen,M.B.A., Ph.D., Founder
Box 2000, Dillon Beach, CA 94929, (707) 878-2900

Werner Erhard and Associates
THE FORUM[1]
765 California Street, San Francisco, CA 94108, (415) 391-9911

THE GOD TRAINING (LRT Spiritual Retreat)
LOVING RELATIONSHIPS TRAINING
Sondra Ray
"Drinking the Divine", Celestial Arts, Berkeley, CA
Rebirthing Center Information
Box 1465, Washington, CT 06793, 1-800-INTL-LRT

INTENSIVE JOURNAL® WORKSHOP
Ira Progoff
Dialogue House
Workshops, Books and Cassette Tapes
80 E. 11th Street, New York, N.Y. 10003, (800) 221-5844

---

[1]In December 1984 the est Training was retired. In January 1985, Werner Erhard and Associates introduced a wholly new program entitled THE FORUM.

384

INWARD BOUND
Alexander Everett
P. O, Box 456, Veneta, OR 97487, (503) 683-2121

RELATIONSHIP TRAINING INSTITUTE
Loy Young
Hotel Costa Rica Surf
Golfito, Costa Rica, 011-506-75-0034

SHAKTI CENTER
Shakti Gawain
"Creative Visualizations", Whatever Publishing , Inc., San Rafael, CA
Workshops, Retreats, Books and Cassette Tapes
P. O. Box 377, Mill Valley, CA 94942, (415) 927-2277

The 6-DAY Advance Training
East Coast Office:
257 Park Avenue South, 3rd Floor, New York, NY 10010
(212) 474-9350

West Coast Office:
765 California, San Francisco, CA 94109, (415) 955-1755

TRANSCENDENTAL MEDITATION (TM)
Check white pages of your telephone book or contact:
Maharishi International University
Fairfield, Iowa 52556 for nearest TM Center

WINGSONG
Lisa deLongchamps
Workshops, Wingsong Consultant's Training and Books
450 Santa Clara Avenue, Oakland, CA 94610
(415) 444-8188

ORGANIZATIONS

THE HOLIDAY PROJECT
Elizabeth G. Russell, Executive Director
1388 Sutter Street, Suite 500, San Francisco, CA 94109
(415) 474-7285

THE HUNGER PROJECT
Joan Holmes, Global Executive Director
1388 Sutter Street, San Francisco, CA 94109
(415) 928-8700

INSTITUTE of NOETIC SCIENCES
Edgar D. Mitchell, Apollo 14 Astronaut and Founder
475 Gate Five Road, Sausalito, CA 94965 (415) 331-5650

A*L*L   P. 144 - Life Path

Divine Principle - Joy 171
If Freedom time - 173
Movies - 213